# Observations On the History and Evidences of the Resurrection of Jesus Christ

Gilbert West

Charles Goring

# OBSERVATIONS
ON THE
# Hiſtory *and* Evidences
OF THE
# RESURRECTION
OF
# *JESUS CHRIST.*

# OBSERVATIONS
ON THE
# History *and* Evidences
OF THE
# RESURRECTION
OF
# *JESUS CHRIST.*

---

By *GILBERT WEST*, Esq;

---

The FOURTH EDITION,
Revised and Corrected by the AUTHOR.

---

*Blame not before thou hast examined the Truth; understand first, and then rebuke.*

ECCLUS. xi. 7.

---

---

*LONDON:*
Printed for R. DODSLEY at *Tully*'s Head in *Pall-mall.*
MDCCXLIX.

# INTRODUCTION.

[illegible] to our purpose [illegible] they have [illegible] Resurrection of Jesus [illegible] Moral Philosophers. [illegible] which, in order to [illegible] of the Evangelists, [illegible] that they [illegible] in the Accounts they have given [illegible]. To this [illegible] two very learned [illegible] ingenious Answers; which [illegible]

# INTRODUCTION.

THE following Obſervations took their Riſe from a Pamphlet entitled, *The Reſurrection of* JESUS *conſidered, in Anſwer to the Trial of the Witneſſes. By a Moral Philoſopher.* The Author of which, in order to overturn the Teſtimony of the Evangeliſts, hath attempted to ſhew that they contradict each other in the Accounts they have given of this Fact. To this Pamphlet there came out two very learned and ingenious Anſwers; which I read with great Satisfaction, as I found in them solid Confutations of many Objections against Christianity started in the first. But I must confess, (though with the utmost Respect to the Knowledge and Abilities of the Authors of the two last-mentioned Pamphlets) that I was not so fully satisfied with their Manner of clearing the *Sacred Writers* from the Contradictions charged upon them. This set me upon reading and examining with Attention the Scriptures themselves; and with no other Biass, than what arose from the Astonishment I was under at finding Writers, who for above these sixteen hundred Years have been reputed holy and inspired, charged with such a Contrariety in their Accounts, as ill agreed with either of those Epithets. Of the Truth of this Charge therefore, I acknowknowledge I had great Difficulty to perſuade myſelf. And indeed it was not long before I diſcovered, as I imagined, the Vanity and Weakneſs of ſuch an Imputation; which however, I cannot ſtile altogether groundleſs, ſince it has an Appearance of being founded in the Words of the Goſpel; though in reality, that Foundation lies no deeper than the Outſide and Surface of the Words. Neither will I call it malicious, ſince having upon farther Inquiry found it to be of a very ancient Date, I know not the firſt Authors of it, and conſequently can form no Judgment of their Intentions. What I have to offer in Defence of the Evangeliſts, is built in like manner upon the ſacred Text; whoſe true Meaning (which upon this Occaſion I ſearched for in vain in the Notes of many eminent Commentators) I have endeavoured to investigate and prove, by comparing their several Accounts with each other, and noting the Agreement and Disagreement of the Circumstances. A Method that hath led me unavoidably into Critical Observations; for the Length and Dryness of which I should however think myself obliged to make some Excuse, did I write only for Amusement, or expect to be read by those, who seek in Books for nothing more solid than Entertainment.

But altho' the clearing the Sacred Writers from the Imputation of contradicting each other, was the principal, and indeed the sole Object I had at first in View; yet having, in the Pursuit of this Object, perceived the Light breaking in upon me still more and more the farther I advanced, and discovering to me almost at every Step some new Circumstances, which tended to illustrate and confirm the Testimony given by those inspired Historians to the Resurrection of *Jesus Christ*, I was induced, by these Discoveries, to go very far beyond my first Design, into a Consideration of the Evidences of this great and important Article, not those only recorded in the sacred Writings, but others arising from subsequent Events and Facts; of which we have, by several Ways, many clear and unquestionable Proofs. The Method in which I have proceeded in this Consideration, is as follows: I have begun with laying down the Order in which the several Incidents related by the Evangelists, appear to have happened; and in the next Place, I have made

made some Observations upon the Method and Manner, in which the Proofs of this astonishing Event were laid before the Apostles, who were appointed to bear Witness of it to all the World. And to these I have, in the third Place, added an exact and rigorous Examination of the Proofs themselves; from all which I have endeavoured to shew, that the Resurrection of *Christ* was most fairly and fully proved to the Apostles and Disciples, those first Converts and Preachers of Christianity.

But as the Resurrection's having been fully proved to the Apostles, tho' absolutely necessary, yet is not of itself sufficient to authorize at this Time, and establish the Faith of a Christian, I imagined that what I had already written, would be imperfect at least, if if not altogether useless, unless I added some Arguments and Reasons I had to offer to induce us, who live at the Distance of seventeen hundred Years from the Date of that miraculous Event, to believe that *Christ* is risen from the Dead. These Reasons therefore I have thought proper to subjoin under two Heads, *viz.* the Testimony of the chosen Witnesses of the Resurrection recorded in the Scriptures, and the Existence of the Christian Religion.

FROM this Account of the Rise, Progress and Design of the following Observations, the Reader will perceive that they were first begun with the single View of obtaining Satisfaction for myself upon some Difficulties in the Evangelical History of the Resurrection; and that they are now published

with

with the Hopes of their being as useful to others, as they have been to me. This is the chief, if not the sole End that a Lay-man can reasonably propose to himself in publishing any thing upon a Subject of this Nature: For I am not ignorant how little Reputation is to be gained by writing on the Side of Christianity, which by many People is regarded as a superstitious Fable, not worth the Thoughts of a wise Man; and considered by more as a meer Political Scheme, calculated to serve the Power and Interest of the Clergy only. How absolutely groundless both these Opinions are, will easily appear to any one, who will take the Pains to examine fairly and impartially the *Proofs* and *Doctrines* of the Christian Religion; *Proofs* established upon *Facts*, the surest Foundations of Evidence; and

*Doc-*

*Doctrines* derived by *Inspiration*, from the great Author of Reason, and Father of *all* Mankind. Whoever hath either neglected, or doth refuse to make this Examination, can have no Right to pass his Judgment upon Christianity, and should methinks for the same Reason be somewhat cautious of censuring those, who acknowledge it to be of divine Institution; especially as he will find in the List of Christians, the great and venerable Names of *Bacon*, *Milton*, *Boyle*, *Locke* and *Newton*; Names to whose Authority every thing should submit but Truth, to whom they themselves thought it not beneath their superior Talents to submit, though she required them to *believe in Christ*.

BUT it may possibly be demanded, why, being a Lay-man, I presume to inter-

intermeddle in a Province commonly thought to belong peculiarly to the Clergy? To which I anſwer, that beſides the Motives above ſuggeſted, this very Prejudice was a powerful Inducement to me to publiſh the following Obſervations, and to prefix my Name to them. The Clergy, I am ſenſible, are both ready and able to maintain the Cauſe of Chriſtianity, as their many excellent Writings in Defence of it ſufficiently demonſtrate; but as the Generality of Mankind is more governed by Prejudice than Reaſon, the Writings of the Clergy are not ſo univerſally read, or ſo candidly received as they deſerve, becauſe they are ſuppoſed to proceed, not from Conſcience and Conviction, but from intereſted Views and the common Cauſe of their Profeſſion; A Suppoſition evidently as partial and inju-

injurious as that would be, which ſhould impute the gallant Behaviour of our Officers to the mean Conſiderations of their *Pay*, and the Hopes of Preferment, excluſive of all the nobler Motives of Gentlemen, *viz.* the Senſe of Honour, and the Love of their Country. But the Clergy, I dare ſay, who, if there be any thing beſides Prejudice in the above-mentioned Imputation upon them, have alone the Right to make this Demand, will readily excuſe my appearing in the Cauſe of Chriſtianity. And the Laity, I hope ſuch of them at leaſt as are Chriſtians not in Name and Profeſſion only, will join with me in declaring againſt the vain Prejudices of Unbelievers, that the Chriſtian Religion is of the utmoſt Importance to all Orders and Degrees of Men; and that the greateſt Service

that

that the moſt zealous Patriot can do his Country, is to promote the Faith, and thereby encourage the Practice of the truly divine Virtues recommended by *Chriſt* and his Apoſtles.

For my own part, if any ſincere Inquirer after Truth, any one honeſt Man ſhall receive the leaſt Benefit from the following Obſervations, I ſhall think I have neither written nor lived in vain.

# OBSERVATIONS UPON THE HISTORY OF THE RESURRECTION of *Jesus Christ*, &c.

## JOHN, Chap. XX.

§. 1. *T*HE *first Day of the Week cometh* Mary, Magdalene *early when it was yet dark, unto the Sepulchre, and seeth the Stone taken away from the Sepulchre. Then she runneth and cometh to* Simon Peter, *and to the other Disciple whom*

Jesus *loved, and saith unto them, They have taken away the Lord out of the Sepulchre, and we know not where they have laid him.* Peter *therefore went forth, and that other Disciple, and came to the Sepulchre. So they ran both together, and the other Disciple did out-run* Peter, *and came first to the Sepulchre; and he stooping down, and* looking in, *saw the Linen Clothes lying, yet went he not in. Then cometh* Simon Peter *following him, and went into the Sepulchre, and seeth the Linen Clothes lie, and the Napkin that was about his Head, not lying with the Linen Clothes, but wrapped together in a Place by itself. Then went in also that other Disciple, which came first to the Sepulchre, and he saw and believed; for as yet they knew not the Scripture that he must rise again from the Dead: Then the Disciples went away again unto their own Homes. But* Mary *stood without at the Sepulchre weeping; and as she wept, she stooped down,* and looked *into the Sepulchre, and seeth two Angels in White, sitting, the one at the Head, and the other at the Feet, where the Body of* Jesus *had lain; and they say unto her, Woman, why weepest thou? She saith unto them, Because they have taken away my Lord, and I know not where they have laid him. And when she had thus said, she turned herself*

*back,*

*back, and saw* Jesus *standing, and knew not that it was* Jesus. Jesus *saith unto her, Woman, why weepest thou? Whom seekest thou? She supposing him to be the Gardener, saith unto him, Sir, if thou hast borne him hence, tell me where thou hast laid him, and I will take him away.* Jesus *saith unto her,* Mary! *She turned herself, and saith unto him, Rabboni! which is to say, Master.* Jesus *saith unto her, Touch me not; for I am not yet ascended unto my Father: But go to my Brethren, and say unto them, I ascend unto my Father and your Father, and to my God and your God.* Mary Magdalene *came and told the Disciples that she had seen the Lord, and that he had spoken these Things unto her.*

FROM this Passage of the Gospel of St. *John*, it is evident, 1st, That *Mary Magdalene* had not seen any Vision of Angels, before she ran to *Peter*; and consequently, that she was not of the Number of those Women, who went into the Sepulchre, and were there told by an Angel that *Jesus* was risen: For had she, before she went to *Peter*, seen any Angels, she would certainly have added so extraordinary a Circumstance to her Account; and had she

 been

been informed by an Angel that *Jesus* was risen, she could not have persisted in lamenting at not being able to find the Body; nor have inquired of him, whom she took to be the Gardener, where he had put it, that she might take it away. It is also farther observable, that when, after her Return to the Sepulchre with *Peter* and *John*, and their Departure from thence, she saw a Vision of Angels, she was standing *without*, at the Sepulchre, weeping; ——that *stooping* down, and looking (not going) into the Sepulchre, she saw two Angels in White, *sitting*, *the one at the Head*, *the other at the Feet*, *where the Body of* Jesus *had lain*, who said no more to her than, *Woman*, *why weepest thou?* To which she answered, *Because they have taken away my Lord, and I know not where they have laid him.* From all which Circumstances it appears, 2dly, That neither after her Return to the Sepulchre with *Peter* and *John*, was she with those Women who went into the Sepulchre, *&c.* that she had not heard any thing of *Christ*'s being risen from the Dead; and that therefore those Women, who were told by an Angel that he was risen, were not at the Sepulchre when she returned

turned thither with *Peter* and *John*. And indeed from the whole Tenor of the above-cited Paſſage of St. *John*'s Goſpel, throughout which no mention is made of any other Woman beſides *Mary Magdalene*, it is more than probable ſhe was alone, when ſhe ſaw the Angels, and when *Chriſt* appeared to her immediately after. That ſhe was alone when *Chriſt* appeared to her, is plainly implied in what St. *Mark* * ſays, who tells us expreſly, that *Chriſt* appeared *firſt* to *Mary Magdalene*, which, had ſhe been accompanied by the other Women, could not have been ſpoken of her with any Propriety of Speech. In the 3d Place, it is plain from the above Relation, that the Angels were not always viſible, but appeared and diſappeared as they thought proper; for *John* and *Peter* going into the Sepulchre ſaw no Angels; but *Mary*, after their Departure, looking in, ſaw two, one ſitting at the Head, and the other at the Feet, where the Body of *Jeſus* had lain.

§. 2. LUKE, Chap. xxiv. 13.

*THE ſame Day two of them* [the Diſciples] *went to a village called* Emmaus, *which was from*

 Jeruſalem

* Chap. xvi. ver. 9.

Jerusalem *about threescore Furlongs, and they talked together of all these Things that had happened. And it came to pass that while they communed together, and reasoned,* Jesus *himself drew near, and went with them; but their Eyes were holden that they should not know him. And he said unto them, What manner of Communications are these, that ye have one to another, as ye walk and are sad? And one of them, whose Name was* Cleopas, *answering, said upon him, Art thou only a Stranger in* Jerusalem, *and hast not known the Things which are come to pass there in these Days? And he said unto them, What Things? And they said unto him, Concerning* Jesus *of* Nazareth, *which was a Prophet mighty in Deed and Word before God, and all the People; and how the Chief Priests and our Rulers deliver'd him to be condemned to Death, and have crucified him. But we trusted that it had been He which should have redeemed* Israel: *And beside all this, to-day is the third Day since these Things were done. Yea, and certain Women also of our Company made us astonished, which were early at the Sepulchre; and when they found not his Body, they came, saying, that they had also seen a Vision of Angels, which said that he was alive: And certain of them which were with us,*

*went*

*went to the Sepulchre, and found it even so as the Women had said; but him they saw not.*

The latter Part of this Passage, which contains an Abridgment of a Report made by some Women to the Apostles before these two Disciples had left *Jerusalem*, suggests the following Observations: 1st, The Angels seen by these Women at the Sepulchre told them that *Jesus* was alive, whence it follows, that this Report was not made by *Mary Magdalene*; for the Angels, which she saw, said no such thing to her. 2dly, As there is no Notice taken of any Appearance of our Saviour to these Women, it is also evident, that this Report could not have been made by the other *Mary* and *Salome*, to whom, as they were going to tell the Disciples the Message of the Angel which they had seen at the Sepulchre, *Jesus* appeared, as I shall presently shew from St. *Matthew*. 3dly, There were therefore several Reports made at different Times to the Apostles, and by different Women. At different Times; for the two Disciples, who, before they left *Jerusalem*, had heard the Report now under Consideration, had not heard those of *Mary Magda-*

*lene*, of the other *Mary* and *Salome*.---By different Women; for it having been juſt now proved, that this Report could not belong to either of the laſt-mentioned Women, it muſt have been made by ſome other; and no other being named by any of the Evangeliſts but *Joanna*, it came in all Likelihood from her, and thoſe that attended her. 4thly, Some of the Diſciples, upon hearing this Report, *went to the Sepulchre, and found it even ſo as the Women had ſaid*; *i. e.* in the moſt obvious Senſe of theſe Words. They ſaw the Body was gone, and they ſaw ſome Angels. But I ſhall not inſiſt upon this Interpretation, but only obſerve, that if *Peter* be ſuppoſed to have been one of thoſe Diſciples, who upon this Information of the Women, went to the Sepulchre, this muſt have been the ſecond Time of his going thither. That *Peter* went a ſecond Time to the Sepulchre I ſhall ſhew more at large, when I come to conſider the former Part of this Chapter of St. *Luke*.

These ſeveral Concluſions being admitted, I think it will be no difficult Matter to defend the Evangeliſts againſt the Imputation of contra-

dicting

dicting each other, in the Accounts they have given of what happened on the Day of the Resurrection. For unless Authors, who relate different and independent Parts of the same History, may, for that Reason, be said to contradict each other, the Evangelists, I will be bold to say, stand as clear of that Charge, at least in that Part of their Writings which we are now examining, as any of the most accurate Historians either ancient or modern; as I shall now endeavour to prove, by considering and comparing the several Relations of this Day's Events in the Gospels of St. *Matthew*, St. *Mark*, St. *Luke*, and St. *John*. That written by St. *John* I have already produced, so that there will be no Occasion for inserting it again in this Place; those of St. *Matthew* and St. *Mark* I shall produce and examine together, for Reasons which will be evident hereafter.

§. 3. MATTH. Chap. xxviii.

*IN the End of the Sabbath, as it began to dawn towards the first Day of the Week, came* Mary Magdalene, *and the other* Mary, *to see the Sepulchre: And behold, there was a great Earth-*

*Earthquake; for the Angel of the Lord descended from Heaven, and came and rolled back the Stone from the Door, and sat upon it: His Countenance was like Lightening, and his Raiment white as Snow; and for fear of him the Keepers did shake, and became as dead Men. And the Angel answered and said unto the Women: Fear not ye; for I know that ye seek* Jesus, *which was crucified: He is not here; for he is risen, as he said; come see the Place where the Lord lay: And go quickly and tell his Disciples that he is risen from the Dead; and behold, he goeth before you into* Galilee, *there shall ye see him: lo, I have told you. And they departed quickly from the Sepulchre with Fear and great Joy, and did run to bring his Disciples Word. And as they went to tell his Disciples, behold,* Jesus *met them, saying, All hail! And they came and held him by the Feet, and worshipped him. Then said* Jesus *unto them, Be not afraid: Go tell my Brethren that they go into* Galilee, *and there shall they see me. Now when they were going, behold, some of the Watch came into the City, and shewed unto the Chief Priests all the Things that were done. And when they were assembled with the Elders, and had taken*

*Counsel,*

*Counsel, they gave large Money unto the Soldiers, saying, Say ye, his Disciples came by Night, and stole him away while we slept. And if this come to the Governor's Ears, we will persuade him, and secure you. So they took the Money, and did as they were taught: And this Saying is commonly reported among the* Jews *until this Day. Then the eleven Disciples went away into* Galilee, *into a Mountain where* Jesus *had appointed them. And when they saw him, they worshipped him: But some doubted.*

MARK, Chap. xvi.

*AND when the Sabbath was past,* Mary Magdalene, *and* Mary *the Mother of* James, *and* Salome, *had bought sweet Spices, that they might come and anoint him; and very early in the Morning, the first Day of the Week, they came unto the Sepulchre at the Rising of the Sun. And they said among themselves, Who shall roll us away the Stone from the Door of the Sepulchre? And when they looked, they saw that the Stone was rolled away, for it was very great. And entering into the Sepulchre, they saw a young Man sitting on the right Side, cloathed in a long white Garment, and they were affrighted. And he saith unto them, Be not affrighted: Ye seek* Jesus *of* Nazareth, *which was crucified: He is risen, he is not here: Behold the Place where they laid him. But go your Way, tell his Disciples and* Peter, *that he goeth before you into* Galilee; *there shall ye see him, as he said unto you. And they went out quickly and fled from the Sepulchre; for they trembled and were amazed; neither said they any thing to any Man; for they were afraid. Now when* Jesus *was risen, early in the first Day of the Week, he appeared first to* Mary Magdalene, *out of whom he had cast seven Devils. And she went and told them that had been with him, as they mourned and wept. And they, when they heard that he was alive, and had been seen of her, believed not. After that he appeared in another Form unto two of them, as they walked and went into the Country. And they went and told it unto the Residue; neither believed they them. Afterward he appeared unto the Eleven, as they sat at Meat, and upbraided them with Unbelief, and Hardness of Heart, because they believed not them which had seen him after he was risen.*

I SHALL range the Obſervations I intend to make upon the ſeveral Particulars contained in theſe two Paſſages, under three Heads. 1ſt, Of ſuch Circumſtances as are related by one of theſe Evangeliſts, but omitted by the other. The 2d, Of ſuch as they both agree in. And the 3d, Of ſuch as ſeem to claſh and diſagree with each other. 1ſt, The ſeveral Particulars of the Earthquake, the Deſcent of the Angel from Heaven, his rolling away the Stone from the Door of the Sepulchre, and ſitting upon it, and the Terror of the Soldiers who guarded the Sepulchre, are related only by St. *Matthew*: As are likewiſe the Appearances of our Saviour to the Women, and to the Eleven Diſciples in *Galilee*, and the Flight of the Guards into the City, and all that paſſed between them and the Chief Prieſts upon that Occaſion. On the other hand, St. *Mark* alone makes mention of the Women's having bought Spices, that they might come and anoint the Body of our Saviour;—of *Salome*'s being one of thoſe Women;—of their entering into the Sepulchre, and ſeeing there a young Man ſitting on the right Side, cloathed in a long

long white Garment;—of the Appearance of *Christ* to *Mary Magdalene*;—to the two Disciples who were going into the Country;—and lastly, to the Eleven as they sat at Meat. As not one of all these Circumstances can be proved to contradict or even disagree with any Particular, which either of these Evangelists has thought fit to mention, no Argument against the Reality or Credibility of them can be drawn from their not having been taken Notice of by both; unless it can be made appear, that a Fact related by one Historian, or one Evidence, must therefore be false, because it is passed over in Silence by another. St. *Matthew* wrote his Gospel first, within a few Years after the Ascension of our Lord; this Gospel St. *Mark*, who wrote his some few Years after, is said to have abridged; tho' this, I think, is said with very little Propriety. For how can that Book be stiled an Abridgment, which contains many Particulars not mentioned in the original Author? That Saint *Mark* relates many Circumstances not taken notice of by St. *Matthew*, will easily appear to any one, who shall take the Pains to compare them together; and of this, to go no farther, we have a plain Inſtance in the two Paſſages before us.

St. *Matthew* wrote his Goſpel at the Requeſt of the *Jewiſh* Converts, who having lived in that Country where the Scene of this great Hiſtory was laid, were doubtleſs acquainted with many Particulars, which, for that Reaſon, it was not neceſſary to mention. This will account for the Conciſeneſs, and ſeeming Defectiveneſs of his Narrations in many Places, as well as for his omitting ſome Circumſtances which the other Evangeliſts thought proper to relate. St. *Mark* compos'd his for Chriſtians of other Nations, who not having the ſame Opportunities of being informed, as their Brethren of *Judæa*, ſtood in need of ſome Notes and Comments to enable them the better to underſtand the Extract, which St. *Mark* choſe to give them out of the Goſpel written by St. *Matthew*. It was therefore neceſſary for St. *Mark* to inſert many Particulars, which the Purpoſe of St. *Matthew* in writing his Goſpel did not lead him to take notice of. Allowing theſe Evangeliſts to have had theſe two diſtinct Views, let us ſee how they

they have pursued them in the Passages now under Consideration.

That the Disciples of *Jesus* came by Night and stole away the Body while the Guards slept, was commonly reported among the *Jews*, even so long after the Ascension of our Lord as when St. *Matthew* wrote his Gospel, as himself * tells us. To furnish the *Jewish* Converts with an Answer to this absurd Story, so industriously propagated among their unbelieving Brethren, and supported by the Authority of the Chief Priests and Elders, this Evangelist relates at large the History of the guarding the Sepulchre, &c. the Earthquake, the Descent of the Angel, his Rolling away the Stone, and the Fright of the Soldiers at his Appearance, who *shook and became as dead Men.*—And indeed, by comparing this Relation with the Report given out by the Soldiers, it will easily appear on which Side the Truth lay. For as there is nothing in the miraculous Resurrection of our Lord, so repugnant to Reason and Probability, as that the Disciples should be able to roll away the Stone which closed

* Chap. xxviii. ver. 15.

closed up the Mouth of the Sepulchre, and carry off the Body of *Jesus*, unperceiv'd by the Soldiers, who were set there on purpose to guard against such an Attempt; so it is also evident, that the Particulars of the Soldiers Report were founded upon the Circumstances of this History. In this Report three Things are asserted, *viz.* That the Disciples stole the Body—that they stole it in the Night,—and that they stole it while the Guards were asleep. That *Jesus* came out of the Sepulchre before the Rising of the Sun, St. *Matthew* informs us, who says that the Earthquake, *&c.* happened at the Time when *Mary Magdalene* and the other *Mary* set out in order to take a View of the Sepulchre, which was just as the Day began to break. This Fact was undoubtedly too notorious for the Chief Priests to venture at falsifying it, and was besides favourable to the two other Articles: This therefore they admitted; and taking the Hint from what the Soldiers told them of their having been cast into a Swoon or Trance *(becoming like dead Men)* at the Appearance of the Angel, and consequently not having seen our Saviour come out of the Sepulchre, they forged the remaining Parts of this Story, that his Disciples came and stole him away while they



slept.

ſlept. They took the Hint, I ſay, of framing theſe two laſt-mentioned Articles from that Circumſtance related by St. *Matthew*, of the *Keepers ſhaking and becoming like dead Men* upon the Sight of the Angel; for throughout this whole Hiſtory there was no other beſides this, upon which they could prevaricate and diſpute. The Stone was rolled away from the Sepulchre, and the Body was gone; this the Chief Prieſts were to account for, without allowing that *Jeſus* was riſen from the Dead. The Diſciples, they ſaid, ſtole it away. What! while the Guards were there? Yes, the Guards were aſleep. With this Anſwer they knew full well many would be ſatisfied, without inquiring any farther into the Matter: but they could not expect that every body would be ſo contented; eſpecially as they had Reaſon to apprehend, that although the Soldiers, who had taken their Money, might be faithful to them, keep their Secret, and atteſt the Story they had framed for them, yet the Truth might come out, by means of thoſe whom they had not bribed; for St. *Matthew* ſays, †, that *ſome* of the Watch went into the City, *and ſhewed unto the Chief Prieſts all the Things that were done.* Some therefore remained be-

† Chap. xxviii. ver. 11.

hind,

hind, who probably had no Share of the Money which the Chief Priests gave to the Soldiers: or if they had, in all likelihood it came too late; they had already divulged the Truth, as well from an Eagerness, which all Men naturally have, to tell a wonderful Story, as from a Desire of justifying themselves for having quitted their Post. The Chief Priests therefore were to guard against this Event also; in order to which nothing could be more effectual, than to counter-work the Evidence of one Part of the Soldiers, by putting into the Mouths of others of them a Story, which, without directly contradicting the Facts, might yet tend to overthrow the only Conclusion which the Disciples of *Jesus* would endeavour to draw from them, and which they were so much concerned to discredit; *viz*, That *Jesus* was risen from the Dead. For if the Disciples and Partizans of *Jesus*, informed by one Part of the Soldiers of the several Circumstances related in St. *Matthew*, should urge these miraculous Events as so many Proofs of the Resurrection of their Master, the unbelieving *Jews* were, by the Testimony of those suborned Witnesses, instructed to answer, that the Earthquake and

 the

the Angel were Illusions of Dreams; ——that the Soldiers had honestly confess'd they were asleep, though some of them, to skreen themselves from the Shame or Punishment such a Breach of Discipline deserved, pretended they were frightened into a Swoon or Trance by an extraordinary Appearance, which they never saw, or saw only in a Dream; —— that while they slept, the Disciples came and stole the Body; for none of the Soldiers, not even those who saw the most, pretend to have seen *Jesus* come out of the Sepulchre; – they are all equally ignorant by what Means the Body was removed; ——when they awaked it was missing; ——— and it was much more likely that the Disciples should have stolen it away, than that an Impostor should rise from the Dead. I shall not go about to confute this Story; to unprejudiced and thinking People it carries it's own Confutation with it: But I must observe, that it is founded entirely upon the Circumstance of the Soldiers not having seen *Jesus* come out of the Sepulchre; a Circumstance, that even those, who told the real Truth, could not contradict, tho' they accounted for it in a different Manner, by saying they were

were frightened into a Swoon or Trance at the Sight of a terrible Apparition, that came and rolled away the Stone, and sat upon it. But this Fact the Chief Priests thought it not prudent to allow, as favouring too much the Opinion of *Christ*'s being risen from the Dead; neither did they thing proper to reject it entirely, because they intended to turn it to their own Advantage; and therefore, denying every thing that was miraculous, they construed this Swoon or Trance into a Sleep, and with a large Sum of Money and Promises of Impunity, hired the Soldiers to confess a Crime, and, by taking Shame to themselves, to cover them from Confusion. And so far, it must be acknowledged, they gained their Point: For, until some farther Proofs of the Resurrection of *Jesus* should be produced, of which at that Time they had heard nothing more, this Story would undoubtedly have served to puzzle the Cause, and hold People in Suspense. Argument and Reason indeed were wholly on the other Side, but Prejudice and Authority were on theirs; and they were not ignorant to which the Bulk of Mankind were most disposed to submit.

BUT as no other than presumptive Arguments in favour of the Resurrection could be drawn from what happened to the Soldiers at the Sepulchre, even tho' the Chief Priests had permitted them to tell the Truth; St. *Matthew*, in his Narration, proceeds to second and confirm those Arguments by positive Evidence; producing Witnesses who had seen and conversed with *Jesus Christ*, after he was risen from the Dead: Of these, as may be gathered from the other Gospels, the Number was very considerable; and very numerous were the Instances of *Christ*'s appearing after his Resurrection: Yet from the latter has St. *Matthew* selected only two, upon each of which I beg leave to make a few Remarks. The first Appearance of *Christ* is to the Women, which happened as they went to tell the Disciples the Message of the Angel that had appeared to them in the Sepulchre. I have already proved, in my Observations upon St. *John*, that *Mary Magdalene* was not one of those Women; and yet the Words of St. *Matthew*, by the common Rule of Construction, seem to import the contrary. For, in the first Place the Pa-

ragraph

ragraph *(and the Angel anſwered and ſaid to the Women)* is, in our Tranſlation, connected with the preceding by the Copulative *And.* 2dly, As in the foregoing Part of this Chapter no Mention is made of any other Women than *Mary Magdalene* and the other *Mary*, and no Hint given of any other Angel than that deſcribed as deſcending from Heaven, *&c.* the Words in this Paragraph *(the Angel*, and *the Women)* muſt be taken to relate to them. To which I anſwer, 1ſt, That this Paragraph is not to be ſo connected with the preceding, as if nothing had intervened; ſince we ſhall find upon a cloſer Examination of it, and comparing it with its Parallel in St. *Mark*, that between the Keepers becoming like dead Men, and the Angels ſpeaking to the Women, *Salome* had joined the two *Maries* in their Way to the Sepulchre; that before they arrived there the Keepers were fled, and the Angel was removed from off the Stone, and was ſeated within the Sepulchre; for which Reaſon the Particle δὲ, inſtead of being rendered by the Copulative *And*, ſhould rather be expreſſed by the Disjunctive *But*, or *Now*, as denoting an Interruption in the Narration, and the Beginning of a new Paragraph. 2dly, I allow the Angel here ſpoken of to be the ſame with that mentioned in the foregoing Verſes, and the other *Mary* to be one of thoſe Women to whom this Angel in the Sepulchre, and afterwards *Chriſt* himſelf appeared, and therefore admit the Words, *the Angel and the Women* in this Verſe relate to them. But this will not remove the Difficulty, and it will be ſaid, that either *Mary Magdalene* was with the other *Mary* in the Sepulchre, or there is an Inaccuracy in the Expreſſion; for the Words, *Women*, and fear not *ye*, being plural, imply there were more than one. I grant it, and St. *Mark* informs us that *Salome* was there.—But then, inſtead of one Inaccuracy to be charg'd upon St. *Matthew*, here are two; *Mary Magdalene*, who was not preſent when the other *Mary* ſaw the Angel, is, by the natural Conſtruction of his Words, ſaid to be there; and *Salome*, who was preſent, he takes no Notice of at all.—I allow it, and let thoſe who are given to object, make the moſt of it: But let it at the ſame Time be remembered, that the greateſt Part of the Evangelical Writers were illiterate Men, not ſkilled in the Rules of Eloquence,

quence, or Grammatical Niceties, against the Laws of which it is easy to point out many Faults in the Writings of most of them. The other Passage I purposed to make some Remarks upon, affords another Instance of the same Kind; it is as follows: *Then the Eleven Disciples went away into* Galilee, *into a Mountain, where* Jesus *had appointed them, and when they saw him, they worshiped him; but some doubted.* Here the Words, *some doubted*, by the strict Rules of Grammar, must be understood of some of the Eleven Disciples, who immediately before are said, when they saw *Jesus*, to have *worshiped* him; which surely is not very consistent with their doubting; neither is it very probable that a Writer, however illiterate, should mean to contradict himself in the Compass of three Words. Another Interpretation therefore, tho' it be not so strictly agreeable to the Grammar Rules, is to be sought after, since it is a less Crime to offend against Grammar than against common Sense. *Some doubted*, must mean some besides the Eleven, who were present upon that Occasion, doubted. And indeed had St. *Matthew*, in the former Part of this Narration, taken notice that

others

others besides the Eleven were there, there would have been no Difficulty in understanding, even according to the strictest Laws of the Syntax, to whom the *some doubted* did belong; *οἱ δὲ*, and *οἱ δὲ* set in Opposition to each other, and signifying *some* and *others*, *these* and *those*, are frequently to be met with in Greek Authors of the greatest Authority; and no Reason can be given, why, according to this Manner of speaking, the *οἱ δὲ ἕνδεκα μαθηταὶ προσεκυνήσαν αὐτῷ — οἱ δὲ ἐδίστασαν*, should not be interpreted *now* or *then*, the Eleven Disciples — worshiped him, but others doubted; but that some Words, to which the second *οἱ δὲ* (others) refer, are wanting.

But these Defects, how grievous soever they may seem to Grammarians, or Cavillers, still more scrupulous and more punctilious than Grammarians themselves, will by no means impeach the Veracity of this Evangelist in the Opinion of those, who in making a Judgment of his Writings, are willing to take into the Account the Purpose he had in composing his Gospel. He wrote, as I observed before,

before, at the Request of the *Jewish* Converts; who, as St. *Chrysostom* informs us, * came to him and besought him to leave in Writing, what they had heard from him by Word of Mouth. His View in writing the Gospel therefore to the *Jews*, was to repeat what he had before preached to them; in doing of which it was not at all incumbent upon him to relate every minute Circumstance, which he could not but know they were well acquainted with, and which the Mention of the principal Fact could not fail to recall to their Memories. Thus in the two Passages above cited (to confine myself to them) it was not necessary for him, writing to the *Jews*, as it was for St. *Mark* who wrote for the *Egyptian* Converts †, to explain the Business that carried *Mary Magdalene* and the other *Mary* to the Sepulchre. It was doubtless known among the *Jews* that they had bought Spices, and went to the Sepulchre in order to embalm the Body of *Jesus*. Neither was it worth while, for the sake of a little Grammatical Exactness, to interrupt the Course of his Narration, to acquaint them that *Salome* joined the two *Maries*.

* Ὑπομνη. περι Ευαγ. † Ibid.

*ries* as they were going to the Sepulchre, and went with them thither; and that *Mary Magdalene* upon seeing the Stone rolled away, ran immediately to inform *Peter* and *John* of it; especially as he did not think proper to take notice of *Christ*'s having appeared to her: And he seems to me to have mentioned *Christ*'s appearing to the other Women, only because it was connected with the principal Fact, the Story of his appearing in *Galilee* to the Eleven Disciples and others. The Disciples going to meet their Master on a Mountain in *Galilee*, where he had appointed them, must needs have made a great Noise among the *Jews*; especially as it did not fall out till above a Week at least after the Resurrection; during which Time he had appeared thrice to his Disciples, † not including his Appearance to *Peter*, to the two Disciples, and the Women. And as above twenty People were Witnesses to one or other of these Appearances, the Fame of them was in all Probability diffused not only through *Jerusalem*, but throughout all *Judea*. It is no wonder therefore, that upon this solemn Occasion, which had been notified so long before,

† See John, Chap. xxii. ver. 14.

fore, not only by an Angel at the Sepulchre, and by *Christ* himself on the Day of his Resurrection, but foretold by him even before his Death; it is no wonder, I say, that upon so solemn an Occasion a great Multitude besides the Eleven, should be got together. St. *Paul* † mentions an Appearance of *Christ* to above five hundred Brethren at once, which cannot, with so good Reason, be understood of any other but this in *Galilee*. And tho' out of so large an Assembly some doubted, as St. *Matthew* says, yet that very Exception implies, that the greatest Number believed; and even those who doubted, must have agreed in some common Points with those who believed. They, as well as the Eleven, saw *Jesus*, but not having had the same sensible Evidences of the Reality of his Body, doubted whether it was himself or his Apparition which they beheld; whilst the latter, who needed no farther Conviction, when they saw him, fell down and worshiped. Here then was a Fact, which could not in all its Circumstances but be very notorious to the *Jews*, and was therefore highly proper to be mentioned by St. *Matthew*.

Here

† 1 Cor. chap. xv. 6.

Here was a Cloud of Witnesses, * the greatest Part of whom were alive when St. *Paul* wrote his Epistle to the *Corinthians* †, and therefore were certainly living when St. *Matthew* composed his Gospel; and many of them probably were of the Number of those Converts, for whom he wrote. Upon any of these Suppositions, and especially the last, it is easy to account for the concise Manner, in which he has related this important Event. It either was, or might easily be known with all its Circumstances by those, to whom he addressed his Gospel. The little attendant Circumstances therefore it was as needless for him to mention, as it was proper to take notice of the Event itself. The Gospel of *Christ* and the Faith of *Christians* are both vain, if *Christ* be not risen from the Dead. It was therefore absolutely necessary for the Apostles and Preachers of the Gospel to prove the Resurrection; this they did as well by their own Testimony, as by that of others, who had seen

* Ibid.

† St. *Paul's* 1st Epist. to the *Corinthians* was written A. D. 57. See Mr. *Lock*, ad locum. The Gospel according to St. *Matthew*, about the Year 53.

seen *Jesus* after he was risen. Thus * St. *Paul* relates several Appearances of *Christ* to *Cephas* and others, and closes all with his own Evidence; adding, *and last of all he was seen of me also.* The Evangelists in like manner produce many Instances of the like Nature. St. *Matthew* speaks of two, St. *Mark* of three, St. *Luke* of as many, and St. *John* of four; each of them selecting such as best suited with the Purpose they had in View when they wrote their Gospels. It is evident at least that St. *Matthew* did so, For in what better Manner could he prove to the *Jews* the Resurrection of *Christ*, than by referring them to the Testimony of some Hundreds of their own Countrymen, who had all seen him after his Death, and were so well convinced of the Reality of his Resurrection, that they believed and embraced his Doctrine? This surely was sufficient to convince those, who required a Number of Witnesses; and was, among the *Jews* at least, the best Answer to those, who on the Credit of a few *Roman* Soldiers, pretended that the Disciples had stolen the Body. Upon this Fact therefore he seems to rest his Cause,

* 1 Cor. xv. 5—8.

Cause, and with it closes his Gospel, adding only the Commission given by *Christ* to the Apostles, and consequently to himself as one of them, *to go and teach all Nations*, and his Promise of *being with them always even unto the End of the World.*

THUS, upon the Supposition that St. *Matthew* wrote his Gospel for the *Jewish* Converts, which St. *Chrysostom* positively asserts, I have endeavoured to account for some Defects and Omissions observable in his Writings, as also for his having given us the History of the Guarding the Sepulchre, *&c.* and of *Christ's* appearing to the Eleven Disciples in *Galilee*, of which the other Evangelists make no mention. I shall now make a few Remarks upon the Particulars related by St. *Mark*, and of which no Notice is taken by St. *Matthew*; but that I may not wander too far from my Purpose, I shall confine them to such only, as belonging to the Facts related by the latter, and having been mentioned only by the former, have induced some People to charge these two Evangelists with contradicting one another. The Circumstances then that I now intend to

con-

consider, are, 1st, That of the Women's *having bought Spices, that they might come and anoint the Body of* Jesus; 2dly, That of *Salome*'s being one of those Women; and 3dly, That of their *entering into the Sepulchre, and seeing a young Man sitting on the right Side clothed in a long white Garment, and their being affrighted.* I have already observed, that St. *Mark* wrote his Gospel for the Use of the *Egyptian Christians*; some say the *Roman*, but whether *Roman* or *Egyptian* is not material to the present Question. It is certain they were *Gentiles*, and Strangers to the *Jewish* Customs and Religion, as may be inferred from several little explanatory Notes dropt up and down in his Gospel. In order therefore to give these Strangers a perfect Intelligence of the Fact, he thought proper to relate, it was necessary for him to begin his Account with that Circumstance of the Women's *having bought Spices*, to anoint the Body of *Jesus*, that they might understand what Business carried them so early to the Sepulchre, and see, by the Preparations made by those Women for the embalming the Body of *Jesus*, and the little Credit given by the Apostles to the Re-

 ports

ports of thoſe, who had ſeen our Lord on the Day of the Reſurrection (which he mentions afterwards) that his Riſing from the Dead, was an Event not in the leaſt expected by any of them, and not believed by the Apoſtles even after ſuch Evidence, as *Jeſus* upbraided them for not aſſenting to; from all which it was natural for them to conclude, that this Fundamental Article of their Faith was neither received nor preached but upon the fulleſt Conviction of its Truth. — But of this laſt Point I ſhall ſpeak more largely hereafter. For his mentioning *Salome* (which was the ſecond Thing propoſed to be conſidered) no other Reaſon can be given, and no better I believe will be required, than that ſhe was there: And as to the third Circumſtance, *viz.* that of their *entering into the Sepulchre, and ſeeing an Angel there ſitting on the right Side,* &c. I ſhall ſhew under the ſecond Head, which I come now to conſider, that tho' St. *Mark* has been more particular in his Relation of it, yet the principal Points are implied in the Account given by St. *Matthew*.

§. 4.

§. 4. THE 2d Head contains the Circumstances in which these two Evangelists agree: And they are these: 1st, The Women's going to the Sepulchre early in the Morning on the first Day of the Week: 2dly, Their being told by an Angel that *Christ* was risen, *&c.* I have nothing to add to the Remarks I have already made upon the first; but upon the second I must observe, that the several Particulars put into the Mouth of this Angel at the Sepulchre by these two Evangelists, are precisely the same, except the Addition of *Peter*'s Name, inserted by St. *Mark*, doubtless for some particular Reason, which it is no Wonder we should not be able to discover at this great Distance of Time. This single Variation will not, I presume, be thought sufficient to overturn the Conclusion I would draw from the exact Agreement of all the other Particulars, that the Fact related by these two sacred Writers is the same; especially if it be considered, that the Circumstance of the Angel's being within the Sepulchre, expressly mentioned by St. *Mark*, is so far from being contradicted by St. *Matthew*, as ſome have imagined, that it is plainly implied by theſe Words, He is not *here.*——*Come* (δεῦτε, which might more properly be tranſlated *come hither) ſee the Place*, where the Lord lay: As is alſo that other Circumſtance of the Women's entering into the Sepulchre, by the *Greek* Term ἐξελθοῦσαι, which ſhould have been rendered *they went out*, inſtead of, *they departed*, as it is in the parallel Paſſage in St. *Mark.* To which let me farther add, that the Deſcription of the Angel's Cloathing, which was a long *white* Garment, according to St. *Mark*, correſponds with the only Particular relating to it taken notice of by St. *Matthew*, which was, its Whiteneſs: *His Raiment was white as Snow.* In the latter indeed this Angel is alſo painted with a *Countenance like Lightning, and the Keepers* are ſaid to have *trembled, &c.* for fear of him. The Purpoſe of this Angel's deſcending from Heaven, ſeems to have been not only to roll away the Stone from the Mouth of the Sepulchre, that the Women who were on their Way thither might have free Entrance into it, but alſo to fright away the Soldiers, who were ſet to guard it; and who,

 had

had they continued there, would certainly not have permitted the Disciples of *Jesus* to have made the necessary Inquiries for their Conviction, could it be supposed that either they, or the Women would have attempted to enter into the Sepulchre, while it was surrounded by a *Roman* Guard. For this End it is not unreasonable to suppose he might not only raise an Earthquake, but assume a Countenance of Terror, and after it was accomplished put on the milder Appearance of a *young Man*, in which Form the Women, as St. *Mark* says, saw him *sitting within the Sepulchre, on the right side*. This Supposition, I say, is neither unreasonable nor presumptuous. For, altho' to argue from the Event to the Design or Intention may, in judging of human Affairs, be deceitful or precarious, yet in the Actions of God, the supreme Disposer of all Events, it is most certain and conclusive. Thus in the present Case, the sudden Appearance of an Angel from Heaven, attended by an Earthquake, * his removing by his single Strength a Stone, which (according to *Beza*'s

 Copy

* See *Whiston* on the Resurrection, &c. according to *Beza*, &c.

Copy of St. *Luke*'s Gospel) twenty Men could hardly roll, his taking his Station upon it, and from thence, with a Countenance like Lightning, blazing and flashing amid the Darkness of the Night, were Circumstances so full of Terror and Amazement, that they could not fail of producing, even in the Hearts of *Roman* Soldiers, the Consternation mentioned by the Evangelist, and driving them from a Post, which a Divinity (for so according to their Way of thinking and speaking they must have stiled the Angel) had now taken Possession of. A Cause so fitted to produce such an Effect, is an Argument of its being intended to produce it; and the Intention being answered by the Event, is a sufficient Reason for varying afterwards the Manner of proceeding. Accordingly the Angel, after he had removed the Stone, and frighted away the Keepers from the Sepulchre, quitted his Station on the Outside, put off his Terrors, and entering into the Sepulchre, sat there in the Form of a *young Man*, to acquaint the Women that *Jesus of Nazareth*, whom they sought in the Grave, was risen from the Dead. That the Angel was not seen by the Women

sitting

sitting on the Stone without the Sepulchre, is evident not only from the Silence of all the Evangelists, with regard to such an Appearance, but also from what has already been observed concerning *Mary Magdalene*, who, tho' she saw the Stone rolled away from the Sepulchre, yet saw no Angel, as I shewed above. Besides, had the Angel remained sitting on the Stone without the Sepulchre, with all his Terrors about him, he would in all Probability, by frightening away the Women and Disciples, as well as the Soldiers, have prevented those Visits to the Sepulchre, which he came on purpose to facilitate. It was necessary therefore either that he should not appear at all to the Women, or that he should appear within the Sepulchre; and in a Form, which altho' more than human, might however not be so terrible, as to deprive them of their Senses, and render them incapable of hearing, certainly of remembering that Message, which he commanded them to deliver to the Disciples. From all which Considerations it may fairly be concluded, that the Appearance of the Angel without the Sepulchre, mentioned by St. *Matthew*, was to the Keepers

 only;

only; and that when he was seen by the Women, he was within the Sepulchre, as St. *Mark* expresly says, and as the Words above-cited from St. *Matthew* strongly imply; so that these two Evangelists agree in relating not only the Words spoken by the Angel, but the principal, and as it were characteristical Circumstances of the Fact, which from this Agreement I would infer to be one and the same. The like Agreement is also to be found in their Account of the Terror of the Women upon seeing the Angel, their speedy Flight from the Sepulchre, and the Disorder and Confusion which so extraordinary an Event occasioned in their Minds; a confused and troubled Mixture of Terror, Astonishment and Joy; which, according to St. *Mark*, was so great as to prevent their telling what had happened, to those they met upon the Way: So must we understand *neither said they any thing to any man.* For it is not to be imagined that they never opened their Lips about it. Their Silence doubtless ended with the Cause of it, *viz.* their Terror and Amazement, and these in all Probability vanished upon their seeing *Christ* himself, who, as St. *Matthew* hath informed

formed us, met them, *as they were going to tell the Disciples* the Message of the Angel; accosted them with an *All hail*, and bade them dismiss their Fears. But of this more hereafter.

§. 5. I COME now under the 3d Head to consider those Particulars, in which these two Evangelists are thought to clash and disagree with each other. But so many of these have been already examined, and, as I hope, reconciled, under the two preceding Divisions, that there remains to be discussed in this but one single Point, arising from the seeming different Accounts of the Time when the Women came to the Sepulchre. St. *Matthew* says, that *Mary Magdalene* and the other *Mary came to see the Sepulchre, as it began to dawn*; St. *Mark*, *They came unto the Sepulchre at the rising of the Sun.* To which I must add St. *John*, who speaking of the same Persons, and the same Fact, says, they came *when it was yet dark*. The σκοτίας ἔτι οὔσης of the latter, and the τῇ ἐπιφωσκούσῃ of St. *Matthew*, that signifying it being yet dark, and this, the Day beginning to dawn, will, I believe, without any

any Difficulty be allowed to denote the ſame Point of Time, *viz.* the Ending of the Night, and the Beginning of the Day; the only Queſtion therefore is, how this can be reconciled with the Time mentioned by St. *Mark*, namely, *the Riſing of the Sun.* But this Queſtion, how perplexing ſoever it may appear at firſt ſight, is eaſily reſolved, only by ſuppoſing that St. *Matthew*, and with him St. *John*, ſpeaks of the Women's ſetting out, and St. *Mark* of their Arrival at the Sepulchre. And indeed the Order of St. *Matthew*'s Narration requires that his Words ſhould be underſtood to ſignify the Time of their ſetting out; otherwiſe, all that is related of the Earthquake, the Deſcent of the Angel, *&c.* muſt be thrown into a Parentheſis, which very much diſturbs the Series of the Story, and introduces much greater Harſhneſſes into the Conſtruction, than any avoided by it. Nay, for my own Part, I confeſs I can ſee no Harſhneſs in the Interpretation now contended for. The *Greek* Word ἦλθε in St. *Matthew*, might as well have been tranſlated *went* as *came*, the Verb ἔρχομαι ſignifying both to *go* and to *come*, and conſequently being capable of either

ther Senſe, according as the Context ſhall require. That in St. *Matthew*, as I ſaid before, requires us to take the Word ἦλθε in the former, for the Sake of Order, and for another Reaſon, which I ſhall now explain. The principal Fact, upon the Account of which the whole Story of the Women's going to the Sepulchre ſeems to have been related, is the Reſurrection of *Chriſt*, and this Fact is abſolutely without a Date, if the Words of St. *Matthew* are to be underſtood to denote the Time of the Women's Arrival at the Sepulchre. When I ſay without a Date, I mean, that it does not appear from any thing in St. *Matthew* or the other Evangeliſts, what Hour of that Night this great Event happened. All the Information they give us is, that when the Women came to the Sepulchre, they were told by Angels he was riſen: But on the contrary, by underſtanding St. *Matthew* to ſpeak of the Time of *Mary Magdalene*'s *ſetting out* to take a View of the Sepulchre, we have the Date of the Reſurrection ſettled, and know preciſely that *Chriſt* roſe from the Dead between the Dawning of the Day and the Sun-riſing. And can

any

any ſubſtantial Reaſon be aſſigned why St. *Matthew*, having thought fit to enter into ſo circumſtantial an Account of the Reſurrection, ſhould omit the Date of ſo important a Fact? or that, not intending to mark it, by mentioning the Time of the Women's going to the Sepulchre, he ſhould place that Fact before another, which in Order of Time was prior to it? All theſe Conſiderations therefore are, in my Opinion, powerful Arguments for underſtanding this Paſſage of St. *Matthew* in the Senſe above expreſt. About St. *Mark*'s Meaning there is no Diſpute. He certainly intended to expreſs the Time of the Women's Arrival at the Sepulchre; his Words cannot be taken in any other Senſe. Thoſe of St. *John* are limited to the ſame Interpretation with thoſe of St. *Matthew*, it having been allowed before that they both ſpeak of the ſame Point of Time.

BEFORE I quit the Examination of theſe Evangeliſts I beg leave to add a few Remarks, on occaſion of a Word made uſe of in this Place both by *Mark* and *John*, the explaining of which will ſet in a proper Light

ſome

ſome Paſſages, that have not hitherto been brought ſufficiently in View. The Word I mean is πρωῒ, which, having by our Tranſlators been rendered by the *Engliſh* Word *early*, hath been limited to that Senſe only; and yet it has a farther Signification, and imports not * *maturè* only, but *prematurè*, *ante conſtitutum tempus*; not only *early*, but *over-early*, *before the appointed time*; and in this Senſe I am perſuaded it was here uſed by the Evangeliſts. For had they intended to denote only the Time of the Women's ſetting out, and arriving at the Sepulchre, the deſcriptive Phraſes *while it was yet dark*, and *at the riſing of the Sun* would have been ſufficient, and the more general Word *early* abſolutely redundant; whereas in the other Senſe it is very ſignificant, and greatly tends to illuſtrate and confirm what I hope more fully to make appear by comparing the ſeveral Parts of this Hiſtory together, that the Women came at different Times to the Sepulchre, and not all at once, as has been imagined. The Buſineſs that carried them all thither was to pay their laſt Reſpects to their deceaſed Maſter, by embalming his Body, for which

* Vid. Scap. Lexicon.

which End they had bought and prepared Unguents and Spices, but were obliged to defer their pious Work by the coming on of the Sabbath, upon which Day *they rested*, says St. *Luke*, *according to the Commandment*. On the Eve of the Sabbath therefore, when they parted, and each retired to their several Habitations, it is most natural to suppose that they agreed to meet upon a certain Hour at the Sepulchre; and as the Errand upon which they were employed required Day-light, the Hour agreed on in all Probability was soon after the Rising of the Sun; their Apprehension of the *Jews*, as well as their Zeal to their Master prompting them to take the earliest Opportunity. But *Mary Magdalene*, it seems, whether from a natural Eagerness of Temper, or a more ardent Affection for her Lord, to whom she had the greatest Obligations, or from a higher Cause, set out together with the other *Mary*, just as the Day began to break, in order *to take a View* of the Sepulchre; and having either called upon *Salome*, or joined her in the Way, came thither together with her, πρωῒ, *early*, *before the Time agreed on*. This, in my Opinion, is a very natural Account of the whole Matter, and points out the Importance of theſe remarkable Expreſſions, went to *ſee the Sepulchre*, in St. *Matthew*, and *who ſhall roll away the Stone for us*, in St. *Mark*. For 1ſt, the Reaſon of theſe two *Maries* ſetting out ſo early is here aſſigned: They went *to take a View* of the Sepulchre, *i. e.* in general; to ſee if all Things were in the ſame Condition, in which they had left them two Days before, that if in that Interval any thing extraordinary had happened, they might report it to their Companions, and in Conjunction with them take their Meaſures accordingly. Hence is it alſo evident in the ſecond Place, why they were ſo few in Number; they came *to view the Sepulchre*, and came before the Time appointed for their Meeting. 2dly, As upon the preſent Suppoſition there were but three Women, who came firſt to the Sepulchre, their Deſign in coming ſo early could be no other than that expreſſed by St. *Matthew*; for they knew that they themſelves were not able to roll away the Stone, which two of them at leaſt (the two *Maries*) had ſeen placed there by

*Joſeph*

*Joseph* of *Arimathea* †, and which they knew could not be removed without a great Number of Hands. Accordingly, *as they drew near they said among themselves, Who shall roll away the Stone for us from the Door of the Sepulchre?* These Words intimate, that one of their chief Views in coming to see the Sepulchre was to survey this Stone, which closed up the Entrance into it, and to consider whether they and the other Women, who were to meet them there, were by themselves able to remove it; or whether they must have Recourse to the Assistance of others. For, *Who shall roll away the Stone for us?* implies a Sense of their own Inability, and of the Necessity of calling in others; after which the only Thing to be considered was whom and how many? This therefore was the Point under Deliberation when they approached the Sepulchre. 2dly, It is also plain from these Words, that they did not expect to find any body there, and consequently that they knew nothing of the Guard, which the High Priest had set to watch the Sepulchre; of which had they received any Intelligence, they would hardly

† Mark xv. 47.

hardly ventured to come at all; or would not have deliberated about rolling away the Stone; as the only or greatest Difficulty.

§. 6. St LUKE, Chap. xxiv.

*NOW upon the first Day of the Week, very early in the Morning, they came unto the Sepulchre, bringing the Spices which they had prepared, and certain others with them: And they found the Stone rolled away from the Sepulchre. And they entered in, and found not the Body of the Lord* Jesus. *And it came to pass as they were much perplexed thereabout, behold two Men stood by them in shining Garments; and as they were afraid, and bowed down their Faces to the Earth, they said unto them, Why seek ye the Living among the Dead? he is not here, but is risen. Remember how he spake unto you, when he was yet in* Galilee, *saying, The Son of Man must be delivered into the Hands of sinful Men, and be crucified, and the third Day rise again. And they remembered his Words, and returned from the Sepulchre, and told all these Things unto the Eleven, and to all the rest. It was* Mary Magdalene, *and* Joanna, *and* Mary *the Mother of* James, *and other Women that were with them, which told these Things unto the Apostles. And their Words seemed to them as idle Tales, and they believed them not. Then arose* Peter *and ran unto the Sepulchre, and stooping down he beheld the Linen Clothes laid by themselves, and departed, wondering in himself at that which was come to pass.*

In this Relation of St. *Luke's* are many Particulars that differ greatly from those mentioned by the other Evangelists. For 1st, The Women entering into the Sepulchre see neither Angel nor Angels; And 2dly, Not finding the Body of the Lord *Jesus*, they fall into great Perplexity. 3dly, In the midst of this Perplexity *there stood by them two Men in shining Garments*; Who, 4thly, Say to them Words very different from those spoken by the Angel in St. *Matthew* and St. *Mark*. 5thly, When those Women return from the Sepulchre, and tell all these Things unto the Eleven and all the rest, St. *Peter* is made to be present, and upon their Report to rise immediately and run to the Sepulchre, *&c.* These Marks of Difference, one would imagine, were sufficient to keep any one from confounding

founding the Stories above-cited of *Joanna* and St. *Peter*, with those concerning the *Maries* and that Disciple related in the other Gospels; especially as they have been observed and acknowledged as well by the Christian as the Infidel; the latter of whom hath produced them to support the Charge of Inconsistency and Contradiction, which he hath endeavoured to fix upon the sacred Writers; while the former, seduced and dazled by some few Points of Resemblance, hath agreed with him in allowing these different Facts to be the same; but denying his Conclusion, hath laboured to reconcile the Inconsistencies, by Rules and Methods of Interpretation, which, as they are strained and unnatural, tend only to discover the Greatness of his Embarrassment. Whereas the true Way, in my Opinion, of answering this Charge, is to shew that it is founded upon a Mistake, by shewing that the Evangelists relate different, but not inconsistent Facts; and that instead of clashing and disagreeing, they mutually confirm, illustrate and support each other's Evidence. This therefore I shall now endeavour to do, by making a few Remarks upon the several Articles above-mentioned. I shall begin with that relating to St. *Peter*, because the settling of that will settle many other Points. *Then arose* Peter, *and ran unto the Sepulchre, and stooping down he beheld the Linen Clothes laid by themselves, and departed, wondering in himself at that which was come to pass.* This Fact has always been taken to be the same with that related by St. *John*, from which however it differs, among other things, in this very material Circumstance, *viz.* That whereas St. *John* expresly says, that *Peter went into* the Sepulchre, while he [*John*] who got thither first, contented himself with barely *stooping down*, and *looking into* it, St. *Luke*, in the Passage before us, tells us, that *Peter stooping down, and looking in* beheld the Linen Clothes laid by themselves, and departed. The Word παρακύψας (stooping down and *looking in*) used by both Evangelists, and in the latter applied only to St. *Peter*, in the former only to St. *John*, is in his Gospel plainly distinguished from the Word εἰσῆλθεν (*entered in*) and set in direct Opposition to it; and that not by the Force of Etymology and Construction only, but by some Particulars resulting refulting from the Actions fignified by thofe two Words, which prove them to be diftinct and different from each other. He who *went into* the Sepulchre, faw more than he, who *ftaying without, only ftooped down and looked in.* Thus *Peter* and *John*, when they *entered* into the Sepulchre, faw *not only* the Linen Clothes lie, *but* the Napkin that was about his Head, not lying with the Linen Clothes, but wrapped together in a Place by itfelf: but when they only *ftooped down and looked in*, they could fee only the Linen Clothes, as is evident from the Words of St. *John*; the whole Paffage runs thus:——Peter *therefore went forth, and that other Difciple, and came to the Sepulchre, and the other Difciple did out-run* Peter, *and came firft to the Sepulchre, and he* ftooping down, and *looking in*, faw the Linen Clothes lying, yet went he not in. *Then cometh* Simon Peter *following him*, and went into the Sepulchre, *and feeth the Linen Clothes lie*, and the Napkin, *that was about his Head*, not lying with the Linen Clothes, but wrapped together in a Place by itfelf. Then went in alfo that other Difciple —— and faw, &c. Now thefe two Actions being

ing by these Marks as clearly distinguished from each other in St. *John*, as the different Places where they were performed can be by the Terms *Entrance* and *Inside* of the Sepulchre, and as so distinguished having been separately performed by that Apostle, they must also necessarily be taken for separate and distinct Actions, when related of St. *Peter*. And if it be reasonable to conclude from St. *John*'s Account that *Peter*, when he came with him to the Sepulchre, did not stop at the Entrance, *stoop down and look in*, but that he *entered* into it; it is no less reasonable to conclude from St. *Luke*'s Narration, that when he came, at the Time mentioned by him, he did not enter in, but *stooping down*, beheld the Linen Clothes and departed, especially if the Force of the *Greek* Word μόνα be considered, and the whole Passage rendered, as it ought to have been, *beheld the* Linen Clothes *only* lying, τὰ ὀθόνια κείμενα μόνα. From all which it evidently follows, that the Fact here related of St. *Peter*, and that related of him by St. *John*, are separate and distinct Facts, and not one and the same, as has been imagined. And as the Facts were different,

different, ſo did they take their Riſe from two different Occaſions, or in other Words, as it is evident from all that has been juſt now ſaid, that *Peter* went twice to the Sepulchre, ſo there are two diſtinct Reaſons for his ſo doing aſſigned in the Goſpels of *Luke* and *John, viz.* the Report of *Mary Magdalene*, and that of *Joanna* and the other Women. By the former having been told that the Body of *Jeſus* was taken out of the Sepulchre, he ran in great Haſte to examine into the Truth of that Account, and in purſuance of this Intent entered into the Sepulchre, that he might receive a thorough Satisfaction upon that Point. In the latter were two additional Circumſtances of Importance ſufficient to awaken the Curioſity of a leſs zealous Diſciple than St. *Peter*, whoſe Affection for his Lord was like his natural Temper, fervent and impetuous. When he heard therefore from *Joanna* and the other Women of a Viſion of Angels, who had appeared to them at the Sepulchre, and informed them that *Chriſt* was riſen, can we wonder at his running thither a *ſecond Time*, in Hopes of receiving ſome Confirmation of the Truth of that Report, which tho' treated by the rest of the Apostles as an idle Tale, he certainly gave Credit to, as the whole Tenor of this Passage implies? I say a *second Time*; because had he gone for the first Time, upon this Report of *Joanna*'s, he could have had no Inducement to have gone to the Sepulchre a second Time from any thing he could learn from the first Report made by *Mary Magdalene*, whose Account contained nothing but what was implied in that given by *Joanna* and the other Women. His Behaviour also upon this Occasion, when he only *stooped down* and looked into the Sepulchre, so different from the former, when he *entered into it*, is very rational, and consonant with the Purpose of this second Visit, which was, to see if the Angels who had appeared to the Women at the Sepulchre, were still there; this could as well be discovered by *looking*, as by *going*, into the Sepulchre, as is plain from the Story of *Mary Magdalene*, who *stooping down and looking in*, saw two Angels sitting, the one at the Head and the other at the Feet where the Body of *Jesus* had lain, as St. *John* tells us.

HAVING

HAVING now, as I hope, proved that this Viſit of St. *Peter*'s to the Sepulchre, mentioned by St. *Luke*, muſt have been his ſecond Viſit, I have cleared this Paſſage from two Objections that lay againſt it; one, that it did not agree with the Relation given by St. *John*; and the other, that it diſturbed and confounded the whole Order of St. *Luke*'s Narration: ſo that notwithſtanding this Verſe is wanting both in the *Greek* and *Latin* Copies of *Beza*, there is no Reaſon for rejecting it, as ſome have propoſed.

THIS Point being ſettled, I beg leave to make a few Inferences from it, in order to explain ſome Paſſages in the preceding Verſes of this Chapter.

FIRST then, it is plain from this and the ninth Verſe, that St. *Peter*, after he had been with St. *John* and *Mary Magdalene* at the Sepulchre, was now got together with the other Apoſtles and Diſciples, whom in all Probability he and *John* had aſſembled upon the

Occaſion

Occasion of *Mary Magdalene*'s Report. *Peter*, I say, and *John*, had in all Probability assembled the other Disciples and Apostles to inform them of what they had heard from *Mary Magdalene*, and of their having been themselves at the Sepulchre to examine into the Truth of her Report. For it is not to be imagined, that these Apostles would not have immediately communicated to the rest an Event of so much Consequence to them all, as that of the Lord's Body being missing from the Sepulchre. And as we now find them gathered together and *Peter* with them, it is no unnatural Supposition that they had been summoned thither by *John* and *Peter*. At least their meeting together so early in the Morning is this Way accounted for. Here then we see the Reason of St. *Luke*'s naming *Mary Magdalene* and the other *Mary* among those, which told these Things to the Apostles. For altho' these two Women were not with *Joanna* and her Set, and consequently could not have joined with them in relating to the Apostles the Vision of the two Angels, &c. yet as the Account of their having found the

Stone

Stone rolled away, and the Body of *Jesus* missing had been reported from them by *Peter* and *John* to the other Apostles, before the Return of *Joanna* from the Sepulchre, St. *Luke* thought fit to set them down as Evidences of some of the Facts related by him; and indeed it was very proper to produce the Testimony of the two *Maries* concerning the Stone's being rolled away, and the Body gone, because they went first to the Sepulchre, and first gave an Account of those two Particulars to the Apostles. I here join the other *Mary* with *Mary Magdalene*; for tho' I think it is pretty plain from St. *John*, that she alone brought this Account; yet it is remarkable that in her Narration she says, *We* know not where they have laid him, speaking, as it were, in the Name of the other *Mary* and her own; and doubtless she did not omit to acquaint them that the other *Mary* came with her to the Sepulchre; so that this Report, tho' made by *Mary Magdalene* alone, may fairly be taken for the joint Report of the two *Maries*, and was probably stiled so by *Peter* and *John*, and therefore represented as such by St. *Luke* in the Passage before us.

SECONDLY,

SECONDLY, From hence alſo I infer, that the Reports of the Women were made ſeparately, and at different Times. For if *Peter* went twice to the Sepulchre, there muſt have been two diſtinct Reaſons for his ſo doing, which Reaſons I have ſhewn to be the Reports of *Mary Magdalene* and *Joanna*: And as there was a conſiderable Interval between his firſt and ſecond Viſit, a proportionable Space of Time muſt have intervened between the two Reports. After *Mary Magdalene*'s he had been at the Sepulchre, had returned from thence to his own Home, and was now got with the other Apoſtles and Diſciples, whom, as I ſaid, he and *John* had in all Probability called together, before *Joanna* and the Women with her came to make theirs.

THIRDLY, As the Reports were made at different Times, and by different Women, as the Facts reported were different, and ſaid to have happened all in the ſame Place, *viz.* at the Sepulchre, and as theſe Facts muſt of Conſequence have happened at different Times; it follows that the Women, who reported thoſe Facts as happening in their Preſence, muſt have been at

the

the Sepulchre at different Times. For had they been all present at each of these Events, no Reason can be given for their differing so widely in their Relations, and pretty difficult will it be to account for their varying so much as to the Time of making their Reports. Here then is a strong Argument in favour of what I have before advanced concerning the Women's coming at different Times to the Sepulchre, and particularly about the *Maries* coming thither earlier than the rest. The Reason for their so doing I have already pointed out in my Observations upon St. *Mark*, and have shewn, that upon the Supposition of that Reason's being the true one, their whole Conduct was proper and consistent: Which leads me to consider that of *Joanna* and the other Women, who came somewhat later, and with another Purpose, to the Sepulchre. The former came to take *a View or Survey of the Sepulchre*, as St. *Matthew* expressly says; the latter came to *embalm or anoint the Lord's Body*, and for that End not only *brought the Spices, which they had prepared*, but were also accompanied by other Women. *Other* Women, must mean some besides

ſides thoſe who followed *Jeſus* from *Galilee*, of whom alone St. *Luke* ſpeaks in the former Part of this Verſe, and the latter Part of the preceding Chapter. By theſe therefore, as contradiſtinguiſhed from the *Galilean* Women, he probably means the Women of *Jeruſalem*, a great Company of whom followed *Jeſus* as he was going to his Crucifixion, bewailing and lamenting him. [See the 27th Verſe of the preceding Chapter.] But what Number of them went upon this Occaſion with the Women of *Galilee*, is not any where ſaid; neither, of theſe, are any named beſides *Joanna*, *Mary Magdalene*, and *Mary* the Mother of *James*, tho' many others followed *Jeſus* from *Galilee* to *Jeruſalem*, as both *Matthew* (c. 27. v. 55.) and St. *Mark* (c. 15. v. 41.) inform us, and were preſent at his Crucifixion. It is therefore very probable that moſt, if not all, of thoſe who were wont to miniſter to him in *Galilee*, who attended him to *Jeruſalem*, and accompanied him even to Mount *Calvary*, contributed to this pious Office of embalming their Maſter's Body, either by buying and preparing the Unguents and Spices, and carrying them to the Sepulchre, or or by going to assist their Companions in embalming the Body and rolling away the Stone, for which Purpose I suppose the Women of *Jerusalem* principally attended, since none of them seem to have made any Purchase of Spices for embalming the Body; and for this last Purpose it is farther probable they thought their Numbers sufficient. Accordingly we do not find them saying among themselves, Who shall roll away the Stone for us, as the *Maries* did; nor do we find the *Maries bringing* the Spices which they had bought, as is here related of *Joanna* and *those with her*; and doubtless the Evangelists had a Meaning in their Use and Application of these Expressions, the former of which is very agreeable to the Purpose that carried the *Maries* so early to the Sepulchre, as is the latter to that of *Joanna*, who coming to embalm the Body, brought with her all that was necessary for performing that Business, *viz.* the Spices, and other Women to assist her in rolling away the Stone, *&c.* The different Conduct of the Women therefore indicates their several Purposes in going to the Sepulchre, and tends to confirm what I have been

all

all along labouring to prove, that they went thither at different Times, and not all together.

And as their having had different Motives was the Cause of their going at different Times, and dividing themselves into different Companies, so from their coming to the Sepulchre in different Bodies, sprang a Subdivision of one of those Companies, which I shall now explain. The two *Maries* and *Salome* came first to the Sepulchre, and as they drew near, lifting up their Eyes, perceived that the Stone, which was very great, was rolled away from the Entrance; upon sight of which, *Mary Magdalene*, concluding that the Body of *Jesus* was taken away, ran immediately to acquaint *Peter* and *John* with it, leaving her two Companions at the Sepulchre. That she was alone when she came to those two Apostles, is strongly implied by the whole Tenor of that Passage in St. *John*, where this Fact is related, as I have already observed; and that she left her Companions at the Sepulchre, is as evident from what St. *Mark* says of their entering into the Sepulchre, &c.

&c. The Reason of which probably was this; she knew that *Joanna* and her Company would not be long before they came thither, and might therefore think it proper to desire the other *Mary* and *Salome* to wait for them there, to inform them that they had found the Stone rolled away, &c. and that she was gone to acquaint *Peter* and *John* with it: But whether this, or any other Reason was the Cause of *Mary Magdalene*'s going by herself to *Peter* and *John*, and the other two Women's staying behind at the Sepulchre, is not very material to inquire; all I contend for is, that so it was; and that hence arose a Subdivision of this Company, that gave Occasion to two Appearances of Angels, and as many of *Christ*, and consequently multiplied the Proofs and Witnesses of the Resurrection.

I HOPE by this time it is sufficiently evident, that the Facts related by the several Women to the Apostles were different and distinct Facts; and therefore I think it unnecessary to enter into any farther Argument upon that Point. And altho' in the Beginning of my Observations upon this Chapter of St.

*Luke*, I noted ſome Particulars wherein this Story of *Joanna* differs from that of the other Women, and promiſed to make ſome Remarks upon them; yet, for the laſt mentioned Reaſon, I dare ſay I ſhall be eaſily acquitted of my Promiſe, eſpecially as thoſe Marks of Difference are ſo obvious and ſtriking, that little more need be done than pointing them out to Obſervation. I muſt however beg leave to obſerve, that the Poſition relating to the Angels appearing and diſappearing as they thought proper, laid down in my Remarks upon St. *John*, is farther proved by the Manner of their appearing mentioned here in Saint *Luke*, which is implied to have been ſudden, not only by the Force and Import of the Expreſſion, but by the remarkable Circumſtance of their not being ſeen by the Women, at their entering into the Sepulchre.

§. 7. THO' the following Paſſage of this Chapter relating to *Chriſt*'s Appearance to the Diſciples at *Emmaus* hath been already produced in part, yet I think it proper to inſert it intire in this Place, that by the Reader's having it all before him at once, he may be better able to judge of the Obſervation I intend to make upon it.

*AND behold two of them went that ſame Day to a Village called* Emmaus, *which was from* Jeruſalem *about threeſcore Furlongs. And they talked together of all thoſe Things that had happened. And it came to paſs that while they communed together, and reaſoned,* Jeſus *himſelf drew near, and went with them; but their Eyes were holden that they ſhould not know him. And he ſaid unto them, What manner of Communications are theſe, that ye have one to another, as ye walk and are ſad? And one of them, whoſe Name was* Cleopas, *anſwering, ſaid unto him, Art thou only a Stranger in* Jeruſalem, *and haſt not known the Things which are come to paſs there in theſe Days? And he ſaid unto them, What Things? And they ſaid unto him, Concerning* Jeſus *of* Nazareth, *which was a Prophet mighty in Deed and Word before God, and all the People; and how the Chief Prieſts and our Rulers delivered him to be condemned to Death, and have crucified him. But we truſted that it had been He which ſhould have redeemed* Iſrael: *And beſide all this, to-day is the third Day since these Things were done. Yea, and certain Women also of our Company made us astonished, which were early at the Sepulchre; and when they found not his Body, they came, saying, that they had also seen a Vision of Angels, which said that he was alive. And certain of them which were with us, went to the Sepulchre, and found it even so as the Women had said: But him they saw not. Then he said unto them, O Fools, and slow of Heart to believe all that the Prophets have spoken! Ought not* Christ *to have suffered these Things, and to enter into his Glory? And beginning at* Moses *and all the Prophets, he expounded unto them in all the Scriptures the Things concerning himself. And they drew nigh unto the Village whither they went, and he made as though he would have gone farther. But they constrained him, saying, Abide with us, for it is towards Evening, and the Day is far spent. And he went in to tarry with them. And it came to pass as he sat at Meat with them, he took Bread and blessed it, and brake and gave to them. And their Eyes were opened, and they knew him; and he vanished out of their Sight. And they said one to another, Did not our Hearts burn within us, while*

*while he talked with us by the Way, and while he opened to us the Scriptures? And they rose up the same Hour, and returned to* Jerusalem, *and found the Eleven gathered together, and them that were with them, saying, The Lord is risen indeed, and hath appeared to* Simon. *And they told what Things were done in the Way, and how he was known of them in breaking of Bread.*

WHOEVER reads this Story over with any Degree of Attention, and considers the Subject of the Conversation, which our Saviour held with the two Disciples upon the Road to *Emmaus*, will perceive that it must have arisen from what the Angels had said to the Women, related in the preceding Verses of this Chapter. To set this Matter in the clearest Light, we will put the several Parts together. The Angels said to the Women, who came to embalm the Body of *Jesus*, *He is not here, but is risen. Remember how he spake unto you, when he was yet in* Galilee, *saying, The Son of Man must be delivered into the Hands of sinful Men, and be crucified, and the third Day rise again.* The Words of our Saviour referred to by the Angels are these (*Luke* xviii. ver. 31—33.) *Then he took unto him the Twelve, and said unto them, Behold we go up to* Jerusalem, *and all Things that are written by the Prophets concerning the Son of Man shall be accomplished. For he shall be delivered unto the* Gentiles, *and shall be mocked, and spitefully entreated, and spitted on; and they shall scourge him, and put him to Death, and the third Day he shall rise again.* The Words of the Angels these two Disciples had heard from the Women, before they left *Jerusalem*; and as they were walking towards *Emmaus*, and talking over all the wonderful Things that had come to pass, they seem at last to have fallen into a Debate upon the Subject of these Words, and the Prophecies referred to by them, just as our Saviour drew near. That they were engaged in some Argument or Disquisition, I infer, not only from the *Greek* Word συζητεῖν, which signifies to discuss, examine, or inquire together; but from our Saviour's Question, who, apparently, having over-heard some Part of their Discourse, asks them, Τινες οἱ λόγοι οὗτοι οὓς ἀντιβάλλετε πρὸς ἀλλήλους; *What Argu-*

*Arguments are these, that ye are debating one with another, while ye walk and are sad?* The Subject of their Argument appears in their Answer to this Question, in which they give him to understand that they were reasoning upon the Things that had come to pass concerning *Jesus of Nazareth, whom,* say they, alluding plainly to the Words of the Angels, *the Chief Priests and our Rulers have delivered to be condemned to Death, and have crucified him.* And hence arises all our Sadness, for *we trusted that it had been He which should have redeemed* Israel; *and over and above all these Things, to-day is the third Day since these Things were done* (another Allusion to the Words of the Angels;) and *to-day some Women of our Company* astonished us with an Account of their having been early at the Sepulchre, and, not finding the Body of *Jesus,* having there been told by Angels that he was risen from the Dead. And some of our Companions, running immediately to the Sepulchre, found the Report of the Women to be true; *but him they saw not.* The Sufferings, and Death, and Resurrection of *Jesus* were the Subjects of their Debates, foretold,

 as

as the Angels bade them remember, out of the Prophets, by *Christ* himself; and the Scope of their Inquiry was how to reconcile these Events with the Prophecies, to which they were referred. Part of them they had seen accomplished in the Sufferings and Death of *Christ*; and that ought to have assured them of the Accomplishment of the other Part. But either from not understanding, or from a Backwardness in believing all that the Prophets had said, they stopped short of this Conclusion. For this Ignorance and Backwardness *Christ* reproves them; asks them whether (according to the Prophets) *Christ ought not to have suffered these Things, and to enter into his Glory*, i. e. to rise again; and then *beginning at* Moses *and all the Prophets, he expounds to them in all the Scriptures the Things concerning himself*. The Connexion is visible; at the Beginning of the Chapter the Angels refer the Disciples for the Proof of the Resurrection to the Prophets; and here, *Christ* joining two of those Disciples on the Road, is, by their Discourse upon that Subject, led to explain those Prophecies, and prove from them that the *Messiah* was certainly risen from the

the Dead. And in the like Manner is the remaining Part of this Chapter to Verse the 49th, connected with this and the preceding. For these two Disciples returning to *Jerusalem*, relate to the Apostles and the rest, whom they found gathered together, what had passed between *Christ* and them upon the Road to *Emmaus*; and while they were speaking, *Christ* himself appears; and after having given them sensible Proofs of his being risen from the Dead, reminds them, as the Angel had done, of the Words which he spake unto them in *Galilee*, saying, *These are the Words which I spake unto you, while I was yet with you, that all things must be fulfilled, which were written in the Law of* Moses, *and in the Prophets, and in the Psalms concerning me. Then opened he their Understanding, that they might understand the Scriptures, and said unto them, Thus it is written, and thus it behoved* Christ *to suffer, and to rise from the Dead the third Day.*

This Connexion and Dependence of the several Parts of this Chapter upon each other, point out to us the Reason that induced St.

*Luke* to relate the Vision of the two Angels to *Joanna* and the other Women; and at the same Time prove that Vision to be distinct and different from those seen by the *Maries*; each of which had, in like manner, its separate and peculiar Reference to other Facts, as will presently be seen.

§. 8. I SHALL now proceed to consider the Appearances of *Christ* to the Women, on the Day of his Resurrection; which, like those of the Angels, have also been confounded, and from the same Cause, *viz.* From the want of attending with due Care to the several Circumstances, by which they are plainly distinguished from each other. And 1st, I observe, that these Appearances of *Christ* are so connected with the Appearances of the Angels, that these having been proved to be distinct, it follows that those are distinct also. 2dly, St. *Mark* expresly tells us, that *Christ* appeared first to *Mary Magdalene*, which, according to all Propriety of Speech, implies that she was alone at the Time of that Appearance, as I have said once before. But I think it best to set down the Passages themselves, of St. *John* and

St.

St. *Matthew*, in which these Appearances are related. *John*, chap. xx. ver. 11. *But* Mary *stood without at the Sepulchre weeping; and as she wept, she stooped down, and looked into the Sepulchre, and seeth two Angels in White, sitting; the one at the Head, and the other at the Feet, where the Body of* Jesus *had lain; and they say unto her, Woman, why weepest thou? She saith unto them, Because they have taken away my Lord, and I know not where they have laid him. And when she had said thus, she turned herself back, and saw* Jesus *standing, and knew not that it was* Jesus. Jesus *saith unto her, Woman, why weepest thou? Whom seekest thou? She supposing him to be the Gardener, saith unto him, Sir, if thou hast borne him hence, tell me where thou hast laid him, and I will take him away.* Jesus *saith unto her,* Mary! *She turned herself, and saith unto him, Rabboni! which is to say, Master.* Jesus *saith unto her, Touch me not, for I am not yet ascended unto my Father: But go to my Brethren, and say unto them, I ascend unto my Father and your Father, and to my God and your God.* Mary Magdalene *came and told the Disciples that she had seen the Lord, and that he had spoken these Things unto her.* Matth. ch. xxviii.

ver.

ver. 9. *And as they went to tell his Disciples, behold,* Jesus *met them, saying, All hail! And they came and held him by the Feet, and worshipped him. Then said* Jesus *unto them, Be not afraid: Go tell my Brethren that they go into* Galilee, *and there shall they see me.*

After having produced these two Passages, it would be wasting both Time and Words, to go about to prove the Appearances therein mentioned to be different. Compare them, and you will find them disagree in every Circumstance; in the Place, the Persons, the Actions, and the Words: Of which last I must observe, that they refer to two different Events, *viz.* the Ascension of *Christ* into Heaven, and meeting his Disciples in *Galilee*, of which they were Prophecies; and by which they, and consequently these Appearances of *Christ* were not long after verified, tho' discredited at first, and treated as idle Tales.

I have now gone over the several Particulars of the History of the Resurrection, related in the four Evangelists, have examined them with all the Attention I am capable of, and with a sincere Desire of discovering and embracing the Truth; and have, as I think, made out the following Points: 1st, That the Women came at different Times, and in different Companies to the Sepulchre: 2dly, That there were several distinct Appearances of Angels: 3dly, That the Angels were not always visible, but appeared and disappeared as they thought proper: 4thly, That these several Facts were reported to the Apostles at different Times, and by different Women: 5thly, That there were two distinct Appearances of *Christ* to the Women: And 6thly, That St. *Peter* was twice at the Sepulchre. These Points being once established, all the Objections against this Part of the Gospel-History, as contradictory and inconsistent, intirely vanish and come to nought. That very learned and ingenious Men have been embarrassed by these Objections is some Excuse for those who first started them, and those who have lately insisted upon them. Their having now received an Answer, (if that will be allow'd) is a clear Proof that it was always possible to answer them, even with a very moderate Share of com-

common Senſe and Learning. The Nature of the Anſwer itſelf, which is founded upon the uſual, obvious, plain Senſe of the Words, without putting any Force, either upon the particular Expreſſions, or the general Conſtruction of the ſeveral Paſſages, is an Evidence of what I now ſay. So that I muſt needs acknowledge that its having been ſo long miſſed, is Matter of far greater Surprize, than its having been hit upon now.

I SHALL here beg leave to ſubjoin a few Obſervations of a very eminent and judicious Perſon, to whoſe Inſpection I ſubmitted theſe Papers; and in whoſe Approbation of them I have great Reaſon to pride my ſelf. They are as follows:

" To prove the Appearances at the Se-
" pulchre to be different, and made to diffe-
" rent Perſons, two Things concur.

" I. THE ſeveral Accounts as given by
" the Evangeliſts.

"II. The Circumſtances which attended "the Caſe.

"The firſt Point is fully conſidered; and of "the ſecond it is very juſtly remarked, That "the Women having agreed to be early at "the Sepulchre, it fell out naturally, *That* "*ſome came before others.* Now there being at "the Place of Meeting ſomething to terrify "them as faſt as they arrived; it accounts al-"ſo for their Diſperſion, and their not meet-"ing at all in one Body. It may help like-"wiſe to account for the Manner of deliver-"ing their Meſſages to the Apoſtles; ſuppo-"ſing the Meſſages not delivered in the ſame "Order in Point of Time, as the Appearances "happened. For the moſt terrified might be "the lateſt Reporters, tho' they received their "Orders firſt. Which Obſervation is favour-"ed by St. *Mark's* ὐδενὶ ὐδὲν εἶπον, *neither* "*ſaid they any thing to any Man.*

"The Difficulty upon ſtating the Appear-"ances to be different, and made to different "Perſons, ariſes chiefly from *Mary Magdalene*

"being

" being mentioned as present by every Evan-" gelist: But there seems to be this Reason " for it; she was at the Head of the Women, " and the chief of those who attended our " Lord, and followed him from *Galilee*; " and *Mary Magdalene and the Women with* " *her*, denotes the Women who came from " *Galilee*, in the same Manner that *the Eleven* " denotes the Apostles.

" THREE Evangelists say expresly that " *many* Women were present at the Crucifixi-" on: Had it been left so generally, we should " have had no Account who they were. " Therefore St. *Matthew* xxvii. 56. adds, ἐν " αἷς ἦν, among whom was *Mary Magdalene*, " *&c.* So it is again *Mark* xv. 40.—St. *Luke* " having said in general Terms, that the Wo-" men, who followed from *Galilee*, were Spec-" tators of the Crucifixion, goes on with the " Account (xxiv. 1.) of their coming to the " Sepulchre, seeing Angels, and returning to " tell the *Eleven* and all the rest. But to give " Credit to their Report, and to correct the " Omission in not describing them before, he " tells us who they were: And how does he

" describe

" describe them? Why, by saying they were " of the Company of *Mary Magdalene*: Ἦσαν " δὲ ἡ Μαγδαληνὴ &c. xxiv. 10. which " Verse admits, perhaps requires, a different " Reading from that in our Translation.

" THESE Considerations seem to account " for *her* being mentioned in the Transactions " of these Women, tho' not always present " herself. St. *Luke* says (xxiv. 1.) that besides " the Women from *Galilee*, there were *other* " *Women there*. To distinguish those, who " make the Report to the Disciples, from *the* " *other Women*, he adds the Words already " referred to *.

G It

* The Words of St. *Luke* deserve a particular Examination; they run thus in the *Greek*:----Καὶ ὑποςρέψασαι ἀπὸ τοῦ μνημείου ἀπήγγειλαν ταῦτα πάντα τοῖς ἕνδεκα ϗ πᾶσι τοῖς λοιποῖς. Ἦσαν δὲ ἡ Μαγδαληνὴ Μαρία ϗ Ἰωάννα ϗ Μαρία Ἰακώβου, ϗ αἱ λοιπαὶ σὺν αὐταῖς, αἳ ἔλεγον πρὸς τοὺς ἀποςόλους ταῦτα. In English, *And turning back from the Sepulchre, they told all these Things to the Eleven, and to all the rest. Now they, who related those Things to the Apostles, were* Mary Magdalene, *and* Joanna, *and* Mary *the Mother of* James, *and the rest with them*, i. e. *of their Company*. As the Acoount of the Proceedings of the *Galilean* Women begins in the foregoing Chapter, and is carried on without any Interruption to the 9th Verse of this Chapter; so that the several Verbs occurring in this and the preceding Verses are all governed by the same Nominative Case, *viz.* γυναῖκες; in ver. 55. of

" IT is remarkable that St. *Mark* says of " the Women, mentioned by him, no more " than that they had *bought* Spices to anoint " the Body; enough to shew with what Intent " they went to the Tomb; ---- that they had " any Spices *with them* he does not say. But " St. *Luke* says of those he mentions, that they " actually *brought* with them the Spices; and " not only so, but that they had *prepared* them; " that is, made them fit for the Use intended. " The several Drugs were bought singly, each " by itself at the Shop, and were necessarily to " be

of the 23d Chapter, it is evident that ταῦτα πάντα, *all these Things*, must be taken to extend to *all* the Particulars mentioned in that Account, and cannot be confined to the Transactions of the Sepulchre only; and the same Observation holds equally to the ταῦτα in the following Verse. The utmost therefore that can be inferred from St. *Luke*'s naming *Mary Magdalene* and the other *Mary*, is, that they were concerned in some or other of these Transactions, and joined in relating some of these Things to the Apostles; which is true, for they *sat over against the Sepulchre*, when *Joseph* laid in it the Body of the Lord, *Matth*. xxvii. 61. *And beheld where he was laid*; *Mark* xv. 47.——They also *had bought sweet Spices, that they might come and anoint him*; *Mark* xvi. 1. And were the first who came to the Sepulchre that Morning, and brought the first Account of the Body's being missing; *Matt*. and *Mark*. And tho' by comparing the Accounts given by the other Evangelists with this

" be mixed, or melted together for Use: And
" I imagine that, tho' all the Women joined in
" buying the Spices, yet the Care of getting
" and preparing them was left particularly to
" the Women mentioned by St. *Luke*: And as
" they were *Galileans*, and not at Home at *Je-*
" *rusalem*, and probably unacquainted with
" the Method of embalming Bodies, that they
" employed some Inhabitants of the Place to
" buy and prepare the Spices, and to go with
" them to apply them to the Body; and these
" are the τινες σὺν ἀυταῖς, *others with them*, in
" Saint *Luke*.



this of St. *Luke*, it appears that neither of these Women went with *Joanna* and her Company to the Sepulchre; yet as they were *Galilean* Women, and bore a Part, and a principal Part too, in what the Women of *Galilee* were then chiefly employed about, namely, the Care of embalming the Body of *Jesus*, there is certainly no Impropriety in St. *Luke*'s naming them with *Joanna* and the rest, as he does in the End of the general and collective Account he gives of what was reported and done by the *Galilean* Women. Neither does his naming them appropriate to *them* any particular Part of that general Account, any more than his not naming them would have excluded them from their Share of those Transactions, and the Report then made to the Apostles. In this Case they would have been included in the general Terms of *Galilean Women*; as by being named, they are distinguished and marked as the most eminent Persons and Leaders of that Company of Women, who followed *Jesus* from *Galilee*, &c.

" THIS will account for St. *Matthew* saying nothing of Spices : --- for *they* had none with them : They set out before those, who were to bring the Spices, to see what Condition the Sepulchre was in : and their Business is properly expressed by θεωρῆσαι τὸν τάφον, *to see the Sepulchre.*

" *MARY Magdalene* was with the first (*Matthew and Mark*) who went to the Sepulchre ; but I think she did not go to the Sepulchre then : As soon as she was in Sight of the Place, lifting up her Eyes [ἀναβλέψασα, *Mark* xvi. 4.] and seeing the Stone removed, she turned instantly [τρέχει οὖν, *John* xx. 2.] to tell *Peter* and *John*. And it is plain by her Behaviour at her second going, that she had no Share in the Fright, that seized those who went on after she left them."

§. 9. HAVING thus cleared the Way, I shall now set down the several Incidents of this wonderful Event, in the Order, in which, according to the foregoing Observations, they seem to have arisen ; after premising that our Sa-

Saviour *Christ* was crucified on a *Friday*, (the Preparation, or the Day before the *Jewish Sabbath)* gave up the Ghost about three o'Clock in the Afternoon of the same Day, and was buried that Evening, before the Commencement of the *Sabbath*, which among the *Jews* was always reckoned to begin from the first Appearance of the Stars on *Friday* Evening, and to end at the Appearance of them again on the Day we call *Saturday*: That some time, and most probably towards the Close of the *Sabbath*, after the Religious Duties of the Day were over, the Chief Priests obtained of *Pilate*, the *Roman* Governor, a Guard to watch the Sepulchre, 'till the third Day was past, pretending to apprehend that his Disciples might come by Night, and steal away the Body, and then give out that he was risen, according to what he himself had predicted while he was yet alive: That they did accordingly set a Guard, made sure the Sepulchre, and to prevent the Soldiers themselves from concurring with the Disciples, they put a Seal upon the Stone, which closed up the Entrance of the Sepulchre.

THE Order, I conceive, to have been as follows:

VERY early on the first Day of the Week (the Day immediately followiug the *Sabbath*, and the third from the Death of *Christ*) *Mary Magdalene* and the other *Mary*, in pursuance of the Design of embalming the Lord's Body, which they had concerted with the other Women, who attended him from *Galilee* to *Jerusalem*, and for the performing of which they had prepared Unguents and Spices, set out in order to take a View of the Sepulchre, just as the Day began to break: And about the Time of their setting out, *there was a great Earthquake: for the Angel of the Lord descended from Heaven, and came and rolled back the Stone from the Door of the Sepulchre, and sat upon it: His Countenance was like Lightning, and his Raiment white as Snow; and for fear of him the Keepers did shake, and became as dead Men*, during whose Amazement and Terror, *Christ* came out of the Sepulchre; and the Keepers being now recovered out of their Trance, and fled, the Angel, who till then sat

upon

upon the Stone, quitted his Station on the Outſide, and entered into the Sepulchre, and probably diſpoſed the Linen Clothes and Napkin in that Order, in which they were afterwards found and obſerved by *John* and *Peter*. *Mary Magdalene*, in the mean while, and the other *Mary*, were ſtill on their Way to the Sepulchre, where, together with *Salome*, (whom they had either called upon, or met as they were going) they arrived at the riſing of the Sun. And as they drew near, diſcourſing about the Method of putting their Intent of embalming the Body of their Maſter in Execution, *they ſaid among themſelves, Who ſhall roll us away the Stone from the Door of the Sepulchre? for it was very great*; and they themſelves (the two *Maries* at leaſt) had ſeen it placed there two Days before, and ſeen with what Difficulty it was done. But in the midſt of their Deliberation about removing this great and ſole Obſtacle to their Deſign (for it does not appear that they knew any thing of the Guard) *lifting up their Eyes*, while they were yet at ſome Diſtance, they perceived it was already rolled away. Alarmed at ſo extraordinary and ſo unexpected a Circumſtance,

*Mary Magdalene* concluding, that, as the Stone could not be moved without a great Number of Hands, ſo it was not rolled away without ſome Deſign; and that they, who rolled it away, could have no other Deſign but to remove the Lord's Body; and being convinced by Appearances that they had done ſo, ran immediately to acquaint *Peter* and *John* with what ſhe had ſeen, and what ſhe ſuſpected, leaving *Mary* and *Salome* there, that if *Joanna* and the other Women ſhould come in the mean time, they might acquaint them with their Surprize at finding the Stone removed, and the Body gone, and of *Mary Magdalene*'s running to inform the two above mentioned Apoſtles of it. While ſhe was going on this Errand, *Mary* and *Salome* went on, and entered into the Sepulchre, *and there ſaw an Angel ſitting on the right Side, cloathed in a long white Garment, and they were affrighted. And he ſaith unto them, Be not affrighted: Ye ſeek* Jeſus *of* Nazareth, *which was crucified: He is riſen, he is not here: Behold the Place where they laid him. But go your Way, tell his Diſciples and* Peter *that he goeth before you into* Galilee; *there*

*ſhall*

*ſhall ye ſee him, as he ſaid unto you. And they went out quickly and fled from the Sepulchre; for they trembled and were amazed; neither ſaid they any thing to any Man; for they were afraid.* After the Departure of *Mary* and *Salome* came *John* and *Peter*, who having been informed by *Mary Magdalene*, that the Body of the Lord was taken away out of the Sepulchre, and that ſhe knew not where they had laid him, *ran both together to the Sepulchre; and the other Diſciple* [John] *out-ran* Peter, *and came firſt to the Sepulchre; and he ſtooping down, and looking in, ſaw the Linen Clothes lying, yet went he not in. Then cometh* Simon Peter *following him, and went into the Sepulchre, and ſeeth the Linen Clothes lie, and the Napkin, that was about his Head, not lying with the Linen Clothes, but wrapped together in a Place by itſelf. Then went in alſo that other Diſciple, which came firſt to the Sepulchre, and he ſaw and* * *believed; for as yet they knew not the Scripture that*

* *Believed.*] Commentators have generally agreed to underſtand by this Word no more than that St. *John* believed, what *Mary Magdalene* ſuggeſted, *viz.* That they had taken away the Lord's Body; and they ſeem to have been

*that he must rise again from the Dead. Then the Disciples went away again unto their own Home. But* Mary *stood without at the Sepulchre weeping; and as she wept, she stooped down, and looked into the Sepulchre, and seeth two Angels in White, sitting, the one at the Head, and the other at the Feet, where the Body of* Jesus *had lain; and they say unto her, Woman, why weepest thou? She saith unto them, Because they have taken away my Lord,*

been led into this Opinion by the Words immediately subjoined, *for as yet they knew not the Scripture that he must rise again from the Dead*; which Words contain a sort of an Excuse for their not believing that he was risen. It is however certain that by the Word *Believe*, when it is put absolutely, the sacred Writers most commonly mean to have, what is called, Faith; and in this Sense it is used no less than three Times in the latter Part of this Chapter. To obviate this Objection, retain the usual Signification of this Verb, and yet reconcile this Verse with the following, it is pretended that *Beza*'s old *Greek* Manuscript says he did not believe, *i. e.* instead of ἐπίστευσεν it has οὐκ ἐπίστευσεν, or ἠπίστευσεν. Instead of entering into an Examination which of these two Readings is to be preferred, I shall only observe, that *Beza* himself in his Comments upon this Passage, takes no notice of the various Reading above mentioned; on the contrary, he contends that St. *John* did believe the Resurrection. These are his Words: *Et credidit,* καὶ ἐπίστευσεν, *Christum videlicet resurrexisse, quanquam tenuis adhuc foret hæc fides, & aliis testimoniis egeret, quibus confirmaretur. Joannes igitur solus jam tum hoc credidit, &c.* See his *Greek* Testament in Fol. printed at *Geneva*, A. D. 1598. And I own I am most inclined to his Opinion, for Reasons which will appear in the Course of this Work.

*Lord, and I know not where they have laid him. And when she had thus said, she turned herself back, and saw* Jesus *standing, and knew not that it was* Jesus. Jesus *saith unto her, Woman, why weepest thou? Whom seekest thou? She supposing him to be the Gardener, saith unto him, Sir, if thou have borne him hence, tell me where thou hast laid him, and I will take him away.* Jesus *saith unto her,* Mary! *She turned herself, and saith unto him, Rabboni! which is to say, Master!* Jesus *saith unto her, Touch me not, for I am not yet ascended unto my Father: But go to my Brethren, and say unto them, I ascend unto my Father and your Father, and to my God and your God.* After this Appearance of *Christ* to *Mary Magdalene*, to whom St. *Mark* says expresly he appeared first, the other *Mary* and *Salome*, who had fled from the Sepulchre in such Terror and Amazement that *they said not any thing to any Man*; (that is, as I understand, had not told the Message of the Angel to some * whom they

* Probably *John* and *Peter*, who were running with *Mary Magdalene* to the Sepulchre, about the Time that these Women were flying from it, might have been discerned by them at a Distance, tho' the Terror they were in might occasion their not recollecting them immediately.——But of this I shall hereafter say something more.

they met, and to whom they were directed to deliver it) were met on their Way by *Jesus Christ* himself, who said unto them, *All hail! and they came and held him by the Feet, and worshiped him. Then said* Jesus *unto them, Be not afraid, Go tell my Brethren that they go into* Galilee, *and there shall they see me.* These several Women and the two Apostles being now gone from the Sepulchre, *Joanna* with the other *Galilean* Women, *and others with them, came bringing the Spices which they had prepared for the embalming the Body of* Jesus, *and finding the Stone rolled away frow the Sepulchre, they entered in; but not finding the Body of the Lord* Jesus, *they were much perplexed thereabout, and behold two Men stood by them in shining Garments; and as they were afraid, and bowed down their Faces to the Earth, they said unto them, Why seek ye the Living among the Dead? He is not here, but is risen. Remember how he spake unto you, when he was yet in* Galilee, *saying, The Son of Man must be delivered into the Hands of sinful Men, and be crucified, and the third Day rise again. And they remembered his Words, and returned from the Sepulchre, and told all*

*these*

*these Things unto the Eleven, and to all the rest. And their Words seemed to them as idle Tales, and they believed them not.* But *Peter*, who upon the Report of *Mary Magdalene* had been at the Sepulchre, had entered into it, and with a Curiosity that bespoke an Expectation of something extraordinary, and a Desire of being satisfied, had observed that the *Linen Clothes*, in which *Christ* was buried, and the *Napkin that was about his Head*, were not only left in the Sepulchre, but carefully wrapped up, and laid in several Places; and who from thence might begin to suspect, what his Companion St. *John* from those very Circumstances seems to have believed: *Peter*, I say, hearing from *Joanna*, that she had seen a Vision of Angels at the Sepulchre, who had assured her that *Christ* was risen, starting up, ran thither immediately, and knowing that the Angels, if they were within the Sepulchre, might be discovered without his going in, he did not as before, enter in, but stooping down looked so far in as to see the *Linen Clothes, and departed, wondering in himself at that which was come to pass*. And either with *Peter*, or about that Time,

went

went ſome other Diſciples, who were preſent when *Joanna*, and the other Women made their Report, *and found it even ſo as the Women had ſaid. The ſame Day two of the Diſciples went to a Village called* Emmaus, *which was from* Jeruſalem *about threeſcore Furlongs. And they talked together of all thoſe Things that had happened. And it came to paſs that while they communed tog.ther, and reaſoned,* Jeſus *himſelf drew near, and went with them; but their Eyes were holden that they ſhould not know him. And he ſaid unto them, What manner of Communications* [Arguments] *are theſe that ye have one to another, as ye walk and are ſad? And one of them, whoſe Name was* Cleopas, *anſwering, ſaid unto him, Art thou only a Stranger in* Jeruſalem, *and haſt not known the Things which are come to paſs there in theſe Days? And he ſaid unto them, What Things? And they ſaid unto him, Concerning* Jeſus *of* Nazareth, *which was a Prophet mighty in Deed and Word before God, and all the People; and how the Chief Prieſts and our Rulers delivered him to be condemned to Death, and have crucified him. But we truſted that it had been He which ſhould have redeemed* Iſrael: *And beſide all this, to-day*

*is*

*is the third Day since these Things were done. Yea, and certain Women also of our Company made us astonished, which were early at the Sepulchre; and when they found not his Body, they came, saying, that they had also seen a Vision of Angels, which said that he was alive. And certain of them which were with us, went to the Sepulchre, and found it even so as the Women had said: But him they saw not. Then he said unto them, O Fools, and slow of Heart to believe all that the Prophets have spoken! Ought not* Christ *to have suffered these Things, and to enter into his Glory? And beginning at* Moses *and all the Prophets, he expounded unto them in all the Scriptures the Things concerning himself. And they drew nigh unto the Village whither they went, and he made as though he would have gone farther. But they constrained him, saying, Abide with us, for it is towards Evening, and the Day is far spent. And he went in to tarry with them. And it came to pass as he sat at Meat with them, he took Bread and blessed it, and brake and gave to them. And their Eyes were opened, and they knew him; and he vanished out of their Sight. And they said one to another, Did not our Hearts burn within us,*

*while*

*while he talked with us by the Way, and while he opened to us the Scriptures? And they rose up the same Hour, and returned to* Jerusalem, *and found the Eleven gathered together, and them that were with them, saying, The Lord is risen indeed, and hath appeared to* Simon. *And they told what Things were done in the Way, and how he was known of them in breaking of Bread.*

THIS is the Order, in which the several Incidents above related appear to have arisen; the Conformity of which with the Words of the Evangelists, interpreted in their obvious and most natural Sense, I have shewn in my Remarks upon the Passages, wherein they are contained: And altho the Reasons there given, are, as I apprehend, sufficient of themselves to justify the Exposition I contend for, yet, for the better Confirmation of what has been advanced, I beg leave to lay before you an Observation or two, suggested by this very Order itself, from whence its Aptness and Tendency to the great End, to which it was in all its Parts directed and disposed by the

the Hand of Providence, *viz.* the Proof of the Reſurrection of *Chriſt*, will manifeſtly appear.

§. 10. FIRST then, by this Order, in which all the different Events naturally and eaſily follow, and as it were riſe out of one another, the Narration of the Evangeliſts is cleared from all Confuſion and Inconſiſtencies. And 2dly, The Proof of the Reſurrection is better eſtabliſhed by thus ſeparating the Women into two or more Diviſions, than upon the contrary Suppoſition, which brings them all together to the Sepulchre; for in the laſt Caſe, inſtead of three different Appearances of Angels to the Women, and two of *Jeſus Chriſt*, we ſhould have but one of each; whereas in the former there is a Train of Witneſſes, a Succeſſion of miraculous Events, mutually ſtrengthening and illuſtrating each other, and equally and jointly concurring to prove one and the ſame Fact; a Fact, which, as it was in its own Nature moſt aſtoniſhing, and in its Conſequences of the utmoſt Importance to Mankind, required the fulleſt and moſt unexceptionable Evidence. And I will venture to say, never was a Fact more fully proved, as I doubt not to make appear to any one, who with me will consider, 1st, The Manner; 2dly, The Matter of the Evidence; and 3dly, The Characters and Dispositions of the Persons whom it was intended to convince. By these I chiefly mean the Apostles, and Disciples of *Jesus*, who were to be the Witnesses of the Resurrection to all the World. By the Manner, I understand the Method and Order in which the several Proofs were laid before them: And by the Matter, the several Facts of which the Evidence consisted.

I SHALL begin with the Apostles and Disciples, for whose Conviction the miraculous Appearances of the Angels, and of *Christ* himself to the Women, were principally designed; and the Knowledge of whose general Characters, as well as of the particular Dispositions of their Minds at that Time, will throw a Light upon the other Points proposed to be considered.

THE

The greateſt Part, if not all, of the Apoſtles and Diſciples of *Jeſus*, thoſe at leaſt who openly and avowedly followed him, were Men of low Birth and mean Occupations, illiterate, and unaccuſtomed to deep Inquiries, and abſtracted Reaſonings; Men of groſs Minds, contracted Notions, and ſtrongly poſſeſſed with the ſelfiſh, carnal, and national Prejudices of the *Jewiſh* Religion, as it was then taught by the *Scribes* and *Phariſees*. And hence, altho' it is evident from ſeveral Paſſages in the Goſpel-Hiſtory, that, convinced by the many Miracles performed by *Jeſus* of *Nazareth*, and the Accompliſhments of many Prophecies in him, they believed him to be the *Meſſiah*, yet their Idea of a *Meſſiah* was the ſame with that of their Brethren the *Jews*; who, by not rightly underſtanding the true Meaning of ſome Prophecies, expected to find in the *Meſſiah*, a Temporal Prince, a Redeemer and Ruler of *Iſrael*, who ſhould never die. And ſo deeply was this Prejudice rooted in the Minds of the Apoſtles, as well as the reſt of the *Jews*, that altho' our Saviour conſtantly diſclaimed the Character of a Temporal Prince, and upon many Occasions endeavoured to undeceive his Disciples, yet they could not wholly give up their Opinion, even after they had seen him risen from the Dead, and received that incontestable Proof of his being the *Messiah*, and of their having mistaken the Sense of that Prophecy about his being never to die. For in one of his Conferences with them after his Resurrection, they ask him, Whether he would at that Time * *restore the Kingdom to* Israel? With so much Obstinacy did they adhere to their former Prejudices. This therefore being their settled Notion of the *Messiah*, can we wonder their former Faith in him should be extinguished, when they saw him suffering, crucified, and dying; and instead of saving others, not able to save himself? To prepare them for these Events, he had indeed most circumstantially foretold his own Sufferings, Death, and Resurrection: But the Apostles themselves assure us that they did not understand those Predictions, 'till some Time after their Accomplishment; and they made this Confession at a Time, when they

* Acts, chap. i, ver. 6.

they were as sensible of their former Dulness, and undoubtedly as much amazed at it, as they now pretend to be, who object it against them; so that their Veracity upon this Point is not to be question'd. Immortality therefore and Temporal Dominion being, in their Opinions, the Characteristicks of the *Messiah*, the Sufferings and Death of *Jesus* must have convinced them before his Resurrection, that he was not the *Messiah*, not that Person, in whom they had trusted as the Redeemer and King of *Israel*. And having, as they imagined, found themselves mistaken in their Faith as to this Point, they might with some Colour of Reason be cautious and backward in believing any Predictions about his Rising from the Dead, had they understood what these Predictions meant. The State of Mind therefore, into which the Apostles fell upon the Death of their Master, must have been a State of Perplexity and Confusion. They could not but reflect upon his miraculous Works, and his more miraculous Holiness of Life, and were not able to account for the ignominious Death of so extraordinary a Person. ---- A State of Dejection and Despair: They had conceived great Expectations from the Persuasion that he was *the Christ of God*: But these were all vanished; their promised Deliverer, their expected King was dead and buried, and no one left to call *him* from the Grave, as *he* did *Lazarus*. With this Life, they might presume, ended his Power of working Miracles; and Death perhaps was an Enemy, he could not subdue, since it was apparent he could not escape it; and hence proceeded their Despair. It was likewise a State of Anxiety and Terror. The *Jews* had just put their Master to Death as a Malefactor and Impostor; what then could his Followers expect from his inveterate and triumphant Enemies, but Insults and Reproaches, and Ignominy, Scourges, Chains, and Death? The Fear of the *Jews* made them desert their Master, when he was first seized; made *Peter*, the most zealous of the Apostles, *deny him thrice*, even with Oaths and Imprecations; and made the Apostles and Disciples, when they met together on the Day of the Resurrection, to confer upon the Accounts they had received of *Christ*'s being risen, retire into a Chamber, and shut the Door, lest they should be disco-

vered

vered by the *Jews*. Such then was the State of the Apoſtles Minds upon the Death of their Maſter, full of Prejudice, Doubt, Perplexity, Deſpair, and Terror: Diſtemperatures that required a gentle Treatment, lenient Medicines, and a gradual Cure. Which leads me to conſider in the next Place the Manner, *i. e.* the Method and Order of that Evidence by which they were recovered into a State of Sanity; and from Deſerters of their Maſter, converted into Believers, Teachers, and Martyrs of the Goſpel.

§ 1. THE firſt Alarm they received was from *Mary Magdalene*, who early in the Morning, on the third Day from the Burial of our Saviour, came running to inform *Peter* and *John*, that ſhe had found the Stone rolled from the Mouth of the Sepulchre, and that the Body of the Lord was taken away. This Information carried thoſe two Apoſtles thither, who entered into the Sepulchre, and found the Linen Clothes, in which his Body had been wrapped, and the Napkin, that was bound about his Head, folded up,

 and

and lying in different Parts of the Sepulchre. These Circumstances, trifling as they may seem at first sight, were, if duly considered, very awakening, and very proper to prepare their Minds for something extraordinary; since nothing but the Resurrection of *Jesus* could, in right Reason, be concluded from them. The Body they saw was gone; but by whom could it be taken away? and for what Purpose? Not by Friends; for then in all Probability they would have known something about it: Not by the *Jews*, for they had nothing to do with it. *Pilate*, to whom alone the Disposal of it belong'd, as the Body of a Malefactor executed by his Orders, had given it to his Disciples, who laid it in the Sepulchre but two Days before; and wherefore should they remove it again so soon? Not to bury it; for in that Case they would not have left the Spices, the Winding-sheet, and the Napkin behind them. Whoever therefore had removed the Body, they could not have done it with a Design to bury it; and yet no other Purpose for the Removal of it could well be imagined. Besides,

ſides, it muſt have been removed in the Night by Stealth, and conſequently in a Hurry: How then came the Winding-ſheet and the Napkin to be folded up, and diſpoſed in ſo orderly a Manner within the Sepulchre? Add to all this, that the Stone was very large, and therefore many People muſt have been concerned in this Tranſaction, not one of whom was there to give an Anſwer to any Queſtions. Theſe, or ſuch-like Reflections could not but riſe in their Minds, and theſe Difficulties could not but diſpoſe them to expect ſome extraordinary Event. His Life, they knew, was a Life of Miracles, and his Death was attended with Prodigies and Wonders; all which could not but come crouding into their Memories; and yet none of them at that Time (excepting *John*) believed that he was riſen from the Dead; *for as yet* (as the Apoſtle aſſures us) *they knew not the Scripture, that he muſt riſe again from the Dead*; that is, they did not underſtand from the Prophets that the *Meſſiah* was to riſe again from the Dead, being on the contrary perſuaded, that theſe very Prophets

phets had foretold the *Messiah* should not die, but *abide for ever.* quainted them with two prizing Particulars, ... That they had their

* The next Information they received was from *Joanna*, and the Women who ac- com-

* I have placed this Report of *Joanna* next to the Relation above-cited made by *Mary Magdalene*, and before the second Report made by her, and that of the other two *Maries*; because, by what the two Disciples, who were going to *Emmaus*, say to *Jesus*, it is evident that they had heard the Report of *Joanna*, and had not, when they left the rest of the Disciples, heard either of the last mentioned Reports. Farther, by their using the first Person plural in speaking of those, to whom this Report was made, as some Women of our Company made us astonished, compared with what St. *Luke* says at the 9th Verse, of the Women returning and telling all these Things to the Eleven and *all the rest*, it looks as if they were of the Number of those, who were present when this Report was made; and that St. *Peter* was of that Number is evident, and so, I think, were all the Eleven, and many other of those called Disciples, assembled together, probably by *John* and *Peter*, as was before observed. These several Points being admitted, it will follow, that the Report of *Joanna and those with her*, was made to the *Eleven and all the rest*, previously to the second Report of *Mary Magdalene*, and that of the other two *Maries*, tho' the Events, which gave occasion to the two latter, were in Order of Time prior to that related by *Joanna*; for if any of those, who were present when *Joanna* related what had happened to her at the Sepulchre, had heard that *Christ* had appeared to *Mary Magdalene* and the two other *Maries*, they would doubtless have mentioned it upon that Occasion, in which Case it must have been heard, and would as certainly have been mentioned by the two Disciples, in their Conversation with

companied her to the Sepulchre, who acquainted them with two new and very surprizing Particulars, *viz.* That they had there seen a *Vision of Angels*, and that those Angels had told them that *Jesus* was risen, and had

more-

with *Jesus* on the Way to *Emmaus*; and even supposing they were not present when *Joanna* made her Report, but received it only from some who were, it is probable that they who told them the Particulars relating to *Joanna*, and *Peter's* second Visit to the Sepulchre, would at the same Time have informed them of the Accounts given by *Mary Magdalene* and the other *Maries*, had they at that Time heard any thing of them. There may indeed be some Difficulty in accounting for this, especially as the Appearance of *Christ* to *Mary Magdalene* was very early; and it is said *John* xx. 18. that she went and told it to the Disciples; and still more expresly by St. *Mark* xvi. 20. and if her Zeal and Haste in carrying the News of the Stone's being removed, and the Warmth of her own Temper, and the express Command of *Christ* to her to acquaint his Disciples, be considered, it will appear very probable that she went on this Errand *immediately*; and it is very natural to think that she went directly to *Peter* this second Time, as she did the first; and that Apostle, when he left her at the Sepulchre, went directly home, as did also *John*, *John* xx. 10. But if he and *Peter* were gone to acquaint the other Disciples with the Lord's Body being missing, as is above supposed, her not finding them immediately is easily accounted for; besides which many other Things might happen unknown to us to bring *Joanna*, and those with her, to *Peter* and the other Disciples, before they saw *Mary Magdalene* after her second Visit to the Sepulchre, and before the other two *Maries* came with their Message, who, notwithstanding their Nearness to the City when *Christ* appeared to them, and

the

moreover reminded them of what himſelf had formerly ſpoken to his Diſciples concerning his Sufferings, his Death, and his Reſurrection on the third Day, being foretold by the Prophets. What various Reflections muſt theſe two amazing Circumſtances immediately ſuggeſt to them! The great Difficulty, about the Body of their Maſter being miſſing, which had ſo much alarmed and puzzled them, was at once ſolved. Angels told the Women he was riſen from the Dead; and to induce them the more eaſily to believe ſo aſtoniſhing an Event, bade them remember that *Chriſt* himſelf had, not only from the Spirit of Prophecy, with which they knew he was indowed, but from the Prophets alſo predicted his own Sufferings, and Death, and Riſing again from the Dead on the third Day.

the early Date of that Appearance, might poſſibly not be enough recovered from their Fright to deliver their Meſſage immediately; or if they were, they might, for the Reaſon above given, miſs that Apoſtle [*Peter*] to whom they were particularly commanded to deliver it; and to whom therefore, in all Probability, they went directly. All theſe Things, however, are mere Conjectures, and as ſuch I ſubmit them to the Judgment of the Reader.

Day. The Words of their Master they well remembered, and were so far convinc'd that the Women spoke Truth. Those Parts also of this Prediction, which related to his Sufferings and Death, they had seen most exactly accomplished; and that was a powerful Argument for their believing that the rest might be so too: Besides, this was the third Day, the very Day on which *Jesus* had told them he should rise from the Dead. The Argument therefore drawn from the Testimony of the Prophets, upon which their Disbelief of the Resurrection was principally founded, was here attacked; and the Interpretation of their Master, verified in most of the Particulars by the Event, was here set up in Opposition to that of the *Scribes* and *Pharisees*, whose Leaven they had so frequently been cautioned against. But then they did not understand what was meant by his Rising from the Dead. Was he once more to live with them upon the Earth? If so, Where was he? No body had as yet seen him, neither the Women, nor those among them, who, upon their Report, had gone to the Sepulchre. By his Rising from the Dead therefore might be meant, that God had taken him into Heaven, as he did *Enoch* and *Elijah*; and could they hope he would return from thence to be the Redeemer and King of *Israel*? To obviate these several Difficulties, and proceed one Step farther towards explaining to them the Meaning of the Resurrection, they were probably acquainted in the next Place by *Mary Magdalene*, that she had seen, not Angels only, but *Christ* himself, who had appeared unto her as she stood weeping at the Sepulchre; that at first indeed she did not know him, taking him for the *Gardener*; that upon his calling her by her Name she knew him; that having offered to embrace him he forbade her, giving her for a Reason that he was *not yet ascended to his Father*: But bidding her go, and tell his Disciples, that in a short Time he should *ascend to his Father, and their Father, his God and their God.* In this Relation of *Mary Magdalene*'s were three Articles of great Importance. 1st, A stronger proof than any they had hitherto received, of *Christ*'s being risen from the Dead: *Mary Magdalene* had seen him. 2dly, He told her he was not yet *ascended to his Father*, by which there seemed to be some

Hopes

Hopes given them, that they also might have the Satisfaction of seeing him. 3dly, The Words, *I ascend to my Father*, &c. plainly referred to a Conversation he had with them before he was betrayed, in which he told them that he should *go to his Father*, &c. By these Words, therefore, they were not only reminded of another Prediction of his, but called upon to expect the great Things, which were to be the Consequence of his *going to the Father*, viz. The *Coming of the Comforter*, a Power of working Miracles; and what would be an Earnest of all these Things, the Joy of seeing him again; all which he had promised them in the Conversation alluded to in this Message.* Yet some Doubts and Difficulties still remained. No body but *Mary Magdalene* had seen him; and she did not know him at first, but took him for the Gardener. Perhaps the whole was Illusion; but allowing it was *Christ* whom she saw, Why was she commanded not to touch him? It was probably an Apparition, and not *Christ* himself. Besides, Wherefore did he not appear to his Disciples, who, according to his own Pro-

* See John xiii. 14.

Promiſe, were to ſee him again? The whole Story therefore might ſtill appear to them an idle viſionary Tale.

To deliver them from theſe Perplexities, nothing could be better calculated than the Account given by the other *Mary* and *Salome*, which imported, that they alſo had been at the Sepulchre, where they had ſeen an Angel, who not only aſſured them that *Chriſt was riſen*, but ordered them to tell his Diſciples, that *they ſhould meet him in* Galilee, agreeably to what he himſelf had ſaid to them in his Life-time: That they were ſo amazed and terrified at this Viſion, that they fled from the Sepulchre with the utmoſt Precipitation, intending to communicate theſe Things to the Apoſtles, as the Angel had commanded them, but were ſo overcome with Fear, that they had not the Power to tell what they had ſeen and heard to ſome, whom they ſaw in the Way: That as they were going, *Jeſus Chriſt* himſelf met them, and ſaluting them with an *All hail! bade them not be afraid, but go and tell his Bretbren that they ſhould go into* Galilee, *and that they ſhould ſee him there*; to which they added, that *they*

*went*

*and held him by the Feet, and worshiped him.*
And farther they informed *Peter*, that the Angel had expresly injoined them to deliver this Message to him in particular. Had the Apostles and Disciples given Credit to this Account of *Mary* and *Salome*, they could have had but one Scruple left. *Jesus* had now appeared to two Women besides *Mary Magdalene*; had permitted those Women to embrace his Feet, and given thereby a sensible Proof that it was himself and not an Apparition, and had also appointed a Place, where they themselves were to see him. The only Scruple therefore, that now remained, arose from their not having seen him themselves; and till they did, they seemed resolved to suspend their Belief of his being risen from the Dead, and treated all these several Visions of the Women as so many idle Tales.

It is observable that all these miraculous Incidents followed close upon the Back of one another, and consequently were crouded into a small Compass of Time; so that we ought to be the less surpriz'd at the Apostles not yielding at once to so much Evidence. Such a Heap of Wonders were enough to amaze and overwhelm their Understandings. They were therefore left for a Time to ruminate upon what they had heard; to compare the several Reports together; to examine the Scriptures; and recollect the Predictions and Discourses of their Master, to which they were referred both by the Angels and himself. But the Examination of the Scriptures was a Work of some Time; and in the Situation in which they then were, their Minds undoubtedly were in too great an Agitation to settle to such an Employment with the Composure and Attention that was necessary. Besides, it must be remembered, they were a Company of illiterate Men, not versed in the Interpretations of Prophecies, nor accustomed to long Arguments and Deductions; and were moreover under the Dominion of an inveterate Prejudice, authorized by the *Scribes* and *Pharisees*, the Priests and Elders, whose Learning and whose Doctrines they had been instructed early to revere. To assist them in their Inquiries, and lead them to the true Sense of the Scriptures, the only rational Means of conquering their Prejudices, *Christ* him-

himself appeared that same Day to *two* of his Disciples, who were going to *Emmaus*; a Village about threescore Furlongs distant from *Jerusalem*, and whom he found discoursing and reasoning as they went, upon those very Topicks. These Disciples, as I have already shewed, had left *Jerusalem* before any of the Women, who had seen *Christ*, had made their Report; at least that Report had not come to their Knowledge. All they had heard was, that some Women who had been early at the Sepulchre, had there been informed by Angels, that he was risen from the Dead, and put in Mind that he himself had formerly predicted his Resurrection, by shewing out of the Prophets that so it was to be. This Argument were they debating, when our Saviour joined them; who questioning them upon the Subject of their Debate, and the Affliction visible in their Countenances; and understanding from the Account they gave, that they were still unsatisfied as to the main Point, and seemed to put the Proof of his being risen from the Dead, upon his shewing himself alive, rebuked them first for their *Ignorance and Backwardness in believing all that the*

*Prophets had ſpoken; and then beginning at* Moſes *and all the Prophets, he expounded to them in all the Scriptures the Things concerning himſelf.* During this whole Converſation they knew him not; *their Eyes were holden,* as St. *Luke* informs us, and for what Reaſon is very plain. The Deſign of *Chriſt* in entering into ſo particular an Expoſition of the Prophets was to ſhew, that, by making a proper Uſe of their Underſtanding, they might, from thoſe very Scriptures, whoſe Authority they allowed, have been convinced that the *Meſſiah ought to have ſuffered,* as they had ſeen him ſuffer, *and to riſe from the Dead on the third Day.* That is, *Chriſt* choſe rather to convince them by Reaſon, than by Senſe; or at leaſt ſo to prepare their Minds, that their aſſenting afterwards to the Teſtimony of their Senſes ſhould be with the Concurrence of their Reaſon. He had proceeded in the ſame Manner with the other Diſciples at *Jeruſalem,* from all of whom he had hitherto with-holden the Evidence of Senſe, having not appeared to any of them, excepting *Peter,* till after the Return of theſe two Diſciples to *Jeruſalem.* This Proceeding, at once ſo becoming the

Lord

Lord of Righteousness and Truth, and the Freedom of Man as a reasonable Being, must have been prevented, had *Christ* discovered himself to them at his first appearing. Wonder and Astonishment in that Case had taken place of Reason, and left them, perhaps, when the first strong Impression was a little worn away, in Doubt and Scepticism. But now having duly prepared them to receive the Testimony of their Senses, he discovered himself to them, and that by an Act of Devotion, *in breaking of Bread*, which among the *Jews* was always attended with Thanksgiving to God, the Giver of our daily Bread. But there seems to have been something peculiar in this Action, upon which Account it was mentioned by St. *Luke* in his Narration of this History, and by the two Disciples themselves, when they related to the Apostles at *Jerusalem*, what had happened to them at *Emmaus*. The Manner undoubtedly of breaking the Bread, and probably the Form of Words in the Thanksgiving, were particular to our Saviour; and these latter perhaps were the very same with those made use of by him at the last Supper. At least, these two Actions are described by St. *Luke* in the same Words, *viz. He took Bread and gave Thanks, and brake it, and gave to them.* If so, how strongly were they called upon by this Action to remember their Lord, who had instituted that very Form in Remembrance of his Death! and how properly did it accompany that Discovery of himself which he now thought fit to make to them! Accordingly they were convinced, and *returned that same Hour to* Jerusalem, where they found the Apostles assembled together and debating, apparently upon the several Reports they had heard that Day, and particularly upon what *Peter* had told them, to whom some Time that Day *Christ* had appeared. But as neither the Time, nor the Particulars of that Appearance are recorded by the Evangelists, I shall not pretend to say any thing more about it, than that the Apostles seem to have laid a greater Stress upon that alone, than upon all those related by the Women, For upon these two Disciples coming into the Chamber, they accost them immediately, without waiting to hear their Story, with *The Lord is risen indeed, and hath appeared to* Simon,

but

but make no mention of any of his Appearances to the Women. After which the two Disciples related what had happened to them in the Way to *Emmaus*, and *how he was known of them in breaking of Bread.* But St. *Mark* says, * they did *not believe these two Disciples* any more than they had done the others, to whom *Christ* had appear'd; which Words seem to contain a sort of a Contradiction to what they themselves seem to acknowledge in saying, *the Lord hath risen indeed, and hath appeared unto* Simon. Let us therefore examine these two Passages with a little more Attention. The whole Passage in St. *Mark* is this: *After that, he appeared in another Form to two of them, as they walked, and went into the Country, and they went and told it unto the Residue, neither believed they them.* To which I must add the following: † *Afterward he appeared unto the Eleven, as they sat at Meat, and upbraided them with their Unbelief and Hardness of Heart, because they believed not them which had seen him after he was risen.* By comparing these Passages in St. *Mark* with the parallel Passage in St. *Luke*, it will appear what the Be-

 lief

* Chap. xvi. 13. † Ver. 14.

lief of the Apostles was, and what their Unbelief. The Parallel to the first has been already considered. The Course of my Narration leads me now to consider that to the second; and in doing of this, I shall take Occasion to observe how they illustrate and explain each other, and thereby vindicate these two Evangelists from the Suspicion of contradicting one another's Account.

THE Apostles, by the several Relations of the Women, which they received early in the Morning, and upon which they had had sufficient Time to comment and reflect (for it was now Night) and afterwards by those of *Peter* and the two Disciples from *Emmaus*, being ripe for Conviction, *Christ* vouchsafed to give them that Evidence they seemed so much to desire, and which having been granted to others, they had some Reason to hope for and expect. Accordingly, as the Disciples from *Emmaus* had just finished their Story, Jesus *himself stood in the midst of them, and saith unto them, Peace be unto you; and they were terrified and affrighted, and supposed they had seen a Spirit.* Here then was their Error, and in

this

this consisted their Unbelief. They acknowledged indeed that *Christ* was risen from the Dead, but did not believe that he had bodily appeared to those, who pretended to have seen him, and to have had sufficient Evidence upon that Point. These, St. *Mark* says, they did *not believe*; and we learn from St. *Luke*, that when he appeared to them, they did *not believe* even their own Eyes, but *supposed they had seen a Spirit*. That this was the Unbelief, for which, as we read in St. *Mark*, our Saviour *rebuked* them, is evident from what follows after in St. *Luke*. *And he said unto them, Why are ye troubled? And why do Thoughts* [Reasonings Διαλογισμα] *arise in your Hearts? Behold my Hands and my Feet! that it is I myself: Handle me and see; for a Spirit hath not Flesh and Bones, as ye see me have. And when he had thus spoken, he shewed them his Hands and his Feet.* We may judge of the Distemper by the Remedy. He bade them feel and see that it was no Spirit, but he himself. Why? Because they doubted of it: And he upbraided them with their *Unbelief and Hardness of Heart*, because they doubted of it, notwithstanding the Testimony

of

of People, whose Veracity they had no Reason to suspect, and who brought Credentials with them, that could not be forged. It being evident from these Passages, thus compared together, that the Unbelief of the Apostles, mentioned by St. *Mark*, and the Belief which they professed, according to St. *Luke*, were both partial, those two Evangelists are thus perfectly reconciled.

BUT if any one should still insist that these Words of the Apostles and Disciples, *The Lord is risen indeed, and hath appeared to* Simon, imply that they then had a full and explicit Belief of the Resurrection of *Christ*, as from the Force of the Word *indeed* I am myself inclined to think, and should demand how they came afterwards to disbelieve the *two Disciples*, and to suspect even that Appearance which themselves saw? I answer, that in the Appearance of *Christ* to the *two Disciples*, and in that afterwards to themselves, were some Circumstances, which at first, and till more satisfactory Proofs were given, might naturally tend to confound and unsettle the

the Faith, which they had taken up upon the Evidence of *Peter*: Because *Christ* appearing first to the two Disciples *in another Form*, and *vanishing* out of their Sight as soon as he was made known to them, seemed better to suit with the Idea of his being a Spirit, than a living Body; and his entering into the Room where they were assembled, *the Doors being shut*, rather confirm'd that Idea, in the first sudden Impression it made upon their Minds; which Mistake, in both Cases, arose from their not attending sufficiently to the miraculous Powers belonging to *Christ*; to the Operations of which his being in the Body was no Impediment. This Inadvertency, and want of due Consideration in the Apostles and Disciples, justifies our Saviour's *rebuking them* for *not believing them which had seen him*. But the Doubts occasioned by it were soon overcome by those farther Proofs of the Reality of his Body, which he afterwards vouchsafed to give them: And by this Explanation, as well as by the former, the Evangelists are cleared from contradicting each other.

How-

However, neither did these Proofs entirely satisfy them; for, as the History goes on, *While they yet believed not for Joy, and wondered,* Christ *said unto them, Have ye any Meat? And they gave him a Piece of a broil'd Fish, and an Honey-comb, and he took it and did eat before them.* So much Compassion did he shew for their Infirmity! and so much Care did he take, that not even a Shadow of a Scruple should remain in their Minds, upon a Point of the utmost Importance to the great Business he came about! And perceiving now that every Doubt was vanished, and they were perfectly convinced, he said to them, (pursuing the Argument begun by the Angels, and carried on by himself with the two Disciples in the Way of *Emmaus) These are the Words which I spake unto you, while I was yet with you, that all Things must be fulfilled, which were written in the Law of* Moses, *and in the Prophets, and in the Psalms concerning me. Then opened he their Understandings, that they might understand the Scriptures, and said unto them, Thus it is written, and thus it behoved* Christ, (i. e. Messiah) *to suffer, and to rise from the Dead on the third Day; and that Repentance, and Remission of Sins should be preached in his Name, beginning at* Jerusalem; *and ye are Witnesses of these Things.*

THE Apostles having now had every kind of Evidence laid before them, that was requisite to convince them of the Reality of the Resurrection of *Christ*; and being moreover enabled by the Gift of that Holy Spirit, which inspired the Prophets, to understand the true Meaning of those sacred Oracles, to which their Master constantly referred them for the Marks and Characters of the *Messiah*, which he affirmed to be found in him, as well in his Sufferings and Death, and Rising again from the Dead on the third Day, as in the miraculous Actions and unspotted Holiness of his Life, were again left to consider and examine at leisure the several Proofs of the Resurrection, which they had heard and seen that Day; and particularly those arising from the Accomplishment of the Predictions contained in the Holy Scriptures. That they might apply themselves to this Examination with that cool, deliberate and sober Attention, that is more especially necessary to the rooting out inveterate and religious Prejudices, and planting in their stead a rational and well-grounded Faith, such as is required of all those who believe in *Christ*, and was particularly necessary for them, who were to be Witnesses of all these Things to all the World, he forbore visiting them any more for eight Days; after which he condescended to submit himself to a farther Examination, in order to remove the unreasonable Scruples of St. *Thomas*, one of the Apostles; who, having not been present when our Saviour appeared to the other Disciples, and consequently not having seen him himself, refused to believe upon the Report of others, so wonderful a Thing as *Christ*'s rising from the Dead: Nay, he was resolved not to be convinced with seeing only. *Except I shall see in his Hands*, says he, *the Print of the Nails, and put my Finger into the Print of the Nails, and thrust my Hand into his Side, I will not believe. Jesus*, when he appeared to his Disciples, *shewed them his Hands and his Feet*, as a Proof of his being the same *Jesus* that was crucified. This Circumstance, among the rest, the Apostles undoubtedly related

lated to St. *Thomas*, as an Evidence by which they were assured that it was their Master, whom they had seen; and upon this Evidence St. *Thomas* also was contented to believe: But first he would be convinced that it was real; he would not only *see* the Print of the Nails, which might be counterfeited, he would *put his Finger into the Print of the Nails, and thrust his Hand into his Side. Eight Days after* therefore, *when his Disciples were again met together in a Chamber, and* Thomas *was with them,* Jesus *came, the Doors being shut, and stood in the Midst, and said, Peace be unto you. Then saith he to* Thomas, *Reach hither thy Finger, and behold my Hands, and reach hither thy Hand, and thrust it into my Side; and be not faithless, but believing.* What could St. *Thomas* do, but yield immediately to the Evidence he had required? And what could he say to one, who appeared to know all his Thoughts, but *my Lord, and my God!* Jesus *saith unto him,* Thomas, *because thou hast seen me, thou hast believed: Blessed are they that have not seen, and yet have believed.*

AFTER

AFTER this there seems to have been no Scruple left in the Minds of any of the Apostles, to whom however *Christ* was still pleased to continue his Visits, * *being seen of them*, as St. *Luke* testifies, *forty Days after his Passion, and speaking of the Things pertaining to the Kingdom of God.* But as hitherto all the Appearances of *Christ* seem to have been intended only for the Conviction of his Apostles; and those that follow rather for their Confirmation and Instruction in the Faith and Doctrines of the Gospel, the sacred Writers, who have been very particular in the Accounts they give us of the former, have mentioned but very few of the latter: I say few; for I think it highly probable that the Appearances of *Christ* to his Apostles for the remaining thirty Days, were more than they have thought proper to record. And the Reason of this different Proceeding is very obvious. The Apostles are to be considered both as *Witnesses* of the Miracles and the Sufferings, the Death and the Resurrection of *Jesus Christ*, and *Teachers and Preachers* of his Doctrine. In the Character of *Witnesses*, a circumstantial Ac-

* Acts, ch. i. ver. 3.

Account of the Means and Opportunities they had of knowing certainly the ſeveral Facts atteſted by them, muſt needs give great Force and Credit to their Evidence; whereas in that of *Preachers* it is ſufficient if their Auditors were ſatisfied in general that the Doctrines taught by them were derived from the Inſtructions, and authorized by the Commiſſion given them by their Maſter *to teach all Nations*; and of this, the various Gifts of the Holy Spirit, poured out not upon the Apoſtles only, but by them upon all Believers, were full and unqueſtionable Proofs. But among the laſt-mentioned Appearances of *Chriſt* there are two, which, by reaſon of their Connexion with the former, ought by no means to have been omitted: The firſt relates to *Chriſt's* meeting his Diſciples in *Galilee*, which was foretold by *Chriſt* himſelf before his Death, repeated by the Angels to the Women at the Sepulchre, and afterwards confirmed to them again by *Chriſt*. The Accompliſhment of this Prophecy, it was certainly neceſſary to ſhew; accordingly we have it in St. *Matthew*, who ſays, *Then the Eleven Diſciples went into* Galilee, *unto a Mountain, where* Jesus *had appointed them, and when they saw him they worshiped him: but others doubted.* The second, in like manner, corresponds with what was spoken by our Saviour to *Mary Magdalene* in these Words: *But go to my Brethren, and say unto them, I ascend unto my Father and your Father, and to my God and your God*; which Words, as I have already observed, referred to a Conversation he had with his Disciples the Night before he was betrayed, wherein he told them, 1st, That he should *go to his Father*; 2dly, That he would come to them before he went to his Father; 3dly, That after he was gone to the Father, he would send them *a Comforter*, even the Spirit of Truth; who would *teach them all Things, and bring all Things to their Remembrance, whatsoever he had said unto them.* And 4thly, That whosoever believed on him should have the Power of working as great, nay greater Miracles than he did. The fulfilling of which several Promises or Prophecies I shall now set down, only premising, that the second Article was abundantly accomplished by the several Appearances above-mentioned, as we have already seen. The first, *viz.* his Ascen-

Ascension into Heaven, came to pass in this Manner :——* *And being assembled together with them, he commanded them that they should not depart from* Jerusalem, *but wait for the Promise of the Father, which*, saith he, *ye have heard of me. For* John *truly baptized with Water, but ye shall be baptized with the* Holy Ghost *not many Days hence. When they therefore were come together, they asked of him saying, Lord, wilt thou at this Time restore the Kingdom to* Israel? *And he said unto them, It is not for you to know the Times or the Seasons, which the Father hath put in his own Power; but ye shall receive Power, after that the* Holy Ghost *is come upon you; and ye shall be Witnesses unto me, both in* Jerusalem, *and in all* Judea, *and in* Samaria, *and unto the uttermost Parts of the Earth. And when he had spoken these Things, while they beheld, he was taken up, and a Cloud received him out of their Sight. And while they looked stedfastly towards Heaven, as he went up, behold two Men stood by them in white Apparel, which said unto them, Ye Men of* Galilee, *why stand ye gazing up into Heaven? This same* Jesus, *which is taken up from you*



* Acts, Ch. i. ver. 4,—14.

*you into Heaven, ſhall ſo come, in like manner as ye have ſeen him go into Heaven.*——The Hiſtory of the Accompliſhment of the third Article is in the next Chapter, and in theſe Words: *And when the Day of Pentecoſt was fully come, they were all with one Accord in one Place; and ſuddenly there came a Sound from Heaven, as of a ruſhing mighty Wind, and it filled all the Houſe where they were ſitting: And there appeared unto them cloven Tongues, like as of Fire, and it ſat upon each of them, and they were filled with the* Holy Ghoſt, *and began to ſpeak with other Tongues, as the Spirit gave them Utterance. And there were dwelling at* Jeruſalem, Jews, *devout Men, out of every Nation under Heaven. Now when this was noiſed abroad, the Multitude came together and were confounded, becauſe that every Man heard them ſpeak in their own Language. And they were all amazed, and marvelled, ſaying one to another, Behold, are not all theſe which ſpeak,* Galileans? *and how hear we every Man in our own Tongue, wherein we are born?* Parthians *and* Medes, *and* Elamites, *and the Dwellers in* Meſopotamia, *and in* Judea, *and* Cappadocia, *in* Pontus, *and* Aſia, Phrygia, *and* Pamphy-

lia,

lia, *in* Egypt; *and in the Parts of* Libya, *about* Cyrene, *and Strangers of* Rome; Jews *and* Proselytes, Cretes *and* Arabians, *we do hear them speak in our Tongues the wonderful Works of God.*—For a Proof of the Completion of the fourth Article, I shall refer the Reader to the History of the Acts of the Apostles, in which he will find numberless Instances of the Power of working Miracles in the Apostles; *by whose Hands* (says the Historian, ch. v. ver. 12.) were *many Signs and Wonders wrought among the People,——in so much that they brought forth the Sick into the Streets, and laid them on Beds and Couches, that at least the Shadow of* Peter *passing by might overshadow some of them. There came also a Multitude out of the Cities round about* Jerusalem, *bringing sick Folks, and them which were vexed with unclean Spirits, and they were healed every one.*

FROM this View of the Method and Order, in which the several Proofs of the Resurrection were laid before the Apostles, it is manifest that, as *Christ* required of them a reasonable and well-grounded Faith, so did he pursue the most proper and effectual

Means for the attaining that End. With this Purpose, instead of bearing down their Reason, and dazzling their Understanding by a full Manifestation of himself all at once, we see him letting in the Light upon them by little and little, and preparing their Minds by the gradual Dawning of Truth, that they might be able to bear the full Lustre of the *Sun of Righteousness* rising from the Grave; to consider and examine, and know that it was he himself, and to assure the World it was impossible they could be deceived. And as, by this Proceeding in general, he intended to open their Understanding by Degrees, and conduct them Step by Step to a full Conviction and Knowledge of the Truth; so by referring them to the Scriptures, and submitting himself to the Scrutiny and Judgment of their Senses, he did not only waive all Authority, but require them in a strong and particular Manner to exercise their Reason in examining the Evidence brought before them; for which Purpose also he both improved their Faculties by the Infusion of his Holy Spirit, and gave them sufficient Time, and frequent Opportunities, *shewing*

*himself*

*himself to them alive after his Passion, by many infallible Proofs,* says the Author of the *Acts*; *being seen of them forty Days; and speaking of the Things pertaining to the Kingdom of God.* And most certainly never was Evidence more fairly offered to Consideration; never was there Inquiry put upon a more rational Method, as indeed there never were any Facts that could better abide the Test. This I shall now endeavour to evince, by considering the Facts themselves, upon which the Proof of the Resurrection, and consequently the Faith of the Apostles, was established.

§. 12. The Facts, of which the Evidence of the Resurrection consisted, may be comprized under three Heads: 1st, The Appearances of the Angels: 2dly, The Appearances of *Christ* to the Women: And 3dly, The Appearances of *Christ* to the Disciples and Apostles.

1st, The Appearances of the Angels at the Sepulchre on the Morning of the Resurrection were many, each differing from the other, and seen by different Persons; as 1st, By

By the *Roman* Soldiers, who kept the Sepulchre; 2dly, By the other *Mary* and *Salome*; 3dly, By *Mary Magdalene*; 4thly, By *Joanna*, and those with her.

The Angel, who appeared to the *Roman* Soldiers, was cloathed with Terror, *His Face was like Lightning, and his Raiment white as Snow.* His Coming was attended with an Earthquake, and his Strength so much beyond that of Mortals, that he singly rolled away the Stone from the Mouth of the Sepulchre; which, according to *Beza*'s Copies, both *Greek* and *Latin*, was so large that twenty Men could hardly roll it. I have already taken notice of the two Purposes, upon which this *Angel of the Lord* descended from Heaven, *viz.* To fright away the Soldiers, and to open the Sepulchre, that the Women who were then on their Way thither, and the others both Women and Disciples, and *Jews*, who were come thither that Day, might have free Entrance into it, and see that the Body of *Jesus* was not there. The Reasonableness of these two Purposes, I

think,

think, every body must acknowledge; and that is a very material Point towards establishing the Credibility of the Fact; especially if we consider that, without the Interposition of Heaven, the Sepulchre would probably not have been opened, nor the Guard removed, till after the Expiration of the third Day, the Day prefixed by *Christ* for his rising from the Dead; in which Case, tho' no earthly Power could have hindered *Christ*, who is the Power of God, from coming out of the Grave, yet the Door of the Sepulchre remaining closed, and the Guard continuing there, must effectually have prevented that Examination into the State of the Sepulchre, which convinced St. *John* that *Christ* was risen; and which, if it did not of itself amount to a clear Proof of the Resurrection, was at least admirably calculated to prepare the Minds, not of the Apostles only, but of all the *Jews* who were at that Time in *Jerusalem*, to admit such other Proofs, as were afterwards offered to their Consideration. For it is not to be imagined, that none but the Disciples of *Jesus* visited the Sepulchre that Day. The Story told by the Soldiers undoubtedly soon spread all over *Jerusalem*; and bare Curiosity, without any other Motive, was surely sufficient to carry Numbers to survey the Scene of so astonishing an Event. A Sepulchre, hewed out of a Rock, closed with a vast Stone, and that Stone but the Evening before sealed up by the High Priests and Elders, and committed to a Guard of *Roman* Soldiers; this Sepulchre, notwithstanding all these Precautions, opened, as one Part of the Soldiers reported, by an Angel from Heaven, or as others said, by the Disciples of *Jesus*; who, as was pretended, *came by Night, and while the Guard slept, stole away the Body of* Jesus, which in Effect was missing. These two different and irreconcileable Reports must have likewise induced others to go, and consider upon the Spot, by examining into the Nature and Situation of the Sepulchre, the Probability of that Report, which charged the Disciples with having stolen away the Body of *Jesus*; for as, upon that Supposition, none but human Means are said to have been employed, in order to know whether those Means were proportioned to the Effects ascribed to them, it was necessary to compare

what

what was done, with the Manner in which it was pretended to be performed. And upon such an Examination, I think, it must have appeared to every considerate Man, if not impossible, at least improbable in the highest Degree, for the Disciples of *Jesus* to have stolen away his Body, while the Guards were at their Posts. For supposing the Disciples to be the Reverse of what they were, bold, enterprising, cunning Impostors, and capable of making so hazardous an Attempt; can it also be supposed, that a Company of *Roman* Soldiers, trained up under the strictest Discipline, and placed there but the Evening before, should be all asleep at the same Time, and sleep so soundly and so long, as not to be awakened, either by rolling away the Stone, (which, as it singly closed up the Mouth of the Sepulchre, must certainly have been very large) or by the carrying off the Body? the former of which required a great Number of Hands, and the latter must have appeared to have been done with some Deliberation, since the *Linen-Clothes* in which the Body was wrapped, and the *Napkin* that was wound about the Head, were folded up and laid in diffe-

I rent

rent Parts of the Sepulchre. The Sepulchre was hewed or hollowed into the ſolid Rock; ſo that they could have no Thought of making a ſecret Paſſage into it, by digging thro' the Rock; and conſequently muſt have gone in by that only Entrance, which was cloſed up by a great Stone, and guarded by a Band of *Roman* Soldiers. Theſe ſeveral Circumſtances duly attended to, were of themſelves ſufficient to invalidate the Teſtimony of thoſe Soldiers, who pretended that the Diſciples ſtole away their Maſter's Body while they were aſleep. But they were on the other hand very ſtrong Arguments for the Credibility of that Account, in which all the Soldiers at firſt agreed, and which Part of them undoubtedly had publiſhed, before the other Story was put into their Mouths by the Chief Prieſts and Elders. For in this Relation a Cauſe is aſſigned proportionable to all the Effects; Effects, which as they were viſible and notorious, as well as extraordinary, could not fail of exciting the natural Curioſity of Mankind to inquire, by what Means they were brought about. The Solution is eaſy and full, *An Angel of the Lord deſcended from*

*Heaven,*

*Heaven, rolled away the Stone from the Mouth of the Sepulchre, and sat upon it: His Countenance was like Lightning, and his Raiment white as Snow.* This accounts for the Terror of the Soldiers, their deserting their Post, their precipitate Flight into the City; for the Stone's being rolled away from the Mouth of the Sepulchre, even while it was surrounded by a *Roman* Guard; for the sepulchral Linen being left in the Grave, folded up, and lying in different Places; and for the Body's being missing; and therefore the Cause here assigned, however wonderful, is most likely to be true.

NOR could the Miracle be an Objection to the Credibility of this Account among the *Jews*; who, upon the Authority of their Lawgiver, their Prophets, and their Historians, were accustomed to think the working Miracles very consistent with the Idea of God, the All-mighty and All-wise Creator of Heaven and Earth; tho' some modern Philosophers have pretended to discover from Reason, that *Miracles are to the common Sense and Understanding of Man utterly impossible, and*

*con-*

*contrary to the Unchangeableness of God.* This Point indeed, if it could be made out, (as most certainly it can not) would of itself be a sufficient Answer to all the Arguments, that can be brought in support of the Credibility, not of this Story only, but of all the Evangelical History, and the *Jewish* Religion also; and would supersede all other Objections to them, as needless and superfluous. Let those then, who upon the Force of this Speculation deny Christianity, here try their Strength: Let them prove that Miracles are utterly impossible, *&c.* or, till they do, let them give leave to those, who are of a contrary Opinion, to insist that in the present Case the Miracle can be no Objection to the Credibility of the Fact; and that, as I have said, it could have been none among the *Jews* in particular; whom from their Infancy had heard, and read, and believed the *mighty Signs and Wonders wrought by God for his People* Israel; had expected to find in the *Messiah* a Power of working Miracles; and had Evidence of many performed among them by *Jesus* and his Disciples. And indeed the Appearance of an Angel, upon this Occasion, so far

from

from being an Objection, was highly proper, I had almost said necessary. *Jesus* had, but two Days before, been put to Death by the Rulers of the *Jews*, as an Impostor; one, who by the Authority of *Beelzebub* cast out Devils, and by assuming the Character of the *Messiah* blasphemed God. His Sepulchre also was guarded by a Band of Soldiers, under the Pretence of preventing his Disciples from carrying on the Imposture begun by their Master, by stealing away his Body, and giving out that he was risen from the Dead, in consequence of what he had said before his Crucifixion. Under these Circumstances the Attestation of Heaven was necessary to shew that God, though he had suffered him to expire on the Cross, had not forsaken him; but on the contrary, had co-operated with him even in his Sufferings, his Death, and Burial, and Resurrection from the Dead on the third Day; having, by the secret Workings of his Providence and his Almighty Power, accomplished in every Point the several Predictions of *Jesus* relating to each of those Events: Events, which at the Time of those Predictions, none but God, or an Eye enlighten'd lighten'd by his omniscient Spirit, could foresee; and which nothing less than his all-controuling Power could bring about. The Descent therefore of *the Angel of the Lord* from Heaven, and his *rolling away the Stone* from the Sepulchre, was a visible Proof that the Finger of God was in the great Work of the Resurrection, was a proper Honour done to him, who claimed to be the Son of God, and unanswerably refuted the impious Calumnies of those, who upon Account of that Claim stiled him an Impostor and Blasphemer.

§. 13. What has been just said of the Propriety and Necessity of an Angel's descending from Heaven, upon the present Occasion, is applicable in general to the several Appearances of Angels seen by the Women, which I shall examine in the next Place, taking it for granted, that the Miraculousness of such Appearances will be no longer urged as an Argument against their Possibility. The only Thing then remaining to be considered in this Examination, is the internal Evidence which these several Visions carry along with them

them of Reality and Truth; for by ſome they have been treated as pure Illuſions, and by others as downright Falſhoods. The principal Argument made uſe of to prove their Falſhood is founded upon a ſuppoſed Contradiction and Inconſiſtency in the ſeveral Accounts given of them by the Evangeliſts; which Argument having been thoroughly diſcuſſed in the foregoing Part of this Diſcourſe, I muſt refer the Reader thither for an Anſwer to it. That theſe Appearances were Illuſions, the Effects of Superſtition, Ignorance and Fear, hath been inſinuated rather than aſſerted; but hath never, that I know of, been attempted to be proved. I ſhall not therefore amuſe myſelf with a vain Search after Arguments, which, I preſume, are not eaſy to be found; or they would have been produced by thoſe, who have laboured with ſo much Diligence to expoſe and ridicule the Faith of *Chriſtians*; but leaving ſuch to make good their Aſſertion, who ſhall think fit to maintain it, I ſhall proceed to lay down a few Obſervations, tending to prove the Reality and Truth of theſe Appearances of the Angels to the Women.

THE Angel first seen by the Women was that described by St. *Mark*, in the Form of a *young Man sitting* [within the Sepulchre] *on the right Side, cloathed in a long white Garment*, at the Sight of whom the Women [*Mary* and *Salome*] discovering great Signs of Fear, he saith unto them, *Be not affrighted; ye seek* Jesus *of* Nazareth, *which was crucified; he is risen, he is not here. Behold the Place where they laid him. But go your Way, tell his Disciples and* Peter, *that he goeth before you into* Galilee; *there shall ye see him, as he said unto you.* That this was a real Vision, and no Phantom of the Imagination, is evident from these Particulars. 1st, As it does not appear from this or any other Account, that the Women, upon their coming to the Sepulchre, were under any such Terrors or Perturbation of Mind, as are apt to fill the Fancy with Spectres and Apparitions. On the contrary, they went thither a little after Day-break, prepared and expecting to find the dead Body of *Jesus* there, and purposing to embalm it; about the doing of which they had been calmly conferring by the Way: So, 2dly, By their coming with

with a Design to embalm the Body, it is plain they had no Notion either of his being already risen, or that he would rise from the Dead; and therefore, 3dly, Had the Angel been only the Creature of a disturbed Imagination, they would scarcely have put into his Mouth a Speech, that directly contradicted all the Ideas, upon which they proceeded but one Moment before. 4thly, It is to be observed farther, that the Illusion must have been double; two Senses must have been deceiv'd, the Hearing and the Sight; for the Angel was heard as well as seen; and tho' this frequently happens in Dreams, and sometimes perhaps in a Delirium, or a Fit of Madness, yet I question whether an Instance exactly parallel in all its Parts, to the Case here supposed, was ever known; for no two People dream together exactly alike, nor are affected in a Delirium with exactly the same Imaginations. 5thly, The Words spoken by the Angel refer to others spoken by *Christ* to his Disciples before his Passion, in which he told them, that after *he was risen, he would go before them to* Galilee. This Promise or Prediction the Angel here reminds them of, bids them tell the Disciples from him to go into *Galilee*, and promises them that *Christ* will meet them there. Now, as not only the Resurrection, but the personal Appearance of *Christ* also, is implied in these Words, the Reason given above under the third Partilar concludes in the present Case more strongly against supposing them to have proceeded only from the Imagination of the Women; for the sudden Change of whose Opinion from a Disbelief of the Resurrection, into a full and explicit Belief of it, no adequate Cause can be assigned. For if it should be allowed that they knew of this Prediction of *Christ*'s, (which however does not appear) yet the Business that brought them to the Sepulchre makes it evident, that till that Instant they did either not recollect, not understand, or not believe it: And if it be farther said, that upon their entering into the Sepulchre, and not finding the Body of *Jesus*, this Prediction might naturally come at once into their Heads, and they might as suddenly, and as reasonably believe *Christ* to be risen, as St. *John* did, whose Faith was built upon no other Evidence than what these Women had now before them; I anſwer, that allowing St. *John*, when he is ſaid to have firſt believed the Reſurrection, had no other Evidence than theſe Women now had, or might have had, yet it is to be obſerved, that St. *John* was in a fitter Diſpoſition of Mind to reflect and judge upon that Evidence, than the Women. St. *John* ran to the Sepulchre, upon the Information given him by *Mary Magdalene*, that the Body of *Jeſus* was removed from thence, and laid ſhe knew not where, nor by whom: And, as the Sepulchre was at ſome Diſtance from his Habitation, many Thoughts muſt naturally have ariſen in his Mind, tending to account for the Removal of the Body; and among the reſt, perhaps, ſome confuſed and obſcure Hope that he might be riſen from the Dead, purſuant to many Predictions to that Purpoſe delivered by him to his Diſciples. But whatever his Thoughts were at the Time of his coming to the Sepulchre, about which it muſt be owned nothing can be offered but mere Conjecture; it is certain he had Leiſure to reflect upon the Predictions of his Maſter, and to examine into the State of the Sepulchre, which both he and

 Peter

*Peter* did, (and that implies ſome Delibera-tion and Preſence of Mind) and that after this deliberate Examination he departed quietly to his own Home. Whereas the Women are repreſented as falling into the utmoſt Terror and Amazement immediately upon their en-tering into the Sepulchre; and continuing un-der the ſame Conſternation till they were met flying from thence by *Chriſt* himſelf. Under ſuch a Diſorder of Mind, can we ſuppoſe them capable of recollecting the Predictions of *Chriſt* about his Reſurrection? conſidering the Proofs of their Accompliſhment ariſing from the State of the Sepulchre? and per-ſuading themſelves at once that he was not only riſen from the Dead, but would perſo-nally appear to his Diſciples? And then im-mediately upon this Conviction fancying they ſaw an Angel, and heard him aſſure them in a diſtinct manner that *Chriſt* was riſen; call them to view the Place where he had been laid, and bid them tell his Diſciples that he would meet them in *Galilee*? In a Word, if this ſuppoſed Illuſion proceeded from a ſtrong Perſuaſion that *Chriſt* was riſen from the

Dead,

Dead, whence arose that Belief? If that Belief arose from a cool Reflexion upon the Predictions of our Saviour, and the State of the Sepulchre, (the Cause of St. *John*'s Faith) Whence came their Terror? Which, if not previous to the Apparition of the Angel, was at least prior to the Words, *Be not affrighted*, with which he first accosted them. If it be urged, that this Terror was of the Nature of those causeless and unaccountable Terrors called Panicks, it may be answered, that this is giving us a Name instead of a Reason, and is, in effect, saying just nothing at all, or saying no more than that they were affrighted, but no body can tell why or wherefore. 6thly, It is observable, that the Speech of the Angel to the Women consists of ten distinct Particulars: As, 1. *Be not affrighted.* 2. *Ye seek* Jesus *of* Nazareth, *who was crucified.* 3. *He is risen.* 4. *He is not here.* 5. *Behold the Place where they laid him.* 6. *But go your way, tell his Disciples,* 7. *And* Peter, 8. *That he goeth before you into* Galilee, 9. *There shall he see him,* 10. *As he said unto you.* The Order and Connexion of which several Particulars, are no leſs remarkable than their Number: and therefore taking both theſe Conſiderations into the Account, I leave any one to judge whether it be conceivable that Women under ſo great a Terror and Diſtraction of Mind, as to fancy they ſaw and heard an Angel when there was no ſuch thing, ſhould be able to compoſe a Speech for this Phantom of their Fear and Imagination, containing ſo much Matter, Order, and Reaſon, and proceeding upon the Suppoſition that they were not then convinced that *Chriſt* was riſen from the Dead, tho' the Belief of his Reſurrection is preſumed not only to have proceeded, but even to have occaſioned this Illuſion.

I HAVE dwelt the longer upon the Examination of this firſt Appearance of the Angel to the Women, becauſe the ſettling the Nature of that will ſave us the Trouble of entering into a particular Diſcuſſion of the reſt; the ſeveral Articles of which will fall under one or other of the foregoing Obſervations. All I ſhall do therefore is, to note the different Circumſtances obſervable in each of them, and from

from thence endeavour to raiſe another Argument for the Truth and Reality of all.

THE Viſion, we have juſt now conſidered, was of one Angel; that ſeen by *Mary Magdalene* was of two; as was likewiſe that reported by *Joanna* and thoſe with her. And whereas the firſt Angel was found by the Women upon their entering into the Sepulchre, ſitting on the right Side, the two laſt-mentioned Appearances were abrupt and ſudden. For the Angels which *Mary Magdalene* diſcovered ſitting, one at the Head, and the other at the Feet, where the Body of *Jeſus* had been laid, were not ſeen by *Peter* and *John*, who juſt before had entered into the Sepulchre, and viewed every Part of it with great Attention; and *Joanna*, and *thoſe with her*, had been ſome time in the Sepulchre before they ſaw any Angels; which Angels ſeem alſo to have appeared to them in a different Attitude from thoſe ſeen by *Mary Magdalene*, and by the other *Mary* and *Salome*. As the Number of the Angels, and the Manner of their Appearance was different, ſo likewiſe were the Words ſpoken

to

to them by the Women, and the Behaviour of the Women upon those several Occasions: *Mary* and *Salome* were touched with Fear, and fled from the Sepulchre in the utmost Terror and Amazement. *Joanna*, and *those with her*, were struck with Awe and Reverence, and bowed down their Faces to the Earth; but *Mary Magdalene* seems to have been so immersed in Grief at not being able to find the Body of the Lord, as to have taken little or no Notice of so extraordinary an Appearance; she sees, hears, and answers the Angels without any Emotion, and without quitting the Object upon which her Mind was wholly fixed, till she was awakened out of her Trance by the well-known Voice of her Master calling her by her Name. But here let us stop a little, and ask a Question or two. Could this Appearance then be an Illusion? Could a Mind so occupied, so lost in one Idea, attend at the same time to the Production of so many others of a different Kind? Or could her Imagination be strong enough to see and converse with Angels, and yet too weak to make any Impression on her, or call off her Attention from a less affecting, less surprising Subject? Real

Angels

Angels indeed ſhe may be ſuppoſed to have ſeen and heard, and not to have regarded them; but Apparitions raiſed by her own Fancy could not have failed engaging her Notice. For although, when we are awake, we cannot avoid perceiving the Ideas excited in us by the Organs of Senſation, yet is it, in moſt Inſtances, in our Power to give to them what Degree of Attention we think fit; and hence it comes to paſs, that when we are earneſtly employed in any Action, intent upon any Thought, or tranſported by any Paſſion, we ſee, and hear, and feel a thouſand Things, of which we take no more Notice, than if we were utterly inſenſible of them, as every one's daily Experience can teſtify: But to the Ideas not proceeding immediately from Senſation, but formed within us by the internal Operation of our Minds, we cannot but attend; becauſe in their own Nature they can exiſt no longer than while we attend to them. Of this Kind are all the Phantoms that haunt our ſleeping or waking Dreams: For ſo all Extaſies, Deliriums, and the Ravings of Madneſs may not improperly be called; and whatever

may

may be the physical Cause, that upon these Occasions sets the Mind to work, and influences her Imagination, she is certainly more than passive in these Productions, and is generally so attentive to them, as to disregard, during her Transports, all the Opportunities of external Objects; or to blend and colour with the prevailing Idea all those arising from the Informations of the Senses. From all which it is evident, that the Mind cannot apply herself to the Contemplation of more than one Object at a Time; which, as long as it keeps Possession, excludes or obscures all others. *Mary Magdalene* therefore, having taken it strongly into her Head, upon seeing the Stone rolled away from the Mouth of the Sepulchre, that some Persons had removed the Body of the Lord; in which Notion she was still more confirmed, after her Return to the Sepulchre with *Peter* and *John*, and grieving at being thus disappointed of paying her last Duty to her deceased Master, whose Body, as *Peter* his most zealous, and *John* his most beloved Disciple, knew nothing of the Removal of it, she might imagine was got into the Hands of his Enemies, to be exposed perhaps

haps once more to fresh Insults and Indignities, or at least to be deprived of the pious Offices, which the Duty and Affection of his Followers and Disciples were preparing to perform. *Mary Magdalene*, I say, falling into a Passion of Grief at this unexpected Distress, and abandoning herself to all the melancholy Reflections that must naturally arise from it, with her Eyes suffused with Tears, and thence discerning more imperfectly, looking as it were by Accident, and while she was thinking on other Matters, into the Sepulchre, and seeing Angels, might, according to the Reasoning above laid down, give but little Heed to them; as not perceiving on a sudden, and under so great a Cloud of Sorrow, the Tokens of any Thing extraordinary in that Appearance. She might take them perhaps for two young Men, which was the Form assumed by those who appeared to the other Women, without reflecting at first that it was impossible they should have been in the Sepulchre without being seen by *John* and *Peter*, and improbable that they should have entered into it after their Departure, without having been observed by her. Intent upon what passed within her own Bosom, she did not give herself Time to consider and examine

amine external Objects; and therefore knew not even *Christ* himself, who appeared to her in the same sudden and miraculous Manner; but, *supposing him to be the Gardener*, begg'd him to tell her, if he had removed the Body, where he had laid it, that she might take it away. By which Question, and the Answer she had made to the Angels immediately before, we may perceive what her Thoughts were so earnestly employed about; and thence conclude still farther, that the Angels were not the Creatures of her Imagination, since they were plainly not the Objects of her Attention. The Appearance therefore of the Angels was real. But to return from this Digression.

If the several Appearances of the Angels examined separately, may be shewn to carry with them evident Marks of Reality and Truth, the considering and comparing them together, will set that Point in a yet stronger Light; such, we presume, as will intirely clear up every Doubt in the Minds of those who seem inclined to believe any thing possible, but that the Gospel should be true. For both the Number, the Manner, the Variety, and Nature of the Circumſtances of theſe Viſions, and their being ſeen by different Perſons at different Times, make it, according to the natural Courſe of Things, utterly incredible that there ſhould have been in them either Illuſion or Impoſture. Many Inſtances perhaps of *Illuſions* in ſingle Perſons, and even in Numbers (for nothing is more contagious than Superſtition and Enthuſiaſm) may be produced; how well authenticated, it will be Time enough to inquire when we know what they are. But I believe it will be generally found, upon a ſtrict Examination, that whenever any Number of People have fallen into ſuch an Illuſion, as, by the Force of Imagination only, to hear and ſee Spectres and Apparitions, the Imagination, or Artifice of ſome one among them hath given Birth to the Phantom; and working upon Minds already diſpoſed to Superſtition, Enthuſiaſm, or Credulity, or cunningly prepared perhaps for that particular Occaſion, hath led them eaſily to ſee and hear Things, that exiſted only in their own prepoſſeſſed and over-heated Fancies. But nothing of all this can be pretended in the preſent Caſe. The Women, by whom theſe different

ferent Visions of Angels were severally seen; had no Communication with each other during the Time of these Appearances, as is evident from the whole Tenor of this History: *Mary* and *Salome* were fled from the Sepulchre before *Mary Magdalene* returned; and *Mary Magdalene* was departed from thence again, before *Joanna*, and *those with her*, came thither; so that they could not catch the Illusion from one another; and that their Minds, at the Time of their coming to the Sepulchre, were very far from being disposed to form Imaginations of *Christ*'s being risen from the Dead, is evident from the Business that carried them thither. They came to perform the last Offices usually paid to the Dead; and by embalming the Body, to compleat the Interment of their deceased Master; which, by the coming on of the Sabbath, they had been obliged to leave unfinished; and when, upon entering into the Sepulchre, they found not the Body, it was more natural for them to think, with *Mary Magdalene*, that some Persons had taken it away, and laid it they knew not where, than to conclude it was risen from the Dead: And it is plain, that *Joanna*, and *those with her*, were in this

Way

Way of Thinking; for *when they entered in, and found not the Body of the Lord* Jeſus, *they*, ſays St. *Luke, were much perplexed thereabout: i. e.* they knew not what was become of the Body, could not account for its being miſſing, and were therefore in great Diſtreſs and Anxiety about it; which would not have happened, had they believed that he had riſen from the Dead.

If, from what has been ſaid, it may ſeem reaſonable to conclude, that the Appearances of the Angels were not the Effects of Illuſion, the Phantoms of a diſtemper'd viſionary Mind, it will, I think, be more eaſily granted, that they were not the Operations of Artifice and Impoſture. For, without examining who could be the Actors, or what the Motives of an Impoſture of this Kind, there are Evidences enough, ariſing from the Circumſtances of theſe ſeveral Appearances, to ſhew, that the Powers that produced them were more than human: Such, for Example, is the Earthquake occaſioned by the Deſcent of the firſt Angel, the amazing Brightneſs of his Countenance, which, St. *Matthew* tells us, *was like Lightning*, and the prodigious Strength, which appeared in his singly rolling away a Stone, that was large enough to close up the Entrance into the Sepulchre; and what was common to all the Angels, the Faculty of becoming visible or invisible as they thought proper. These certainly were characteristical Marks of an Agent endowed with Privileges and Powers superior to the limited Abilities of Man, whose Operations cannot go farther than his Knowledge of the Laws and Powers of Nature; and how far short of such wonderful Effects as these that Knowledge would carry him, I leave the most ingenious Professor of natural Magic to determine.

2. I come now, in the second Place, to consider the Appearances of *Christ* himself to the Women, which were two, the first to *Mary Magdalene*, the second to the other *Mary* and *Salome*. But I shall not have Occasion to dwell long upon this Head, since the Appearances of the Angels having been proved to be real, put these Appearances of *Christ* more out of Doubt and Suspicion. The Angels affirmed that he was *risen* from the Dead; and if he was risen,

risen, it was natural to expect he would appear. The main Difficulty consisted in his getting loose from the Bands of Death, and breaking the Prison of the Grave; and therefore, whoever upon the Testimony of the Angels believed the Resurrection (as all those must have done who acknowledged them to be real Angels) would not, if they saw *Christ* himself, be very apt to call in question the Reality of his Appearance. But tho' the Testimony of Angels, affirming that *Christ* was risen from the Dead, renders his appearing afterwards less liable to Doubt and Question; yet before we admit the Reality of every such Appearance as may be pretended, I grant it is reasonable to expect some farther Proofs, tho' perhaps not so many or so strong, as if no such previous Evidence had been given. And in the Case of *Mary* and *Salome* it may be suggested, that their very Belief of the Resurrection of *Christ*, joined to the Disorder and Amazement they were then under, might help to convince them too easily of the Reality of his Appearance, tho' at the same time it might be nothing but a Spectre of their Imagination, and a meer Illusion: Let us therefore examine what Evi-

 dence

dence may be collected from the Account given of this Appearance, to induce us to think, that these Women were not deceived; and the Evidence, I believe, will be found sufficient. They had the Attestation of their Sight, their Hearing, and their Feeling: By the two first the Voice and Countenance of their Lord might be known; and by the last they might be assured, that it was no Spectre that they heard and saw, but a Body consisting of Flesh and Bones. One of these Proofs indeed was wanting to *Mary Magdalene*, *Christ* forbade her to touch him; and yet, any one, who considers with due Attention the Circumstances of this Appearance, will find *sufficient* Reason to be persuaded that it was *Christ* himself who appeared to her. For first, he had stood by her some time, had spoken to her, and she had answered him, before she knew him to be *Christ*; on the contrary, she took him for the Gardener: By all which it is manifest, that the Spectre, if it was one, was not of her creating. * Her Mind was otherwise engaged; and had it been either at leisure, or disposed to raise Apparitions, it is most likely she

* See the preceding Article.

ſhe would have called up ſome Perſon, with whom ſhe had more Acquaintance and Concern than a Keeper of a Garden, whom probably ſhe had never known nor ſeen before. 2dly, He called her by her Name; by which it appeared that he knew her, ſo did ſhe, it ſeems, diſcover him; for turning immediately about, ſhe accoſted him with the reſpectful Title of *Rabbouni*, my Maſter; and, as may be inferred from the enſuing Words of *Chriſt*, offered to embrace him. His Voice and his Countenance convinced her that it was *Chriſt* himſelf. 3dly, In theſe Words, *Touch me not, for I am not yet aſcended to my Father; but go to my Brethren, and ſay to them, I aſcend to my Father and your Father, to my God and your God*, is contained a moſt clear Proof that it was *Chriſt* himſelf who uttered them. To underſtand this, it muſt be remembered, that theſe Words allude to a long * Diſcourſe which our Saviour held to his Diſciples the very Night in which he was betrayed; wherein he told them, that he ſhould leave them for a ſhort Time (*a little while and ye ſhall not ſee me*) and that he would come to them again,

 tho'

* See John, Chap. xiv. xv. and xvi.

tho' but for a ſhort Time (*and again a little while, and ye ſhall ſee me*) *becauſe* (added he) *I go to my Father*. By the Phraſe *I go to my Father*, *Chriſt* meant his final quitting the World, as he himſelf explained it to his Diſciples, who did not then underſtand either of the above-cited Expreſſions. * *I came forth from the Father*, ſays he, *and am come into the World: Again, I leave the World and go to the Father*. But leſt they ſhould fall into Deſpair at being thus forſaken by him, for whom they had forſaken all the World, he at the ſame Time promiſed to ſend them a *Comforter*, even the Holy Spirit, who ſhould † *teach them all Things, bring to their Minds whatſoever he had ſaid unto them*; *ſhould guide them into all Truth*, ‡ *ſhew them Things to come, and abide with them for ever*; and that *whoever believed in him ſhould be able to do greater Works* [*i. e.* Miracles] *than he did, becauſe he was to go to the Father*; and that finally, tho' they for a Seaſon ſhould be ſorrowful, yet ſhould § *their Sorrow be turned into Joy, and that Joy ſhould no Man take from them*. Theſe were magnificent Promiſes; Promiſes,

* John xvi. 28. † Ibid. xiv. 26. ‡ Ch. xvi. 13. Ibid. xvi. 16. § Ch. xvi. 20.——22.

miſes, which, as the Diſciples could not but remember *Chriſt* had made to them, ſo they might be aſſured that no one but *Chriſt* was able to make them good; and therefore, when they came to reflect ſeriouſly upon the Import of theſe Words, *Touch me not, for I am not yet aſcended to my Father; but go to my Brethren, and ſay to them, I aſcend to my Father and your Father, to my God and your God,* it was impoſſible for them to conclude otherwiſe than that it was *Chriſt* himſelf who appear'd and ſpoke to *Mary Magdalene*. For as the latter Expreſſion, *I aſcend to my Father*, &c. implied a Remembrance, and conſequently a Renewal of thoſe Promiſes, which were to take Place after his Aſcenſion to the Father; ſo did the former, *I am not aſcended to the Father*, give them Encouragement to expect the Performance of that other Promiſe of his coming to them again before his Aſcenſion, by giving them to underſtand, that he had not yet quitted this World: And I take *Chriſt*'s forbidding *Mary Magdalene* to *touch* [or embrace] him, to have been meant as a Signification of his intending to ſee her and his Diſciples again; juſt as in ordinary Life, when one Friend ſays to another, "Don't take leave, for I am not go- "ing yet," he means to let him know that he purposes to see him again before he sets out upon his Journey. That this is the true Import of the Words *Touch me not*, is, in my Opinion, evident, not only from the Reason subjoined in the Words immediately following, *For I am not yet ascended to my Father*; (by which Expression, as I have shewed above, *Christ* meant he had not finally quitted the World;) but from these farther Considerations: *Christ*, by shewing himself first to *Mary Magdalene*, intended, doubtless, to give her a distinguishing Mark of his Favour, and therefore cannot reasonably be supposed to have designed at the same time to have put a Slight upon her, by refusing her a Pleasure which he granted not long after to the other *Mary* and *Salome*; and yet this must be supposed, if *Touch me not* be understood to imply a Prohibition to *Mary Magdalene* to embrace him, for any Reason consistent with the Regard shewn to the other Women, and different from that now contended for, namely, because he intended to see her and his Disciples again. On the contrary, if these Words be taken to signify only

only a Put-off to ſome fitter Opportunity, they will be ſo far from importing any Unkindneſs or Reprehenſion to *Mary Magdalene*, that they may rather be looked upon as a gracious Aſſurance, a kind of friendly Engagement to come to her again; and in this Senſe they correſpond exactly with *Chriſt*'s Purpoſe in ſending this Meſſage by her to his Diſciples; which, as I have obſerved before, was to let them know that he remembered his Promiſe of coming to them again, and was ſtill in a Condition to perform it, not having quitted this World; and of his Intention to perform it, this his refuſing to admit the affectionate or reverential Embraces of *Mary Magdalene*, *who loved much, for much had been forgiven to her*, was an Earneſt, as his coming to them again would be a Pledge of his Reſolution to acquit himſelf in due Time of thoſe Promiſes which were not to take Effect, till after his final Departure out of this World. And thus will this whole Diſcourſe of our Saviour to *Mary Magdalene* be in all its Parts intelligible, rational, and coherent; whereas, if it be ſuppoſed that *Mary Magdalene* was forbidden to *touch Chriſt* for ſome myſtical Reaſon, contained

tained in the Words, *for I am not yet ascended to the Father*, it will be very difficult to understand either the Meaning or Intent of that Message, which she was commanded to carry to the Disciples; and still more difficult to account for his suffering, not long after, the Embraces of the other *Mary* and *Salome*. To the same, or even greater Difficulties, will that Interpretation of this Passage be liable, which supposes that the Prohibition to *Mary Magdalene* was grounded upon the spiritual Nature of *Christ*'s Body, which, it is presumed, was not sensible to the Touch or Feeling. And indeed, both these Reasons for the Behaviour of *Christ* to *Mary Magdalene* are overturned, by his contrary Behaviour to the other *Mary* and *Salome*. But if the Sense I contend for be admitted, it will be no difficult Matter to account for this Difference of his Behaviour on those two Occasions. Why he forbade *Mary Magdalene* to touch him, has already been explained; why he permitted the other *Mary* and *Salome to hold him by the Feet and worship him*, I shall now endeavour to shew. These last-mentioned Women, as * St. *Mark* informs

* Chap. ult.

forms us, were so terrified and amazed at the Sight and Words of the Angel, who appeared to them in the Sepulchre, that, altho' they * ran with a Design to tell the Disciples what they had heard and seen, as the Angel had commanded them, yet, thro' the Greatness of their Confusion and Disorder, they had neglected to deliver this important Message to † some whom they saw in their Way; for so, with

* Matt. xxviii. 8.

† That these Words, *Neither said they any thing to any Man*, must be limited to some certain Time, will, I believe be readily allowed; for it cannot be imagined, that after all the other Appearances of the Angels, &c. were published, these Women only *never* opened their Lips *to any Man* about what they had seen and heard at the Sepulchre: The Question then will be, How long they may be supposed to have forborn speaking of it? And this, I think, was no longer than during the Time of their flying from the Sepulchre, and till they were met by *Christ* himself; because the only Reason here assigned for their *not saying any thing to any Man*, viz. *For they were afraid*, (or affrighted rather) being removed by *Christ*'s appearing to them, &c. it is reasonable to believe (if it is not implied) that their Silence lasted no longer, than the only Cause of it, their Terror. Besides, as St. *Mark* breaks off the Narration of what happened to these Women very abruptly, short of *Christ*'s appearing to them, in order to relate his Appearance to *Mary Magdalene*, which indeed was previous to it, tho' subsequent to the Appearance of the Angel seen by these Women at the Sepulchre, what he says of their *not saying any thing to any Man*, cannot be taken to extend beyond the Period where he chose to break off his Narration, without supposing him guilty of a needless Impropriety. And if these Words, *Neither said they any thing to any Man*, be construed to signify that they did

with all the Commentators, I understand these Words of St. *Mark*, *neither said they any thing to any Man, for they were afraid.* That this Testimony therefore of the Angel to the Resurrection of *Christ*, and the Assurance given to the Disciples, that they should see their Master in *Galilee*, might not be lost either by the Women's forgetting, thro' the Greatness of their Amazement, what the Angel had said to them, or thro' a Suspicion of its having been a meer Illusion,

did not tell what they had seen and heard to some, whom they saw as they were flying from the Sepulchre, it seems rational to conclude, that *these* were some of the Disciples, to whom they were ordered to deliver the Message of the Angel, and to whom they would probably have delivered it, had they not been under so great a Terror and Amazement. For had the Persons, whom they saw, been any other than the Disciples of *Jesus*, it is not likely that St. *Mark* would have taken any Notice of their *not saying any thing to any Man*, since it is reasonable to imagine they would not, even tho' they had not been affrighted, have told the Message of the Angel, &c. to any but the Disciples: And as the Time of *Peter* and *John*'s running to the Sepulchre, upon the first Report of *Mary Magdalene*, co-incides with that of these Women flying from it, it is no improbable Conjecture, that these were the Persons whom they saw in their Way, at a Distance perhaps, and coming by a different Road to the Sepulchre; especially if it be considered that, as the Words of St. *Mark*, *Neither said they*, &c. seem to carry with them an Imputation of Neglect upon these Women, tho' he at the same time both accounts for it, and excuses it, by adding, *for they were affrighted*; so the same Evangelist hath before acquainted us (Ver. 7.) that they were ordered by the Angel to deliver the Message he gave them to *Peter* in particular.

Illuſion, neglecting or ſcrupling to tell it; *Chriſt* himſelf thought proper to appear to them, to calm their Minds, diſperſe their Terror, obviate their Doubts. With this View he firſt accoſts them with the gracious Salutation of *All hail!* then ſuffers them not only to approach him, but to *hold him by the Feet and worſhip him*; and laſtly, bidding them diſmiſs their Fears, orders them, in Confirmation of what the Angel had ſaid to them, to tell his Diſciples from him to *go into Galilee*, aſſuring them with his own Mouth, *that they ſhould ſee him there.* Every Word, we ſee, tended to inſpire them with Courage and Confidence; and the gracious Influence of every Word upon their Minds, could not but be rendered ſtill more powerful and efficacious by his ſuffering them to embrace him. After this familiar Inſtance of his Favour and Complacence, and this ſenſible Proof of his being really and bodily riſen from the Dead, there could be no Room left for Doubt or Terror: Conviction, Certainty, and Joy muſt have baniſhed thoſe uneaſy Paſſions for ever from their Breaſts. And hence it appears, that the different Conduct of *Chriſt* on theſe two Occaſions, was owing to the different Circumstances attending them; to which it was most wisely suited. *Mary Magdalene's* Grief (the only Disorder of Mind she then laboured under) for the supposed Loss of her Master's Body, was soon dispersed, upon her hearing him call her by her Name, and seeing him stand by her; she was immediately convinced that it was *Christ*, and testified her Conviction by giving him the Title of *Rabbouni*, my Master. She wanted not (and therefore there was no Need of giving her) any farther Proofs; but satisfied with what she had seen and heard, she went to the Disciples, and told them she *had seen the Lord*; and that he had said such and such Things to her. But Terror, the most untractable of all Passions, when excessive, had seized upon the other *Mary* and *Salome*; a Terror, which, had it proceeded from the unexpected and supernatural Appearance of an Angel, was more likely to be confirmed, than removed by the like Appearance of *Christ*, had he not proceeded gently with them, and by his gracious Words and Demeanour given them Encouragement and Permission to familiarize themselves with him by Degrees, and take,

in

in their own Way, what Proofs they thought proper to remove their Fears or Doubts, and convince them that their affectionate and beloved Maſter was in reality reſtored to them again from the Grave.

BUT beſides the Aſſurance given by *Chriſt* to his Diſciples in the Words here ſpoken by *Mary Magdalene*, of his Intention to perform his Promiſes of coming to them again, *&c.* I cannot help thinking he had a farther Meaning, which, tho' not ſo obvious, is however, in my Opinion, equally deducible from thoſe Words with the other juſt now mentioned. That remarkable Expreſſion, *I aſcend to my Father*, *Chriſt* undoubtedly made uſe of upon this Occaſion to recall to his Diſciples Minds the Diſcourſe he held to them three Nights before, in which he explained ſo clearly what he meant by *going to his Father*, that they ſaid to him, *Lo! now ſpeakeſt thou plainly, and ſpeakeſt no Parable* *. But this was not the only Expreſſion that puzzled them; they were as much in the Dark as to the Meaning of, *a little while and ye ſhall not ſee me, and again a little while and ye ſhall ſee me,* which they likewiſe confeſſed they did not

2 under-

* John xvi. 29.

understand. But *Christ* did not think fit to clear up their Doubts at that Time, and left those Words to be expounded by the Events to which they severally related, and which were then drawing on apace. For that very Night he was betrayed, and seized, and deserted by his Disciples, as he himself had foretold but a very few Hours before, upon their professing *to believe that he came forth from God:* The next Day he was crucified, expired upon the Cross, and was buried. Upon this melancholy Catastrophe the Disciples could be no longer at a Loss to understand what *Christ* meant, when he said to them, *A little while and ye shall not see me:* He was gone from them, and, as their Fears suggested, gone for ever, notwithstanding he had expresly told them, that he would come to them again; and to those Words, *A little while and ye shall not see me,* he added, *And again a little while and ye shall see me.* This latter Expression, one would think, was full as intelligible as the former; and as the one now expounded by the Event, was plainly a Prophecy of his Death, so must the other be understood as a Prophecy of his Resurrection from the Dead. But if they understood it in that Senſe, they were very far from having a right Notion of the Reſurrection from the Dead; as is evident from their imagining, when *Chriſt* firſt ſhewed himſelf to them after his Paſſion, that they ſaw a Spirit; even tho' they had juſt before declared their Belief *that he was riſen indeed, and had appeared to* Simon. The Reſurrection of the Body, it ſhould ſeem from this Inſtance, made no Part of their Notion of the Reſurrection from the Dead: To lead them therefore into a right underſtanding of this moſt important Article of Faith, *Chriſt*, in ſpeaking to *Mary Magdalene*, and by her to his Diſciples, makes uſe of Terms, which ſtrongly imply his being really, that is bodily, riſen from the Dead. *I am not yet*, ſays he, *aſcended to my Father; but go unto my Brethren, and ſay unto them, I aſcend unto my Father*, &c. The Words *I go to my Father*, *Chriſt*, as has already been obſerved, explained by the well-underſtood Phraſe of leaving the World; and to this Explanation the Words immediately foregoing give ſo great a Light, that it is impoſſible to miſtake his Meaning. The whole Paſſage runs thus, *I came forth from the Father, and am come into the World; and again I leave the World, and go to the Father.* By the Expreſſion, *I am come into the World, Chriſt* certainly meant to ſignify his being and converſing viſibly and bodily upon Earth; and therefore by the other Expreſſion, *I leave the World,* he muſt have intended to denote the contrary to all this, *viz.* his ceaſing to be and converſe viſibly and bodily upon Earth; and ſo undoubtedly the Diſciples underſtood him to mean, when they ſaid to him, *Now ſpeakeſt thou plainly, and ſpeakeſt no Parable.* But as they very well knew that the uſual Road, by which all Men quitted this World, lay through the Gates of Death, and were aſſured their Maſter had trodden that irremeable Path, they might naturally conclude, that what he had ſaid to them about *leaving the World and going to his Father,* was accompliſhed in his Death; and conſiſtently with that Notion might imagine that, by his coming to them again, no more was intended, than his appearing to them in the ſame Manner as many Perſons have been thought and ſaid to appear after their Deceaſe. To guard againſt this double Error, which *Chriſt,* to whom the

Thoughts

Thoughts of all Hearts are open, perceived in the Minds of his Disciples, he plainly intimates to them in the Words, *I am not yet ascended to my Father, but------ I do* (or shall) *ascend to my Father*, that his dying, and his final leaving of the World were distinct things; the latter of which was still to come, tho' the former was past: He had indeed died like other Mortals, and had, like them, left the World for a Season, as he himself had often foretold them should come to pass; but he was now risen from the Dead, returned into the World, and should not leave it finally till he ascended to his Father. Of his being returned into the World, his appearing to *Mary Magdalene* was doubtless intended for a Proof; and yet of this it could be no Proof at all, if what she saw was no more than what is commonly called a Spirit; since the Spirits of many People have been thought to appear after their Decease, who notwithstanding are supposed to have as effectually left this World by their Death, as those who have never appeared at all. *Lazarus*, like *Christ*, had died, and was by his quickening Word recalled to Life, which consists in the

Animation of the Body by its Union with the Soul. Now had *Christ* called up nothing but the Spirit of *Lazarus*, and left his Body to putrify and perish in the Grave, would not *Lazarus*, I ask, have still been reputed dead, and consequently considered as out of this World, tho' his Spirit had appeared to a thousand different People? If *Christ* therefore was risen from the Dead, as the Angels affirmed he was; if he had not yet finally left the World, as the Words, *I am not yet ascended to my Father*, plainly import; and if his appearing to *Mary Magdalene* was intended for a Proof of those two Points, as undoubtedly it was; it will follow that he was really, that is bodily, risen from the Dead; that he was still in the World in the same Manner, as when he *came forth from the Father, and came into the World*; and that it was he himself, and not a Spirit without Flesh and Bones, that appeared to *Mary Magdalene*.

Before I conclude this Argument, I must beg leave to make one Observation more upon the Term *Ascend*, twice used by our Saviour in the Compass of these few Words.

Words. In the Discourse here alluded to by *Christ*, he told his Disciples that he should *go* to his Father, and he now bids *Mary Magdalene* tell them that he should *ascend* to his Father; a Variation in the Phrase, which I am persuaded had its particular Meaning, and that not very difficult to be discovered. For as by the former Expression he intended, as we have seen, to signify in general his final Departure out of this World, so by the latter is the particular Manner of that Departure intimated; and doubtless with a View of letting his Disciples know the precise Time, after which they should no longer expect to see and converse with him upon Earth, but wait for the Coming of that *Comforter*, which he promised to send them in his room; and who, unless he departed from them, was not to come. *Jesus* made frequent Visits to his Disciples after his Passion, * *being seen of them*, says St. *Luke*, *forty Days*, *and speaking of the Things pertaining to the Kingdom of God*. Between some of these Visits were pretty long Intervals, † during which he seems to have

 dis-

* Acts, ch. i. & iii. † See John xx. 21.

disappeared, *i. e.* not to have resided upon Earth. Had *Christ* therefore left his Disciples without any Mark or Token, by which they might be able to distinguish his final Departure, from those that were only temporary, they would probably have taken each Visit for the last; or have lingered after his final Departure, in a fruitless Expectation of seeing him again; either of which States of Uncertainty, and especially the last, were liable to many Inconveniencies, to Doubts and Jealousies, and Fears, which it was Goodness, as well as Wisdom in our Saviour to prevent. Nor was the preventing these Evils the only Advantage that flowed from this early Intimation of the Manner of *Christ*'s final Departure out of this World, implied in the Words, *I ascend to my Father*, and verified in his Ascension into Heaven. For as this could not have been effected without the Power of God co-operating with him, so neither could it have been fore-known by him, without the Communication of that Spirit, which only knows the Counsels of God. When the Disciples therefore beheld their Master * *taken*

*up*

* Acts, ch. i. ver. 9. See *Whitby* on this Place.

*up* into Heaven, *and received out of their Sight by a Cloud* of Glory, they could not but know aſſuredly that this was the Event foretold about forty Days before to *Mary Magdalene*; and knowing that, could no longer doubt whether it was *Chriſt* himſelf who appeared and ſpoke thoſe prophetick Words to her; how little Credit ſoever they had given to her, when ſhe firſt told them ſhe *had ſeen the Lord*.

And thus, (as I have endeavoured to make appear) in theſe comprehenſive Words of *Chriſt* ſpoken to *Mary Magdalene*, *Touch me not, for I am not yet aſcended to my Father, but go to my Brethren, and ſay to them, I aſcend to my Father*, are implied three Particulars. 1ſt, A Renewal of the ſeveral Promiſes made by him to his Diſciples, the Night in which he was betrayed; one of which was the Promiſe of coming to them again before his final Departure out of this World. Of his Intention to perform which Promiſe, I take his forbidding *Mary Magdalene* to touch or embrace him, to be an Earnest or Token. 2dly, An Intimation, that as his Death and his final Departure out of the World were two distinct Things, the latter of which was yet to come; so by his rising from the Dead, they were to understand his returning and being in the World, in the same Manner with those, who have not yet quitted the World by Death, and consequently that he was really, that is bodily, risen from the Dead, of which his appearing to *Mary Magdalene* and saying those Words, was an undoubted Evidence. And 3dly, A prophetical Account of the Manner of his departing finally out of the World, *viz.* By ascending into Heaven. From which several Particulars it was impossible, as I said before, for the Disciples to draw any other Conclusion than that it was *Christ* himself who appeared and spoke to *Mary Magdalene.* I do not say the Disciples must necessarily have perceived, at the very first hearing these Words, the several Inferences which I have drawn from them; but when they came to consider them attentively, to reflect upon what their Master had said to

them

them the Night in which he was betrayed, (to which these Words evidently referred) and when, after having handled his Feet and Hands, they were by their own Senses convinced that he was bodily risen from the Dead; and lastly, when they had seen those Words, *I ascend to my Father*, verified in his ascending into Heaven before their Eyes; then, I think, they could hardly avoid perceiving the several Inferences, and drawing from them the Conclusion above mentioned. For if it was not *Christ*, who appeared to *Mary Magdalene*, it must have been either some Spirit good or bad; or some Man, who, to impose upon her, counterfeited the Person and Voice of *Christ*; or lastly, the Whole must have been forged and invented by her. The first of these Suppositions is blasphemous; the second absurd; and the third improbable. For allowing her to have been capable of making a Lye, for the carrying on an Imposture, from which she could reap no Benefit, and to have been informed of what our Saviour had spoken to his Disciples the Night in which he was betrayed, which does not appear, it must have

been

been either extreme Madneſs or Folly in her to put the Credit of her Tale upon Events, ſuch as the appearing of *Chriſt* to his Diſciples, and his aſcending into Heaven, which were ſo far from being in the Number of Contingencies, that they were not even within the Powers and Operations of what are called natural Cauſes.

The ſame Anſwer may be made to the Suppoſition, that the Appearance of *Chriſt* to the other *Mary* and *Salome* was likewiſe a Forgery of thoſe Women; and with this I ſhall conclude the ſecond Head.

§. 15. 3dly, Of the many Appearances of *Chriſt* to his Diſciples, for the forty Days after his Paſſion, the ſacred Writers have mentioned particularly but very few; imagining, doubtleſs, thoſe few ſufficient to prove that fundamental Article of the Chriſtian Faith, the Reſurrection of *Jeſus*. And indeed whoever attends to the Nature and Variety of the Evidence contained even in thoſe few Particulars, which they have tranſmitted to us, cannot, I think, but acknowledge that thoſe, who were appointed to be the Witneſſes of the

the Resurrection, had every kind of Proof, that in the like Circumstances, either the most Scrupulous could demand, or the most Incredulous imagine. This I doubt not but to be able to make appear, in the Course of the following Observations; in which I shall confine myself to the Examination of those Appearances only, whose Circumstances the Evangelical Historians have thought proper to record, and upon which the Faith of the Apostles was principally established.

The first of these, though but barely mentioned by * St. *Mark*, is very particularly related by † St. *Luke*, in the following Words: *And behold two of them went the same Day to a Village called* Emmaus, *which was from* Jerusalem *about threescore Furlongs; and they talked together of all these Things which had happened; and it came to pass, that while they communed together, and reasoned,* Jesus *himself drew near, and went with them: But their Eyes were holden that they should not know him. And he said unto them, What manner of Communications are these, that ye have one to another, as ye walk*

* Ch. xvi. † Ch. xxiv.

*walk and are ſad? And one of them, whoſe Name was* Cleopas, *anſwering, ſaid to him, Art thou only a Stranger in* Jeruſalem, *and haſt not known the Things which are come to paſs there in theſe Days? And he ſaid unto them, What Things? And they ſaid unto him, Concerning* Jeſus *of* Nazareth, *which was a Prophet mighty in Deed and Word before God, and all the People; and how the Chief Prieſts and our Rulers delivered him to be condemned to Death, and have crucified him. But we truſted that it had been He which ſhould have redeemed* Iſrael: *And beſide all this, to-day is the third Day ſince theſe Things were done. Yea, and certain Women alſo of our Company made us aſtoniſhed, which were early at the Sepulchre; and when they found not his Body, they came, ſaying, that they had alſo ſeen a Viſion of Angels, which ſaid that he was alive. And certain of them which were with us, went to the Sepulchre, and found it even ſo as the Women had ſaid: But him they ſaw not. Then he ſaid unto them, O Fools, and ſlow of Heart to believe all that the Prophets have ſpoken! Ought not* Chriſt *to have ſuffered theſe Things, and to enter into his Glory? And beginning at* Moſes

*and*

*and all the Prophets, he expounded unto them in all the Scriptures the Things concerning himself. And they drew nigh unto the Village whither they went, and he made as though he would have gone farther. But they constrained him, saying, Abide with us, for it is towards Evening, and the Day is far spent. And he went in to tarry with them. And it came to pass as he sat at Meat with them, he took Bread and blessed it, and brake and gave to them. And their Eyes were opened, and they knew him; and he vanished out of their Sight. And they said one to another, Did not our Hearts burn within us, while he talked with us by the Way, and while he opened to us the Scriptures? And they rose up the same Hour, and returned to* Jerusalem, *and found the Eleven gathered together, and them that were with them, saying, The Lord is risen indeed, and hath appeared to* Simon. *And they told what Things were done in the Way, and how he was known of them in breaking of Bread.*

Two Objections have been made to the Credibility of this Fact: 1st, That these Disciples knew not *Jesus* during the whole Time

Time of his walking, conversing, and sitting at Meat with them: 2dly, That when upon his breaking Bread, &c. their Eyes were opened, and they are said to have known him, he vanished so suddenly out of their Sight, that they seem not to have had Time enough to satisfy those Doubts, which must have arisen from their having conversed with him so long without knowing him. To the first of these Objections the Evangelist himself furnishes us with an Answer, telling us, that *their Eyes were holden that they should not know him*; which, as it will not be pretended to be above the Operation of Him, whom the Apostle of the *Gentiles* stiles * *the Power of God*, so have I already shewed it to be a Proceeding not unworthy of Him, whom the same inspired Writer, in the same Place, calls also *the Wisdom of God.* He threw a Mist before their corporeal Eyes, that he might, by the pure and unprejudiced Light of Reason only, remove from before their internal Sight, that strong Delusion, which held their Understanding from knowing the true Import of those Types and Prophecies, by which his Suf-

ferings,

* Vide sup.

ferings, Death and Resurrection were foreshewn. He disguised himself, but laid open the Scriptures; which till then had *appeared to them in another Form*; and having by an Exposition of *Moses* and the Prophets, which made *their Hearts burn within them*, stript off those Veils and Colours, which the worldly and carnal-minded Scribes and Pharisees had laid over them, and set them before their Eyes in their genuine Shape and Lustre, he in the next Place disclosed himself, and left them convinced, as well from the Scriptures, as from their Senses, that he was risen from the Dead. Which leads me to consider the 2d Objection, founded on his vanishing out of their Sight so soon after his discovering himself to them.

AND here I shall observe, 1st, That it appears they had no doubt but that the Person, who joined them in the Way to *Emmaus*, and opened the Scriptures to them, was the same, whom, upon his breaking of Bread, &c. they took to be *Jesus*. 2dly, That upon their taking him to be *Jesus*, they must have been sensible of some Alteration, either in themselves or in him, by which they were enabled to discover the Mistake they were under while they knew him not. 3dly, That Alteration must to them have appeared super-natural and miraculous, as it is implied to have been in this Phrase, *their Eyes were opened, and they knew him*; as must also his vanishing (or disappearing) from their Sight. And as from these Particulars it could not but be evident to them, that the Person, whom, when *their Eyes were opened*, they, from his Countenance, *&c.* knew to be *Jesus*, was endowed with Powers more than human; so was it impossible for them to conclude it to be any other than *Jesus* himself, without blasphemously supposing that God would permit any Spirit, whether good or bad, to assume the Person of his beloved Son, with a View of countenancing and carrying on a Falshood and Imposture; especially, as in the Conversation he had held with them by the Way, he had opened the Scriptures, and had shewn them from *Moses* and all the Prophets, that *Christ* was to suffer and die, and rise again from the Dead. But besides the clearing up all their Doubts, arising from his Sufferings and Death, which had staggered their Faith

in him, whom till then *they trusted to be Him who should redeem* Israel, it is very probable, from what they say about *their Hearts burning within them, while he opened to them the Scriptures*, that they perceived, either in his Manner or his Doctrine, some lively Marks and Characters of that Dignity and Authority, which was wont to distinguish him so much from the ordinary Teachers of *Israel*, the Scribes and Pharisees. And, not to repeat what I have said before, about the Probability of *Christ*'s having upon this Occasion made use of some Gesture or Phrase peculiar to himself, in breaking and blessing the Bread, I shall only add one Remark from * *Grotius*, *viz.* that since it was the Custom among the *Jews* for the Master of the Feast, or the most honourable Guest, immediately after blessing the Cup, to take the Bread, give Thanks over it, break it, and after eating a Bit of it, to distribute it round the Table, *Christ* by this Action declared himself something more, than what those Disciples had hitherto taken him for, a Stranger and Traveller whom they had picked up by the Way, and *constrained to abide*



* In locum. See also Drusius, ibid.

with them; and by that Declaration awakened their Attention to that Diſcovery of himſelf, which followed immediately upon it; and to which this ſolemn and religious Act was certainly no improper Introduction. The Inference that is naturally deducible from theſe ſeveral Obſervations, is, that theſe two Diſciples, even upon the Suppoſition that *Chriſt* diſappeared, immediately after their Eyes were opened, and they knew him, had ſufficient Reaſon to be aſſured that it was he himſelf, who had walked, converſed, and ſat at Meat with them; and conſequently that he was riſen from the Dead, according to what the Angels had told the Women, who had been that Morning at the Sepulchre.

§. 16. THE next Appearance of *Chriſt*, that I ſhall take notice of, and that to which all thoſe before mentioned were preparatory, was to the Eleven, and thoſe with them, on the Evening of the ſame Day. This Appearance is mentioned by three of the Evangeliſts, one relating one Particular, and another another; out of each of whoſe Goſpels I ſhall therefore take ſuch Circumſtances

as

as are not related by the others, and putting the ſcattered Parts together, compoſe from all of them one intire Relation.

* *Then the ſame Day*, (*viz.* the Day of the Reſurrection) *at Evening, being the firſt Day of the Week, when the Doors were ſhut, where the Diſciples were aſſembled for fear of the* Jews, † *while they ſat at Meat*, [immediately after the two Diſciples from *Emmaus* had finiſhed their Relation] *came* Jeſus *and ſtood in the Midſt, and ſaith unto them, Peace be with you.* || *But they were terrified and affrighted, and ſuppoſed that they had ſeen a Spirit.* ‡ *And he (upbraiding them with their Unbelief and Hardneſs of Heart, becauſe they believed not them, who had ſeen him after he was riſen) ſaid to them,* ⸸ *Why are you troubled, and why do Thoughts ariſe in your Hearts? Behold my Hands and Feet, that it is I myſelf: handle me and ſee, for a Spirit hath not Fleſh and Bones as ye ſee me have. And when he had thus ſpoken, he ſhewed them his Hands and his Feet. And while they yet believed not for Joy, and wondered, he ſaid to them, Have ye here any Meat? And they gave him a Piece of a broiled Fiſh,*



* John xx. ver. 19. † Mark xvi. ver. 14.
|| Luke xxiv. 36. ‡ Mark xvi. 14. ⸸ Luke xxiv. 38.

*Fish, and of an Honey-comb; and he took it; and did eat it before him.* * *Then were the Disciples glad when they saw the Lord.* † *And he said to them, These are the Words which I spake unto you, while I was yet with you, that all Things must be fulfilled which were written in the Law of* Moses, *and in the Prophets, and in the Psalms concerning me. Then* (‖ *breathing on them, and saying, Receive ye the Holy Ghost*) *opened he their Understandings, that they might understand the Scriptures; and said to them, Thus it is written, and thus it behoved* Christ *to suffer; and to rise from the Dead the third Day.* -----*And ye are Witnesses of these Things.*

To this I shall add the Appearance of *Christ* to St. *Thomas*, that I may bring all the Proofs of the Resurrection under one View.

‡ *But* Thomas, *one of the Twelve, called* Didymus, *was not with them when* Jesus *came. The other Disciples therefore said to him, We have seen the Lord: But he said to them, Except I shall see in his Hands the Print of the Nails,*

* John xx. 20. † Luke xxiv. 44. ‖ John xx. 22.
‡ John xx. 24.

*Nails, and put my Finger into the Print of the Nails, and thrust my Hand into his Side, I will not believe. And after eight Days, again his Disciples were within, and* Thomas *with them; then came* Jesus, *the Doors being shut, and stood in the Midst, and said, Peace be unto you. Then said he to* Thomas, *Reach hither thy Finger, and behold my Hands; and reach hither thy Hand, and thrust it into my Side; and be not faithless, but believing. And* Thomas *answered and said unto him, My Lord, and my God!* Jesus *saith unto him,* Thomas, *because thou hast seen me, thou hast believed: Blessed are they that have not seen, and yet have believed.*

THE Proofs of *Christ*'s being risen from the Dead, here exhibited to the Disciples, as set forth in the above-cited Passages, may be comprized under four Heads. 1st, The Testimony of those *who had seen him after he was risen.* 2dly, The Evidences of their own Senses. 3dly, The exact Accomplishment of the *Words which he had spoken to them, while he was yet with them.* And 4thly, The *fulfilling of all the Things which were written in the*

*Law of* Moses, *and in the Prophets, and in the Psalms, concerning him.* The Conclusiveness of all which Proofs I shall endeavour to shew in some Observations upon each of them. Upon the First I have nothing to add to what I have written already under the second general † Head, and the Beginning of this, excepting that our Lord, by *upbraiding his Disciples for not believing those who had seen him after he had risen,* took from them all Possibility of doubting afterwards of the Truth and Reality of those Appearances, thus confirmed and verified by his own irrefragable Testimony. Under the Words, *those who had seen him after he was risen,* is comprehended likewise his Appearance to *Simon,* mentioned both by * St. *Luke* and ‡ St. *Paul,* as also that to the two Disciples on the Way to *Emmaus.* Upon the second Head, (*viz.* the Evidence of their own Senses) it might, one would imagine, be thought sufficient to observe, that the Disciples had the

† See the 2d Head, Of the Appearances of *Christ* to the Women; and the 3d, Of his Appearance to the two Disciples on the Way to *Emmaus.*

* Chap. xxiv. 34. ‡ 1 Cor. xv. 5.

the ſame * *infallible Proofs* (as the Author of the *Acts* calls them) of *Chriſt*'s being alive after his Paſſion, as they had ever had of his being alive before it. They ſaw him, ſaw the particular Marks of Identity in his Perſon and Countenance, in his Hands, Feet, and Side, which had been pierced at his Crucifixion; and one of them, who had refuſed to believe *except he put his Finger into the Print of the Nails, and thruſt his Hand into his Side*, had that farther Satisfaction, unreaſonable as it was, granted him; they ſaw him alſo eat, what they themſelves gave him, *a Piece of a broiled Fiſh and an Honey-comb*; they heard him ſpeak, and were by him commanded to *handle him*, and ſee that he had Fleſh and Bones; a Command † which, doubtleſs, they obeyed. And yet all theſe infallible Tokens or Proofs, theſe Τεκμήρια, *certa & indubitata ſigna*, have been ſet aſide by ſome pretended



Phi-

* Acts i. 3. ἐν πολλοῖς τεκμηρίοις, by many certain and undoubted Proofs or Tokens. *Quintilian* from *Ariſtotle* ſays, Τεκμήρια are *indubitata & certiſſima ſigna*, as the Actions of ſpeaking, walking, eating, and drinking are the Τεκμήρια [undoubted Signs] of Life.

† The Words, *as ye ſee me have*, ſtrongly imply, that they had received the Satisfaction offered them by feeling his Hands and Feet.

Philosophers and philosophizing Divines, upon no better Grounds, than their own vain Inferences from these Words of St. *John*, *Then came* Jesus, *the Doors being shut, and stood in the Midst:* For taking it for granted, what as Philosophers it better became them to have proved, that it is suggested in these Words that *Jesus* passed thro' the Walls, or Doors, while they remained shut, without either suffering in his own Body, or causing in them any Change, during his so passing; and having discovered, "that "for one solid or material Body to pass thro' "another solid or material Body, without injuring the Form of either, both the passive and passing Body remaining the same, "is contrary to all the Laws of Nature," they have concluded, that the Body of *Christ* was not real, *i. e.* a material Body, and consequently was incapable of being felt by St. *Thomas*, *&c.* From whence it will follow, that the whole Story is absurd and false.

In answer to this, I deny that the Words, Jesus *came, the Doors being shut, and stood in the Midst,* imply that *Jesus passed through the*

*Walls*

*Walls or Doors, while they remained ſhut, without either ſuffering in his own Body, or cauſing in them any Change during his ſo paſſing.* They ſeem, indeed, to imply, that he came in miraculouſly, though not by a Miracle that contains a Contradiction or Impoſſibility; and I am perſuaded that had not St. *John* intended to ſignify that he came in miraculouſly, he would not twice have mentioned that otherwiſe trifling Circumſtance of *the Doors being ſhut*. But tho' a Denial without Proof be a proper and ſufficient Anſwer to an Aſſertion without Proof, yet I will give ſome Reaſons why the Interpretation contended for by theſe Philoſophers cannot be the true one. 1ſt, It is not to be preſumed, that St. *John*, who with the other Diſciples had received ſenſible Evidence of the Reality, *i. e.* the Materiality of *Chriſt*'s Body, ſhould be abſurd enough to imagine at the ſame time, that it was a ſpiritual Body; which he muſt have done, had he thought that *Jeſus* paſſed through the Walls or Doors, while they remained ſhut, without either ſuffering in his own Body, or cauſing in them any Change,

during

during his ſo paſſing; it requiring no great Depth of Philoſophy to underſtand it to be impoſſible, even to Omnipotence, to cauſe the Body of a Man to penetrate thro' a Wall or Door, without cauſing ſome Change or Alteration in the one or the other. Neither (2dly,) is it to be preſumed, that St. *John*, intending, as it is plain he did, by relating the Story of St. *Thomas*, to acquaint the World, that he [*Thomas*] as well as the other Diſciples, had by feeling and examining his Maſter's Body, ſenſible Evidence of his being really, *i. e.* bodily, riſen from the Dead, ſhould be weak enough to inſert in his Relation a Circumſtance, which tended to prove that the Body which St. *Thomas* is ſuppoſed to have felt, was not a material but a ſpiritual Body, and conſequently incapable of being felt and handled. Contradictions and Abſurdities are not to be preſumed in any Writer. On the contrary, as it is ſuppoſed that every Man in his Senſes has ſome Meaning in what he ſpeaks or writes, ſo by that Meaning only (which is beſt collected from the Drift and Tenor of the whole Diſcourſe) is the Senſe of any ambiguous Word or Sentence in it to be determined; and every Interpretation of ſuch ambiguous Word or Sentence, as can be ſhewn to be inconſiſtent with the plain Meaning of the Speaker or Writer, is, for that Reaſon, to be rejected. This Juſtice, Candour, and Common Senſe require. 3dly, By the Way of Reaſoning made uſe of upon this Occaſion by theſe free-reaſoning Philoſophers, the Spirituality of the Walls, or Doors, may as well be inferred as the Spirituality of *Chriſt*'s Body; for *Chriſt*'s Body being proved to be Material, by being handled by his Diſciples, *&c.* and it being admitted that he penetrated through the Walls or Doors, while they remained ſhut, without ſuffering, *&c.* it will follow that the Walls or Doors had ſpiritual Bodies; ſince it is contrary to the Laws of Nature, that one ſolid or material Body ſhould paſs, *&c.* An Argument which would have very well become the Philoſophical Anſwer to the *Tryal of the Witneſſes*, as being ſophiſtical, ludicrous, and abſurd.

HAVING now given my Reaſons for rejecting, as falſe, the Interpretation above mentioned,

mentioned, which ſome have endeavoured to fix upon theſe Words of St. *John*, Jeſus *came, the Doors being ſhut, and ſtood in the Midſt*; and having alſo allowed, that thoſe Words naturally ſuggeſt the Entrance of our Saviour to have been miraculous; I ſhall in the next Place attempt to ſhew that the Miracle here wrought by *Jeſus*, inſtead of awakening in the Minds of the Diſciples any Suſpicion, that their Senſes might have been impoſed upon, in the Examination they took of their Lord's Body, becauſe it is as eaſy for a Power, that can controul the Law of Nature, to excite in us the Ideas of hearing, ſeeing, and feeling, without the real Exiſtence of any Object of thoſe Senſations, as to open a Paſſage for a Human Body through Walls or Doors, without making any viſible Breach in them; this Miracle, I ſay, inſtead of raiſing any ſuch Suſcipion in the Diſciples, tended on the contrary to remove all their Doubts, and convince them effectually, that it was *Jeſus* himſelf in a Body conſiſting of Fleſh and Bones, and not a Spirit, which appeared to them.

THE

THE Disciples, during their Conversation with *Christ* before his Passion, had been accustomed to see him work Miracles of various Kinds, cast out Devils, heal all manner of Diseases, give Light to the Blind, Elocution to the Dumb, Legs and Nerves to the Lame and Paralytick, and Life to the Dead; and all this by a Word, which they had also seen even the Winds and Seas obey. From this extensive Power of controuling the Laws of Nature, established by the great Creator himself, joined to the more than human Purity of his Life and Doctrine, the Disciples most rationally concluded that he *came forth from God*. And therefore, as on the one hand, the Power of working Miracles was a characteristical Mark of *Jesus*, and consequently his working Miracles after his Resurrection was one Evidence of the Identity of his Person; so, on the other hand, was the Assurance of his coming *forth from the God of Truth*, founded upon his doing such Works, *as no Man could do, unless God was with him*, an infallible Security to the Disciples, against the Suspicion of his intending to impose upon them. From whence it will follow, that when, upon their fancying they saw a Spirit, he assured them it was he himself, and no Spirit, which (says he) *hath not Flesh and Bones, as* they, by feeling and handling him, *saw he had*, they could have no Shadow of a Pretence either for disbelieving his Word, or distrusting their own Senses. For, in reality, doth not his appealing to their Senses for a Confirmation of what he asserted, (*viz.* that it was he himself, and not a Spirit) imply an Affirmation that their Senses were the proper Judges of the Point in Question, and that he therefore left the Determination of it to them? And are not both the Parts of this Affirmation absolutely false, if it be supposed that the Body here assumed by *Christ* was a spiritual, *i. e.* an immaterial Body? And if, instead of the Object upon which they were to judge, (*viz.* a material Body, capable of exciting such and such Sensations) a very different Thing was substituted, namely, a mere Idea of such an Object, occasioned by the illusory and suborned Evidence of Sensations imprinted on their Minds by a miraculous Power; would not, I say, an Appeal to the Judgment of their Senses in this Case, have been a Mockery?

ery? And would not the impoſing upon their Senſes, after ſuch an Appeal, have been fraudulent and diſhoneſt? And would not ſuch a Proceeding have been abſurd as well as diſhoneſt? For, if it be allowed that *Jeſus* had the Power of impoſing miraculouſly upon the Senſes of his Diſciples, it will not ſurely be denied that he had the Power of entering miraculouſly into the Chamber, where they were aſſembled, while *the Doors were ſhut*. The latter of theſe two Miracles renders the firſt unneceſſary. For if *Jeſus* could in his Human Body enter into the Chamber, while the Doors were ſhut, there was no Occaſion for him to impoſe upon the Senſes of his Diſciples. And if he had it in his Option to work which ever of thoſe Miracles he pleaſed, would it not have been abſurd (with Reverence be it ſpoken) in him to chuſe that, which was inconſiſtent with the Character of one who *came forth from the God of Truth*, and directly oppoſite to the Deſign of his appearing to his Diſciples after his Paſſion; which was, by offering his Body to the Examination of their Senſes, to convince them that he was really, *i. e.* bodily, riſen from the Dead?

The Disciples therefore, who by the mighty Signs and Wonders done by him before his Passion, were convinced that God was with him, could not, upon this Occasion, but draw the same Conclusion from his entering miraculously into the Room while the Doors were shut, and as miraculously perceiving the secret Doubts and Reasonings of their Hearts: And tho', not understanding what was meant by rising from the Dead, they had at first suspected him to be a Spirit; yet having been satisfied of the contrary by handling his Body, they had no more Reason to distrust the Evidence of their Senses, than they had formerly, when after having seen him *walk upon the Waves* *, and having from thence fallen into the like Imagination of his being a *Spirit*, they had been convinced of their Mistake by the same Kind of Proofs, *viz.* by seeing, hearing, and feeling him, eating and conversing with him in the same Manner as with other Men. And indeed there is no Intimation in the sacred Writers of their having had, upon either of these Occasions, any Suspicion of Fraud or Imposture.

* Matth. xiv.

Imposture. They were simple plain Men, Strangers to vain and visionary Speculations; and went upon those Grounds, upon which all Men *act*, however some may *talk*, who have reasoned themselves out of all the Principles of Reason. Having therefore throughout all their past Lives trusted to the Information of their Senses, they could not avoid believing them upon the present Occasion, especially when they were commanded to believe them, by one whose transcendent Knowledge and Power manifested him to have a thorough Insight into the Frame of Man, as well as a supreme Authority over the Laws of Nature.

§. 17. 3dly, The exact Accomplishment of the Words, in which our Saviour foretold to his Disciples his Sufferings, Death and Resurrection, will evidently appear by comparing the Words of those Prophecies with the several Circumstances of those Events. And therefore, to enable the Reader to make this Comparison with the greater Ease, I shall first set down the several Particulars of the Passion, and Death, &c. of *Christ*, and then produce the Prophecies corresponding to them.

THE Sufferings of *Jesus*, properly so called, took their Beginning from the Treachery of * *Judas, one of the Twelve, who*, (as it is related by the Evangelists) *having received a Band of Soldiers, &c. from the Chief Priests*, with whom he had bargained *for thirty Pieces of Silver* to deliver him up, *went with them to a Garden, whither he knew* Christ *was accustomed to resort*, and there by the Sign agreed on *(a Kiss)* having pointed him out, put him into their Hands, who seizing on him immediately, *carried him before the High Priest, &c.*

THIS Fact was several Times foretold by *Jesus*; at first more obscurely, as in these Words, † *Have not I chosen you Twelve, and one of you is a Devil*, Διάβολος, an Informer; and in these, ‖ *The Son of Man shall be betrayed into the Hands of Men*; and in others of the same general Import; then more plainly at the last Supper, to his Disciples, who, upon his

* Matt. xxvi. Mark xiv. Luke xxii. John xviii.
† John vi. 70. ‖ Matt. xvii. 22.

his ſaying, * *Verily I ſay unto you that one of you ſhall betray me*, were *exceeding ſorrowful, and began every one of them to ſay to him, Lord is it I?* In anſwer to which he ſaid, *He that dippeth his Hand with me in the Diſh, the ſame ſhall betray me.* Theſe Words, as *Grotius* † obſerves, muſt be taken to come ſomewhat nearer to a Declaration of the Perſon who was to betray *Jeſus*, than thoſe others, *One of you ſhall betray me*: " Wherefore, adds that learned " Commentator, I am perſuaded that *Judas* " ſat near to *Chriſt*, ſo as to eat out of the " ſame Diſh or Meſs with him, there being " ſeveral Diſhes or Meſſes on the Table." This Conjecture is indeed very probable, and gives great Light to this whole Matter: Upon which we may obſerve ſtill farther, that as the Diſciples, even after this Declaration, were ſtill in Doubt of whom he ſpake, it is evident there muſt have been others beſides *Judas*, who ‖ *dipped their Hands in the ſame Diſh with Jeſus*, otherwiſe that Deſcription had ſufficiently made him known, and there had been no Occaſion for *Simon Peter* to have *beckoned to*

 *that*

* Matth. xxvi. 21. Mark xiv. 18. Luke xxii. 21.
† See Grot. in loc. ‖ John xiii. 22.

*that Diſciple, who was leaning on the Boſom of Jeſus*, that he ſhould aſk him of whom he ſpoke? In compliance therefore with this Demand made to him by St. *John* in the Name of all his Diſciples, and to put an End at once to all their Doubts, *Jeſus* told them he would point out the very Perſon to them, ſaying, *He it is, to whom I ſhall give a Sop when I have dipped it; and when he had dipped the Sop, he gave it to Judas Iſcariot the Son of Simon*; who appearing ſurprized at being thus pronounced a Traitor, either for his farther Satisfaction, or to diſſemble the Wickedneſs of his Heart, himſelf aſked *Jeſus*, if it was He: To whom *Jeſus* anſwered, *Thou ſayeſt*. "And "thus (concludes *Grotius*) *Chriſt* gave Proofs "of his Fore-knowledge by Degrees; firſt in-"cluding the future Traitor in the Number "of the Twelve; then in the leſſer Number of "thoſe who ſat next to him; and laſtly, by "certain and preciſe Marks, pointing out the "very Perſon himſelf." To which I muſt add, that in order to imprint this Prophecy ſtrongly on the Minds of his Diſciples, he introduced it with applying to himſelf a Paſſage of the Pſalms,

Pſalms, * *He that eateth Bread with me, hath lift up his Heel againſt me*; and with theſe remarkable Words, *Now I tell you before it come, that when it is come to paſs you may believe that I am he.*

2. The next Incident is the Deſertion of the Diſciples, who, as we learn both from St. *Matthew* † and St. *Mark* ‡; upon their Maſter's being ſeized by the Soldiers and Servants of the Chief Prieſt, who came with *Judas*, *all* immediately *forſook him and fled.*

Of this their Deſertion *Jeſus* had forewarned them but a very ſhort Time before it came to paſs, and that in the very Pride and Confidence of their Faith upon their profeſſing to believe, that *he came forth from God:* ‖ *Then ſaith* Jeſus *to them, All ye ſhall be offended becauſe of me this Night*, or (as it is in St. *John*) *ſhall be ſcatter'd every Man to his own Home; for it is written, I will ſmite the Shepherd, and the Sheep of the Flock ſhall be ſcattered abroad.*



* Pſal. xli. 9. † Matth. xxvi. 56. ‡ Mark xiv. 50. ‖ Matth. xxvi. 31. Mark xiv. 27. compared with John xvi. 32.

3. THE third Particular is *Peter*'s disowning *Christ*, recorded in all the Evangelists; by whose Accounts it appears, that *Peter*, following *Christ* at a distance to the Palace of the High Priest, was let into the Court by the Means of St. *John*, who *spake to her that kept the Door, and brought in Peter*; where standing among the Croud while his Master was under Examination, he was three several Times charged by some that were about him with belonging to *Christ*, which he as often denied, affirming *with Oaths and Imprecations*, that he did not so much as know him; and immediately after his third Denial the Cock crew; * *and then the Lord turned, and looked upon* Peter, *and* Peter *remembered the Word of the Lord—and went out and wept bitterly*. The Prophecy is as follows: † *Verily I say to thee* [Peter,] *this Day, even this Night, before the Cock crow twice thou shalt deny* [or disown] *me thrice*. Here we see the Nature, the Time, and the Repetitions of *Peter*'s Offence precisely defined and limited. And I take the Suddenness and Sincerity of his Return to his former Faith

* Luke xxii. 61. † Mark xiv. 31.

Faith in his Maſter, implied in his *weeping bitterly* upon the Recollection of his Crime, and of his Maſter's Words, to be fore-ſignified in this Paſſage of St. * *Luke, And the Lord ſaid,* Simon, Simon, *behold* Satan *hath deſired to have you, that he may ſift you as Wheat; but I have prayed for thee, that thy Faith fail not, and when thou art converted* [ἐπιστρέψας, returned back again to the Faith,] *ſtrengthen thy Brethren.*

4. THE fourth Event foretold by *Chriſt,* is his being delivered to the High Prieſts, and by them to *Pontius Pilate* the *Roman* Governor, together with many Particulars of his Sufferings from that Time to his Crucifixion. All which Things are related by the Evangeliſts, as follows:

† *AND they that had laid hold on* Jeſus, *led him away to* Caiaphas *the High Prieſt,* where the Scribes and the Elders were aſſembled; who, after having examined ſome Witneſſes, from whoſe Evidence nothing criminal could be



* Ch. xxii. 31, 32. † Mat. xxvi. 57. Mar. xiv. 53.

be made out against him, at length *adjured him by the living God to tell them, Whether he was the* Christ, *the Son of God.* To him *Jesus* saith, *Thou hast said. Then the High Priest rent his Cloaths, saying, He hath spoken Blasphemy, What farther Need have we of Witnesses? Behold now you have heard his Blasphemy; What think ye? They answered and said,* He is guilty of Death. *Then did they spit in his Face, and buffeted him, and others smote him with the Palms of their Hands, saying, Prophecy to us, thou* Christ, *who is he that smote thee.*

*AND when they had bound him, they led him away to* Pontius Pilate, *the* (Roman) *Governor*; who, overcome by the Clamours of a tumultuous Multitude, at last delivered him to be crucified, after having declared him innocent five several Times, and endeavoured in vain to prevail upon the *Jews* to let him go free, or to be contented with his having scourged him. * *Then the Soldiers of the Governor took* Jesus *into the common Hall, and gathered to him the whole Band of Soldiers; and they stripped him, and put on him a Scarlet Robe;*

* Mat. xxvii. 27.

*Robe; and when they had platted a Crown of Thorns, they put it upon his Head, and a Reed in his Right Hand. And they bowed the Knee before him, and mocked him, ſaying, Hail King of the* Jews. *And they ſpit upon him, and took the Robe off from him, and put his own Raiment on him, and led him away to crucify him.*

THE Words in which many of theſe Particulars were foretold, are theſe. * *Behold, we go up to* Jeruſalem, *and the Son of Man ſhall be betrayed to the Chief Prieſts, and to the Scribes, and they ſhall condemn him to Death. And ſhall deliver him to the* Gentiles *to mock, and to ſcourge, and to crucify him.* † In St. *Mark* it is, *They* [the *Gentiles*] *ſhall mock him, and ſhall ſcourge him, and ſhall ſpit upon him, and ſhall kill him.* || In St. *Luke, For he ſhall be delivered to the* Gentiles, *and ſhall be mocked, and ſpitefully entreated, and ſpit on, and they ſhall ſcourge him and put him to Death.* Of his Sufferings from the Elders and Chief Prieſts he ſpoke in theſe Words: ‡ *From that Time*

* Mat. xx. 18. † Ch. ix. 34. || Ch. xviii. 32.
‡ Mat. xvi. 20.

*Time forth began* Jesus *to shew to the Disciples how he must go to* Jerusalem, *and suffer many Things of the Elders and Chief Priests, and Scribes, and be killed*, &c.

5. His Crucifixion and Death are mentioned in every one of the last cited Passages, and in many others up and down the Evangelists, either in express Words, or in Figures and Allusions, which I think it is not necessary to insert, no more than the Relation of those Events, which are too well known to be disputed.

One Proof however of his Death I shall here beg leave to mention, because it has not been much attended to by common Readers. St. *John*, Chap. xix. ver. 33, 34, after having related that the Soldiers *brake the Legs of the two Thieves*, who were crucified with *Jesus*, adds, *But when they came to* Jesus, *and saw that he was dead already, they brake not his Legs; but one of the Soldiers with a Spear pierced his Side, and forthwith came thereout Blood and Water; and he that saw it, bare Record, &c.* Upon these Words *Beza* makes the following

lowing Observation. Among the Reasons that induced St. *John* to assert this Fact with so much Emphasis, this ought not to be passed over, which *Erasmus* also touches upon; namely, that by this Wound the Death of *Christ* is fully proved. For the Water flowing out of that Wound in the Side, was an Indication of the Spear's have penetrated the *Pericardium*, in which that Water is lodged, and which being wounded, every Animal must necessarily die immediately. This Fact therefore was inserted to obviate the Calumnies of the Enemies of the Truth, who might otherwise pretend that *Jesus* was taken down from the Cross before he was dead, and thence call in question the Reality of his Resurrection from the Dead.

6. OF his Rising from the Dead I need not here again produce the Proofs, having set them forth so copiously in all the preceding Parts of this Discourse; but concerning the Evidence of his rising precisely on *the third Day*, I think it proper here to add an Observation or two. That he did not rise before

before the third Day, is evident from what St. *Matthew* relates of the Watch or Guard being set at the Door of the Sepulchre. The Passage is this: * *Now the next Day, that followed the Day of the Preparation, the Chief Priests and Pharisees came together to* Pilate, *saying, Sir, we remember that that Deceiver said, whilst he was yet alive, After three Days I will rise again: Command therefore that the Sepulchre be made sure* until the third Day, *lest his Disciples come by Night and steal him away, and say to the People, he is risen from the Dead; so the last Error shall be worse than the first*, &c. From these Words I observe, 1st, That the Watch or Guard was set at the Sepulchre the next Day after the Death and Burial of *Christ*. 2dly, It is most probable this was done on what we call, the Evening of that Day; because that was a *High-day*, not only a *Sabbath*, but the *Passover*; and it can hardly be imagined that the Chief Priests, and especially the Pharisees, who pretended to greater Strictness and Purity than any other Sect of the *Jews*, should, before the Religious Duties of the Day were over, defile themselves by going to

* Chap. xxvii. 63.

to *Pilate*; for that they were very ſcrupulous upon that Point appears from what * St. *John* ſays of their not entering into the Hall of Judgment (the *Prætorium*, where *Pilate*'s Tribunal was) the Day before, *leſt they ſhould be defiled*, and ſo kept from eating the Paſſover. And if it ſhould be ſaid, that the Paſchal Lamb being always eaten in the Night, all their Scruples upon that Account were over, and they at Liberty to go to *Pilate* in the Morning, or at what other Time they pleaſed; I anſwer, that allowing the Objection, it is ſtill farther to be conſidered that this was the Sabbath Day; and can it be ſuppoſed that the Phariſees, who cenſured *Jeſus for healing, and his Diſciples for plucking and eating the Ears of Corn on the Sabbath Day*, would profane that Day, and defile themſelves, not only by going to *Pilate*, but with the Soldiers to the Sepulchre of *Chriſt*, and ſetting a Seal upon the Door of the Sepulchre, before the Religious Duties of that ſolemn Day were paſt? eſpecially as they were under no kind of Neceſſity of doing it before the Evening; though it was highly expedient for them not to

* Ch. xviii. 28.

to delay it beyond that Time. Both which Points I ſhall now explain.

*JESUS* had ſaid, whilſt he was yet alive, that he ſhould riſe again from the Dead on *the third Day*; which Prophecy would have been equally falſified by his riſing on the firſt, or ſecond, as on the fourth. If his Body therefore was not in the Sepulchre *at the Cloſe of the ſecond Day*, the Chief Prieſts and Phariſees would gain their Point, and might have aſſerted boldly, that he was an Impoſtor; from whence it will follow, that it was time enough for them to viſit the Sepulchre at *the Cloſe of the ſecond Day*. On the other hand, as he had declared he ſhould riſe on the *third Day*, it was neceſſary for them, (if they apprehended what they gave out, that his Diſciples would come and ſteal him away) to guard againſt any ſuch Attempt on that Day, and *for that Day only*. And, as the third Day began from the Evening or Shutting-in of the ſecond, according to the Way of computing uſed among the *Jews*, it was as neceſſary for them not to delay viſiting the Sepulchre, and ſetting their Guard, till after the

Be-

Beginning of that third Day; for if they had come to the Sepulchre, though ever so short a Time after the *third Day was begun*, and had found the Body missing, they could not from thence have proved him an Impostor. And accordingly St. *Matthew* tells us they went thither on the *second Day*, which was the Sabbath; and though the going to *Pilate*, and with the *Roman* Soldiers, to the Sepulchre, and sealing up the Stone, was undoubtedly a Profanation of the Sabbath, in the Eyes of the ceremonious Pharisees, yet might they excuse themselves to their Consciences, or (what seems to have been of greater Consequence in their Opinions) to the World, by pleading the Necessity of doing it that Day. And surely nothing could have carried them out on such a Business, on such a Day, but the urgent Necessity of doing it *then*, or *not at all*. And as I have shewn above, that this urgent Necessity could not take place till the *Close of the second Day*, and just, though but one Moment, before the Beginning of the third; it will follow, from what hath been said, that in the Estimation of the High Priests and Pharisees, the Day on which they set their

Guard was the *second* Day: and the *next* Day consequently was the *third*; to the End of which they requested *Pilate* to command that the Sepulchre might be made sure. Here then we have a Proof, furnished by the Murderers and Blasphemers of *Christ* themselves, that he was not risen before the third Day; for it is to be taken for granted, that before they sealed up the Sepulchre, and set the Guard, they had inspected it, and seen that the Body was still there. Hence also we are enabled to answer the unlearned Cavils that have been raised upon these Expressions, *three Days and three Nights*, and *after three Days*. For it is plain that the Chief Priests and Pharisees, by their going to the Sepulchre on the Sabbath Day, understood that Day to be the *second*; and it is as plain by their setting the Guard from that Time, and the Reason given to *Pilate* for their so doing, *viz. lest the Disciples should come in the Night, and steal him away*, that they construed that Day, which was just then beginning, to be the Day limited by *Christ* for his Rising from the Dead, *i. e.* the third Day. For had they taken these Words of our Saviour, *The Son of Man shall*

*be*

*be three Days and three Nights in the Heart of the Earth*, in their ſtrict literal Senſe, they need not have been in ſuch haſte to ſet their Guard; ſince, according to that Interpretation, there were yet *two Days* and two *Nights* to come; neither, for the ſame Reaſon, had they any Occaſion to apprehend ill Conſequences from the Diſciples coming *that Night* and ſtealing away the Body of their Maſter. So that, unleſs it be ſuppoſed that the Chief Prieſts and Phariſees, the moſt learned Sect among the *Jews*, did not underſtand the Meaning of a Phraſe in their own Language; or that they were ſo impious or impolitick as to profane the Sabbath and defile themſelves without any Occaſion; and ſo ſenſeleſs and impertinent as to aſk a Guard of *Pilate* for watching the Sepulchre *that Night and Day*, to prevent the Diſciples ſtealing away the Body of *Chriſt* the Night or the Day following; unleſs, I ſay, theſe ſtrange Suppoſitions be admitted, we may fairly conclude, that in the Language, and to the Underſtanding of the *Jews*, *three Days and three Nights*, and *after three Days*, were equivalent to *three Days*, or *in three Days*. That he roſe on the *third* Day, the Teſtimony of the Angels, and his own Appearances to the Women, to *Simon*, and to the two Diſciples on the Way to *Emmaus*, which all happened on that Day, are clear and ſufficient Proofs.

THE Predictions of *Chriſt*, relating to this miraculous Event, are many; ſome of which only I ſhall here ſet down, for Brevity's ſake.

* *AND as they* [the three Diſciples] *came down from the Mountain* [where *Chriſt* had been transfigured] *Jeſus charged them, ſaying, Tell the Viſion to no Man, until the Son of Man be riſen again from the Dead.*

† *BUT after I am riſen, I will go before you into* Galilee.

‡ *FROM that Time forth began* Jeſus *to ſhew to his Diſciples, how that he muſt go to* Jeruſalem, *and ſuffer many Things of the Elders and Chief Prieſts and Scribes, and be killed; and be raiſed again the third Day.*

BE-

* Mat. xviii. 9. † Chap. xxvi. 32. ‡ Chap. xvi. 22.

* *BEHOLD, we go up to* Jerusalem, *and the Son of Man shall be betrayed to the Chief Priests, and to the Scribes, and they shall condemn him to Death, and shall deliver him to the Gentiles, to mock, and to scourge, and to crucify him, and the third Day he shall rise again.*

I SHALL defer what Remarks I have to make upon these Predictions, and their Accomplishment, till I come to consider the Prophecies contained in the Writings of *Moses*, and the *Prophets*, and the *Psalms*, relating to the Sufferings, and Death, and Resurrection of *Christ*; for those only belong to the present Subject.

§. 18. *4thly*, THE fourth Evidence appealed to by our Saviour, was the Testimony of the Scriptures; in which are contained, not only the Promises of a Messiah, and Saviour of the World, but the Marks and Descriptions by which he was to be known. Of these there are many, and those so various, so seemingly incompatible in one and the same



* Matth. xx. 18, 19.

Perſon, and exhibited under ſuch a Multitude of Types and Figures, that as it was abſurd for a meer Mortal to pretend to anſwer the Character of the Meſſiah in all Points, ſo was it difficult to thoſe, who by ſome Expreſſions of the Prophets were filled with the Idea of a glorious, powerful, and triumphant Deliverer, to underſtand the Intimation given in others of his Sufferings and Death. But this Difficulty proceeds rather from the Prejudices and Blindneſs of the Interpreters, than from any Degree of Obſcurity in the latter more than in the former. His Sufferings and Death, and his offering himſelf up as a Sacrifice for Sin, are as plainly ſet forth in the Writings of the Prophets, and in the Types of the *Moſaical* Ceremonies, as his Power and his Prieſthood: And if the *Jews*, and even the Diſciples, poſſeſſed with the like vain and carnal Imaginations, turned their Views and Expectations to the one, and over-looked the other, it was owing to their miſtaking the Nature of his Kingdom, and the End and Deſign of his Prieſtly Office. This, I doubt not, might be made appear by comparing the ſeveral Types and Prophecies together, but would carry me too far from my preſent Purpoſe, which is only to ſhew, that the Sufferings, and Death, and Reſurrection of *Chriſt*, were foretold in the Types and Predictions contained in the Books of *Moſes*, in the *Prophets*, and in the *Pſalms*; and to derive from thence another Proof in favour of the Reſurrection.

THE firſt Prophecy relating to this Subject in the Books of *Moſes*, and the firſt indeed that was ever given to Man, is that recorded in the third Chapter of *Geneſis*, and the 15th Verſe, in theſe Words, *And I will put Enmity between thee* [the Serpent] *and the Woman, and between thy Seed and her Seed. It ſhall bruiſe thy Head, and thou ſhalt bruiſe his Heel.*

UPON this Prophecy, I ſhall beg leave to quote a Paſſage out of the preſent Biſhop of *Saliſbury*'s moſt admirable Diſcourſes, *Of the Uſe and Intent of Prophecy in the ſeveral Ages of the World*, Diſc. III. p. 57.---" Let us con-" ſider the Hiſtory of *Moſes*, as we ſhould do " any other ancient *Eaſtern* Hiſtory of the " like Antiquity: Suppoſe for Inſtance, that " this Account of the Fall had been preſerved

" to us out of *Sanchoniatho*'s *Phœnician* Hi-
" story: We should in that Case be at a Loss
" perhaps to account for every Manner of
" *Representation*, for every *Figure* and *Ex-
" pression* in the Story; but we should soon
" agree that all these Difficulties were impu-
" table to the *Manner* and *Customs* of his *Age*
" and *Country*; and should shew more Re-
" spect to so *venerable* a Piece of *Antiquity*,
" than to charge it with *Want* of *Sense*, be-
" cause we did not understand every minute
" Circumstance: We should likewise agree,
" that there were evidently *four Persons* con-
" cerned in the Story; the *Man*, the *Wo-
" man*, the *Person* represented by the *Serpent*,
" and *God*. Disagree we could not about their
" several Parts. The *Serpent* is evidently the
" *Tempter*; the *Man* and the *Woman* are the
" *Offenders*; *God* the *Judge* of all three. The
" Punishments inflicted on the *Man* and *Wo-
" man* have no Obscurity in them; and as to
" the *Serpent*'s Sentence, we should think it
" reasonable to give it such a Sense as the
" whole Series of the Story requires.

" 'Tis no unreasonable Thing surely to
" demand the same Equity of you in inter-
" preting

" preting the Sense of *Moses*, as you would " certainly use towards any other ancient Wri- " ter. And if the same Equity be allowed, " this *plain Fact* undeniably arises from the " History; That Man was tempted to Diso- " bedience, and did disobey, and forfeited " all Title to Happiness, and to Life itself; " That God judged *him* and the *Deceiver* like- " wise under the *Form* of a *Serpent*. We re- " quire no more; and will proceed upon this " Fact to consider this Prophecy before us.

" THE Prophecy is Part of the Sen- " tence passed upon the Deceiver: The " Words are these: *I will put Enmity between* " *thee and the Woman, and between thy Seed* " *and her Seed: It shall bruise thy Head, and* " *thou shalt bruise his Heel*; Gen. iii. 15. " Christian Writers apply this to our blessed " Saviour, emphatically stiled here *the Seed of* " *the Woman*, and who came in the Fulness " of Time to *bruise the Serpent's Head*, by de- " stroying the Works of the Devil, and re- " storing those to the Liberty of the Sons of " God, who were held under the Bondage " and Captivity of Sin. You'll say, What

" unreasonable Liberty of Interpretation is " this? Tell us by what Rules of Language " *the Seed of the Woman* is made to denote " *one* particular *Person*, and by what Art you " discover the Mystery of *Christ*'s miraculous " Conception and Birth in this common Ex- " pression? Tell us likewise, how bruising " the Serpent's Head comes to signify the " destroying the Power of Sin, and the " Redemption of Mankind by *Christ*? 'Tis " no Wonder to hear such Questions, from " those who look no farther than to the " third Chapter of *Genesis*, to see the Ground " of the Christian Application. As the Pro- " phecy stands *there*, nothing appears to point " out this particular Meaning; much less to " confine this Prophecy to it. But of this " hereafter. Let us for the present lay aside " all our own Notions, and go back to the " State and Condition of Things, as they were " at the Time of the Delivery of this Pro- " phecy; and see (if haply we may discover " it) what God intended to discover at that " Time by this Prophecy, and what we may " reasonably suppose our first Parents under- " stood it to mean.

" THEY

" They were now in a State of Sin, " ſtanding before God to receive Sentence for " their Diſobedience, and had Reaſon to ex- " pect a full Execution of the Penalty threat- " ened, *In the Day thou eateſt thereof thou ſhalt* " *ſurely die*. But God came in Mercy as well " as Judgment, purpoſing not only to puniſh, " but to reſtore Man. The Judgment is aw- " ful and ſevere; the Woman is doom'd to " Sorrow in Conception; the Man to Sorrow " and Travail all the Days of his Life; the " Ground is curſed for his Sake; and the " End of the Judgment is, *Duſt thou art, and* " *to Duſt thou ſhalt return*. Had they been left " thus, they might have continued in their " Labour and Sorrow for their appointed " Time, and at laſt returned to Duſt, with- " out any well-grounded Hope or Confi- " dence in God: They muſt have looked up- " on themſelves as rejected by their Maker, " delivered up to Trouble and Sorrow in this " World, and as having no Hope in any " other. Upon this Foot, I conceive, there " could have been no Religion left in the " World; for a Senſe of Religion, without " Hope,

" Hope, is a State of Phrenzy and Diſtrac-
" tion, void of all Inducements to Love and
" Obedience, or any thing elſe that is Praiſe-
" worthy. If therefore God intended to pre-
" ſerve them as Objects of Mercy, it was
" abſolutely neceſſary to communicate *ſo much*
" *Hope* to them, as might be a *rational*
" *Foundation* for their future Endeavours to
" reconcile themſelves to him by a better
" Obedience. This ſeems to be the *primary*
" Intention of this firſt divine Prophecy; and
" it was neceſſary to the State of the World,
" and the Condition of Religion, which
" could not poſſibly have been ſupported
" without the Communication of ſuch Hopes.
" The Prophecy is excellently adapted to
" this Purpoſe, and manifeſtly conveyed ſuch
" Hopes to our firſt Parents. For let us con-
" ſider, in what Senſe we may ſuppoſe them to
" underſtand this Prophecy. Now they muſt
" neceſſarily underſtand the Prophecy, either
" according to the literal Meaning of the
" Words, or according to ſuch Meaning as
" the whole Circumſtance of the Tranſaction,
" of which they are a Part, does require.
" If we ſuppoſe them to underſtand the
" Words

" Words literally, and that God meant them " ſo to be underſtood, this Paſſage muſt ap- " pear ridiculous. Do but imagine that you " ſee *God* coming to *judge* the *Offenders*; *Adam* " and *Eve* before him in the *utmoſt Diſtreſs*; " that you hear *God* inflicting *Pains*, and " *Sorrow*, and *Miſery*, and *Death* upon the " firſt of Human Race; and that in the " midſt of all this Scene of Woe and great " Calamity, you hear *God* foretelling with " great *Solemnity* a *very trivial* Accident, that " ſhould ſometimes happen in the World; " That Serpents would be apt to bite Men " by the Heels, and that Men would be apt " to revenge themſelves by ſtriking them on " the Head. What has *this Trifle* to do with " the *Loſs of Mankind*, with the *Corruption* " of the *natural* and *moral* World, and the " *Ruin* of all the *Glory* and *Happineſs* of the " Creation? Great Comfort it was to *Adam*, " doubtleſs, after telling him that his Days " ſhould be ſhort and full of Miſery, and " his End without Hope, to let him know, " that he ſhould now and then knock a " Snake on the Head, but not even that, " without paying dear for his poor Victory,

" for

" for the Snake should often bite him by " the Heel. *Adam*, surely, could not un- " derstand the Prophecy in this Sense, tho' " some of his Sons have so understood it; " a plain Indication how much more some " Men are concern'd to maintain a literal " Interpretation of Scripture, than they are " to make it speak common Sense. Leaving " this therefore as absolutely absurd and ridi- " culous, let us consider what Meaning the Cir- " cumstances of the Transaction do necessarily " fix to the Words of this Prophecy. *Adam* " tempted by his Wife, and she by the Ser- " pent, had fallen from their Obedience, and " were now in the Presence of God expect- " ing Judgment. They knew full well at " this Juncture, that their *Fall* was the " *Victory* of the *Serpent*, whom by Expe- " rience they found to be an *Enemy* to *God* " and to *Man*; to Man, whom he had *ruin-* " *ed* by seducing him to Sin; to God, the " noblest Work of whose Creation he had " defaced. It could not therefore but be " some Comfort to them to hear the Serpent " first condemned, and to see that however " he had prevailed against them, he had

" gained

" gained no Victory over their Maker, who " was able to assert his own Honour, and " to punish this great Author of Iniquity. " By this Method of God's Proceeding they " were secured from thinking that there was " any evil Being equal to the Creator in Power " and Dominion. An Opinion which gain- " ed Ground in After-times thro' the Pre- " valency of Evil; and is, where it does " prevail, destructive of all true Religion. " The Condemnation therefore of the Serpent " was the Maintenance of God's Supremacy; " and that it was so understood, we have, if " I mistake not, a very antient Testimony " in the Book of *Job: With God is Strength* " *and Wisdom, the Deceived and the Deceiver* " *are his*: i. e. equally subject to his Com- " mand; *Job* xii. 16. The Belief of God's " supreme Dominion, which is the Founda- " tion of all Religion, being thus preserved, " it was still necessary to give them such " Hopes as might make them capable of Re- " ligion toward God. These Hopes they " could not but conceive, when they heard " from the Mouth of God that the Serpent's " Victory was not a compleat Victory over

" even

" even themselves; that they and their Pos-
" terity should be enabled to contest his Em-
" pire; and though they were to suffer much
" in the Struggle, yet finally they should
" prevail and bruise the Serpent's Head, and
" deliver themselves from his Power and Do-
" minion over them. What now could they
" conceive this Conquest over the Serpent to
" mean? Is it not natural to expect that we
" shall recover that by Victory, which we
" lost by being defeated? They knew that
" the Enemy had subdued them by Sin;
" could they then conceive Hopes of Victory
" otherwise than by Righteousness? They lost
" thro' Sin the Happiness of their Creation;
" could they expect less from the Return
" of Righteousness than the Recovery of the
" Blessings forfeited? What else but this could
" they expect? For the certain Knowledge
" they had of their Loss when the Serpent
" prevailed, could not but lead them to a
" clear Knowledge of what they should re-
" gain by prevailing against the Serpent. The
" Language of this Prophecy is indeed in
" part Metaphorical, but 'tis a great Mistake
" to think that all Metaphors are of un-

" certain

" certain Signification; for the Design and " Scope of the Speaker, with the Circum- " stances attending, create a fixed and deter- " minate Sense. Were it otherwise, there " would be no Certainty in any Language; " all Languages, the *Eastern* more especially, " abounding in Metaphors.

" LET us now look back to our Subject, " and see what Application we are to make " of this Instance.

" THIS Prophecy was to our first Parents " but very obscure; it was, in the Phrase of " St. *Peter*, but *a Light shining in a dark* " *Place*; all that they could certainly con- " clude from it was, that their Case was not " desperate; that some Remedy, that some " Deliverance from the Evil they were un- " der, would in Time appear; but *when*, or " *where*, or by *what Means*, they could not " understand: Their own Sentence, which " returned them back again to the Dust of " the Earth, made it difficult to apprehend " what this Victory over the Serpent should " signify, or how they, who were shortly to

" be

" be Duſt and Aſhes, ſhould be the better " for it. But after all that can be urged up- " on this Head to ſet out the Obſcurity of " this Promiſe, I would aſk one Queſtion : " Was not this Promiſe or Prophecy, tho' " ſurrounded with all this Obſcurity, a Foun- " dation for Religion, and Truſt and Confi- " dence towards God after the Fall, in Hopes " of Deliverance from the Evils introduced " by Diſobedience? If it was, it fully an- " ſwered the Neceſſity of their Caſe, to whom " it was given, and manifeſted to them all " that God intended to make manifeſt. " They could have had towards God no " Religion, without ſome Hopes of Mercy : " It was neceſſary therefore to convey ſuch " Hopes; but to tell them how theſe Hopes " ſhould be accompliſhed, at what Time " and Manner preciſely, was not neceſſary " to their Religion. And what is now " to be objected againſt this Prophecy? " It is very obſcure you ſay; ſo it is; but " 'tis obſcure in the Points, which God did " not intend to explain at that Time, and " which were not neceſſary then to be known. " You ſee a plain Reaſon for giving this

" Prophe-

" this Prophecy, and as far as the Reaſon for " giving the Prophecy extends, ſo far the Pro- " phecy is very plain: 'Tis obſcure only where " there is no Reaſon why it ſhould be plain; " which ſurely is a Fault eaſily to be forgiven, " and very far from being a proper Subject " for Complaint.

" But if this Prophecy conveyed to our " firſt Parents only a general Hope and Ex- " pectation of Pardon and Reſtoration, and " was intended by God to convey no more " to *them*, how came we their Poſterity to find " ſo much more in this Promiſe than we ſup- " poſe them to find? How is it that we pre- " tend to diſcover *Chriſt* in this Prophecy, to " ſee in it the Myſtery of his Birth, his Suffer- " ings, and his final Triumph over all the " Powers of Darkneſs? By what new Light " do we diſcern all theſe Secrets? By what " Art do we unfold them?

" 'Tis no Wonder to me, that ſuch as come " to the Examination of the Prophecies ap- " plied to *Chriſt*, expecting to find in each of " them ſome expreſs Character and Mark of

" *Christ*, plainly to be understood as such antecedently to his Coming, should ask these, or any other the like Questions; or that the Argument from antient Prophecy, should appear so light and trivial to those who know no better Use of it.

" *KNOWN unto God are all his Works from the Beginning*; and whatever Degree of Light he thought fit to communicate to our first Parents, or to their Children in After-times, there is no doubt but that He had a perfect Knowledge at all Times of all the Methods by which he intended to rescue and restore Mankind; and therefore all the Notices given by him to Mankind of his intended Salvation, must correspond to the great Event, whenever the Fulness of Time shall make it manifest. No Reason can be given why God should at all Times, or at any Time clearly open the Secrets of his Providence to Men; it depends meerly upon his good Pleasure to do it in what Time and in what Manner he thinks proper. But there is a necessary Reason to be given why all such Notices as God thinks fit to give

" should

" should answer exactly in due Time to the " Completion of the great Design: It is ab- " surd therefore to complain of the antient " Prophecies for being obscure; for it is chal- " lenging God for not telling us more of his " Secrets. But if we pretend that God has " at length manifested to us by the Re- " velation of the Gospel the Method of his " Salvation, it is necessary for us to shew that " all the Notices of this Salvation given to " the old World do correspond to the Things " which we have seen and heard with our Eyes. " The Argument from Prophecy therefore is " not to be formed in this Manner: *All the* " *antient Prophecies have expresly pointed out* " *and characterized* Christ Jesus. But it must " be formed in this Manner: *All the Notices* " *which God gave the Fathers of his intend-* " *ed Salvation, are perfectly answered by the* " *Coming of* Christ. He never promised or " engaged his Word in any Particular relating " to the common Salvation, but what he has " fully made good by sending his Son to our " Redemption. Let us try these Methods " upon the Prophecy before us. If you de- " mand that we should shew you *à priori Christ-*

" *Jesus* set forth in this Prophecy, and that " God had limited himself by this Promise " to convey the Blessings intended by sending " his own Son in the Flesh, and by no other " Means whatever, you demand what I can- " not shew, nor do I know who can. But if " you enquire whether this Prophecy, in the " obvious and most natural Meaning of it, in " that Sense in which our first Parents, and " their Children after, might easily understand " it, has been verified by the Coming of " *Christ*, I conceive it may be made as clear as " the Sun at Noon-day, that all the Expec- " tation raised by this Prophecy, has been " completely answered by the Redemption " wrought by *Jesus Christ*. And what have " you to desire more than to see a Prophecy " fulfilled exactly? If you insist that the Pro- " phecy should have been more express, you " must demand of God why he gave you no " more Light; but you ought at least to sus- " pend this Demand till you have a Reason " to shew for it.

" I KNOW that this Prophecy is urged far- " ther, and that Christian Writers argue from " the

" the Expressions of it to shew that *Christ* is
" therein particularly foretold: He properly
" is the *Seed of a Woman* in a Sense in which
" no other ever was; his Sufferings were well
" prefigured by the *bruising of the Heel*, his
" complete Victory over Sin and Death by
" *bruising the Serpent's Head*. When Unbe-
" lievers hear such Reasonings, they think
" themselves intitled to laugh; but their Scorn
" be to themselves. We readily allow that the
" Expressions do not imply necessarily this
" Sense: We allow farther, that there is no
" Appearance that our first Parents understood
" them in this Sense, or that God intended
" they should so understand them: But since
" this Prophecy has been plainly fulfilled in
" *Christ*, and by the Event appropriated to
" him only; I would fain know how it comes
" to be conceived to be so ridiculous a thing
" in us, to suppose that God, to whom the
" whole Event was known from the Begin-
" ning*, should make choice of such Ex-

R 3 pressions,

* *Remember the former Things of old; for I am God, and there is none else; I am God, and there is none like me; declaring the End from the Beginning, and from antient Times the Things that are not yet done, saying, My Counsel shall stand, and I will do all my Pleasure.* Isa. xlvi. 9, 10.

The

" pressions, as naturally conveyed so much " Knowledge as he intended to convey to our " first Parents, and yet should appear in the " Fulness of Time to have been peculiarly " adapted to the Event, which he from the " Beginning saw, and which he intended the " World should one Day see; and which " when they should see, they might the more " easily acknowledge to be the Work of his " Hand, by the secret Evidence which he had " inclosed from the Days of old in the Words " of Prophecy. However the Wit of Man " may despise this Method, yet there is no- " thing in it unbecoming the Wisdom of " God. And when we see this to be the Case, " not only in this Instance, but in many other " Prophecies of the Old Testament, it is not " without Reason we conclude, that under the " Obscurity of antient Prophecy there was an " Evidence of God's Truth kept in Reserve, " to be made manifest in due Time."

The exquisite and masterly Sense, Clearness and Force of Reason, which is so conspicuous

*The Works of the Lord are done in Judgment from the Beginning; and from the Time he made them, he disposed the Parts thereof.* Ecclus. xvi. 26.

culous in this Passage, that every common Reader must perceive, and every judicious one admire it; and the Pertinency of it to the present Subject, will, I doubt not, sufficiently atone for the Length of the Quotation.

In all the Books of *Moses* I find no other Prophecy but this, relating to the Death and Sufferings of *Christ*; I shall therefore, according to the Method pointed out in the Words of our Saviour, proceed in the next Place to the Prophets; and first produce one out of *Isaiah*, whose Application to the Messiah the most obstinate Enemies of the Gospel have not been able to deny.

Isaiah, Ch. liii. *Who hath believed our Report? And to whom is the Arm of the Lord revealed? For he shall grow up before him as a tender Plant, and as a Root out of a dry Ground: He hath no Form nor Comeliness, and when we shall see him, there is no Beauty that we should desire him.* " *He is despised and rejected of Men,* " *a Man of Sorrows, and acquainted with Grief;* " *and we hid as it were our Faces from him. He was despised, and we esteemed him not. Surely he*

 *hath*

*hath borne our Griefs, and carried our Sorrows: Yea we did esteem him stricken, smitten of God and afflicted. But he was* wounded *for our Transgressions, he was* bruised *for our Iniquities: The Chastisement of our Peace was upon him, and with his* Stripes *we are healed. All we like Sheep have gone astray: We have turned every one to his own Way, and the Lord hath laid on him the Iniquity of us all. He was* oppressed *and he was* afflicted, *yet he "opened not his Mouth. He is "brought as a Lamb to the Slaughter, and as a "Sheep before her Shearers is dumb, so he opened "not his Mouth." He was taken from* * *Prison and from Judgment: And who shall declare his Generation? For "he was cut off out of the "Land of the Living;" for the Transgression of my People he was stricken. "And he made "his Grave with the Wicked, and with the "Rich in his Death; because he had done no Vio-"lence, neither was any Deceit in his Mouth." Yet it pleased the Lord to bruise him, he hath put him to Grief: When thou shalt make his Soul an Offering for Sin, he shall see his Seed, he shall prolong his Days, and the Pleasure of the Lord shall prosper in his Hands. He shall see of the Travel*

* The Margin of the Bible has it, *He was taken away by Distress and Judgment.*

*Travel of his Soul, and shall be satisfied: By his Knowledge shall my righteous Servant justify many: For he shall bear their Iniquities. Therefore will I divide him a Portion with the Great, and he shall divide the Spoil with the Strong; because he poured out his Soul unto Death,* " *and he was* " *numbered with the Transgressors,*" *and he bare the Sin of many, and* " *made Intercession for* " *the Transgressors.*"

It is impossible for any one, who is the least acquainted with the History of *Christ*, not to perceive many Circumstances of his Life, his Sufferings and his Death, plainly pointed at in this Prophecy; and indeed so apparently and so completely was it fulfilled in *Christ*, that the later Rabbins, to avoid the Conclusions which the *Christians* might draw from this and other Prophecies in favour of the Gospel, have invented a Distinction of a double Messias; " one * who was to redeem us, and " another who was to suffer for us; for they " say, that there are two several Persons pro- " mised under the Name of the Messias; one " of the Tribe of *Ephraim*, the other of the " Tribe

* See *Pearson* on the Creed, p. 185.

" Tribe of *Judah*; one the Son of *Joseph*, the " other the Son of *David*; the one to pre- " cede, fight, and suffer Death; the other to " follow, conquer, reign, and never to die." But Bishop *Pearson*, from whom I have borrowed this Remark, has clearly shewed this Distinction to be not only false in itself, but advantageous to the Christian Faith, as admitting a suffering Messias to be foretold by the Prophets; and has also proved, * that the antient Rabbins did understand this Fifty-third Chapter of *Isaiah* to be a Description of the Messias, without any Intimation of a double Messias, an Invention introduc'd by the modern *Jews*, to favour their vain Expectations of a temporal Prince and Deliverer.

For what is farther to be considered out of the other Prophecies, and especially the *Psalms*, relating to this Subject, I cannot do better than to give it to the Reader in the Words of the same Bishop *Pearson*, whose Observations upon the several Articles concerning the Sufferings, &c. of *Jesus*, I would wish him to consider.

" All

* *Pearson* on the Creed, p. 57.

" * ALL which [the Predictions of his Sufferings, and particularly this Fifty-third Chapter of *Isaiah*, compared with his Life]
" if we look upon in the Gross, we must
" acknowledge it fulfilled in Him [*Jesus*]
" to the highest Degree imaginable, *that he*
" *was a Man of Sorrows and acquainted with*
" *Grief*. But if we compare the particular
" Predictions with the historical Passages of
" his Sufferings, if we join the Prophets and
" Evangelists together, it will most manifestly
" appear the Messias was to suffer nothing
" which *Christ* hath not suffered. If *Zachary*
" say, † *They weighed for my Price thirty Pieces*
" *of Silver*; St. *Matthew* ‡ will shew, that *Judas* sold *Jesus* at the same Rate; for the Chief
" Priests *covenanted with him for thirty Pieces*
" *of Silver*. If *Isaiah* say, ‖ *That he was*
" *wounded*; if *Zachary*, § *they shall look upon*
" *me whom they have pierced*; if the Prophet
" *David* yet more particularly, :: *they pierced*
" *my Hands and my Feet*; the Evangelists will
" shew how he was fastened to the Cross, and
" *Jesus* himself ** *the Print of the Nails*. If
" the *Psalmist* tell us, they should †† *laugh him*
" to

* *Pearson* on the Creed, p. 88. † Zach. xi. 12.
‡ Mat. xxvi. 15. ‖ If. liii. 5. § Zach. xii. 10.
:: Pf. xxii. 16. ** John xx. 25. †† Pf. xxii. 7, 8.

" *to Scorn, and ſhake their Head, ſaying, He*
" *truſted in the Lord that he would deliver him;*
" *let him deliver him, ſeeing he delighted in him;*
" St. *Matthew* will deſcribe the ſame Action,
" and the ſame Expreſſions: For * *they that*
" *paſſed by reviled him, wagging their Heads,*
" *and ſaying, He truſted in God, let him deliver*
" *him now if he will have him; for he ſaid, I*
" *am the Son of God.* Let *David* ſay, † *My*
" *God, my God, why haſt thou forſaken me?*
" and the Son of *David* will ſhew in whoſe
" Perſon the Father ſpoke it, *Eli, Eli, lama*
" *ſabacthani?* Let *Iſaiah* foretell, § *He was*
" *numbered with the Tranſgreſſors*, and you
" ſhall find him ‡ *crucified between two Thieves,*
" *one on his Right-hand, the other on his Left.*
" Read in the *Pſalmiſt*, ‖ *In my Thirſt they*
" *gave me Vinegar to drink*; and you ſhall
" find in the Evangeliſt, ** *Jeſus, that the*
" *Scripture might be fulfilled, ſaid, I thirſt: And*
" *they took a Spunge, and filled it with Vinegar,*
" *and put it on a Reed, and gave him to drink.*
" Read farther yet, †† *They part my Garments*
" *among them, and caſt Lots upon my Veſture;*
" and

* Mat. xxvii. 39, 43. † Pſ. xxii. 1. Mat. xxvii. 46.
§ Iſ. liii. 12. ‡ Mark xv. 27. ‖ Pſ. lxix. 21.
** John xix. 28. Mat. xxvii. 48. †† Pſ. xxii. 18.

" and to fulfill the Prediction, the Soldiers " ſhall make good the Diſtinction, † *Who took " his Garments, and made four Parts, to every " Soldier a Part, and alſo his Coat: Now the " Coat was without Seam, woven from the " Top throughout. They ſaid therefore among " themſelves, Let us not rend it, but caſt Lots " for it, whoſe it ſhall be.* Laſtly, let the " Prophets teach us, ‖ *that he ſhall be brought " like a Lamb to the Slaughter, and be cut off " out of the Land of the Living*; all the *E-" vangeliſts* will declare how like a Lamb he " ſuffered, and the very *Jews* will acknow-" ledge that he was cut off."

These Inſtances, I imagine, are ſufficient to ſhew, that according to the Prophets, *thus it behoved Chriſt to ſuffer, and to die.* That his Burial alſo, and his Reſurrection, were in like manner foretold, will appear by the following Paſſages.

*ISAIAH*, in the above-quoted Chapter, Ver. 9. ſpeaks of his Burial in theſe Words, *And he made his Grave with the Wicked, and with*

† John xix. 23, 24. ‖ Iſ. liii. 7, 8.

*with the Rich in his Death*, the circumstantial Accomplishment of which is too remarkable not to be taken notice of.

* THE Power of Life and Death had been taken from the *Jews* and lodged in the Hands of the *Roman* Governor, from the Time that *Augustus* annexed *Judea* to the Province of *Syria*; which was done some Years after the Birth of *Christ*. The Chief Priests therefore and Rulers of the *Jews* were obliged to apply to *Pontius Pilate*, not only to put *Jesus* to Death, but for Leave to take down his Body and those of the two Malefactors executed with him, *that they might not remain upon the Cross on the Sabbath-day*. For among the *Romans*, (with whom Crucifixion was the usual capital Punishment for Slaves, Robbers, &c. under the Degree of *Roman* Citizens) it was customary to let the Carcass hang on the Cross till it was either consumed by Time, or devoured by Birds and Beasts. Upon a Petition however of the executed Person's Friends or Relations, Leave to bury them was seldom or never refused; and hence *Pilate* without any

* See *Pearson* on the Creed, Article 4.

any Difficulty yielded to the Application of the *Jews* for taking down the Bodies, and gave Permiſſion to *Joſeph* of *Arimathæa* to bury that of *Jeſus*. What became of the Bodies of the two Thieves after they were taken down from the Croſs is not mentioned by any of the Evangeliſts. That they were buried is almoſt certain; becauſe not only the Cuſtom of the *Jews*, but the expreſs Words of *Moſes* † required, *If a Man have committed a Sin worthy of Death, and he be put to Death, and thou hang him on a Tree, his Body ſhall not remain all Night upon the Tree, but thou ſhalt in any wiſe bury him that Day, that thy Land be not defiled.* Which Precept was doubtleſs the Reaſon of their petitioning *Pilate* to have the Bodies taken from the Croſs that Day, enforced by the additional Conſideration of the particular Solemnity and Sanctity of the Paſchal Sabbath then immediately enſuing. And that they were buried in or near the Place of Crucifixion is, I think, moſt probable for the following Reaſons. Firſt, The Place where they were executed was called *Golgotha*, i. e. * *a Place of a Skull*, a Name in all likelihood derived

† Deut. xxi. 22, 23. * Matth. xxvii. 33.

derived to it from the Number of Skulls, which (if it was the usual Place of Execution, as from this Instance it is most reasonable to conclude it was) might frequently have been found there, either fallen from Bodies left to putrify on the Cross, or turned up by the opening the Ground for such Malefactors as the Governor permitted to be buried. Secondly, The Paschal Sabbath * was drawing on apace. For as among the *Jews* the Day was always reckoned to commence from the Evening, so, for the greater Caution, were they accustomed to begin the Sabbatical Rest from all kind of Work an Hour before Sun-set; but on this Day, which was the Preparation of the Passover, the holy Hours (if I may so speak) began still earlier; because the ‖ Paschal Lambs were always slain between the ninth and eleventh Hours, within which Space of Time the whole Multitude of *Jews* repaired to the Temple ‡, where alone the Passover was killed, and having there offered the Blood and Entrails of the Paschal Victims, they brought back the remaining Carcass to dress

* Grotius, ad ver. 58. 27. Mat. ‖ Ibid. xxvi. Mat. 2.
‡ Lamy Dissert. de Pasch.

drefs and eat it at their own Homes, according to the *Mofaical* Inftitution. The *Jews* could not then be much preffed in Time, for the ninth Hour was begun before our Saviour expired, and the Soldiers coming after that Time to the two Malefactors, found them not yet dead; and therefore by a cruel kind of Mercy to put an End to a painful Life, and to difpatch them the more fpeedily, broke their Legs, the *Coup de Grace* obtained for thofe miferable Wretches of the *Roman* Governor by the *Jews*, and intended likewife for him, who, though innocent, and delivered up by their Malice to that infamous and horrid Death, yet, with a Benevolence and Generofity unparallelled, interceded for them even upon the Crofs, in thefe compaffionate Terms, *Father*, * *forgive them, for they know not what they do!* Now as *Jefus*, and confequently the two Thieves, did not expire till after the ninth Hour, as the *Jews* were obliged to repair to the Temple before the eleventh Hour, at the Expiration of which the Sabbatical Reft from all kinds of Work began; and as they were folicitous that the Bodies fhould be ta-

S ken

* Luke xxiii. 34.

ken down and buried before the Commencement of that high and solemn Day; it is most likely they buried them at or near the Place where they were crucified; because they had not Time to carry them to any great Distance; because *Golgotha*, from its Name, seems to have been a Place of Burial for those who had been executed there; and because the Want of Time is the very Reason given in the Evangelist for laying the Body of *Jesus* in the Sepulchre of *Joseph* of *Arimathæa*; which was near adjoining, as St. *John* tells us in these Words: * *Now in the Place where he was crucified there was a Garden, and in the Garden a new Sepulchre, wherein was never Man yet laid.* There laid they *Jesus* therefore because of the *Jews* Preparation, for the Sepulchre was nigh at Hand. Here then we may see and admire the exact Completion of this famous Prophecy of *Isaiah*: *He made his Grave with the Wicked, and with the Rich in his Death.* He was buried like the *Wicked* Companions of his Death under the general Leave granted to the *Jews* for taking down their Bodies from the Cross; and was like them buried

in

* Chap. xix. 41, 42.

in or near the Place of Execution. But here the Distinction foreseen and foretold many hundred Years before, took place in favour of *Jesus*, who, though *numbered with the Transgressors, had done no Violence, neither was there any Deceit in his Mouth*: For *Joseph* of *Arimathæa* *, *a rich Man, and an honourable Counsellor, and* Nicodemus †, *a Man of the* Pharisees, *a Ruler of the* Jews, *a Master of* Israel, *conspired* ‡ *to make his Grave with the Rich*, *by wrapping his Body in Linen-clothes, with a mixture of Myrrh and Aloes, about an hundred Pound Weight, and laying it in a new Sepulchre* hewed or hollowed into a Rock, which *Joseph* of *Arimathæa* had caused to be made for his own Use; Circumstances which evidently shew, that he was not only buried *by* the Rich, but *like* the Rich also according to the Prophecy.

The Words of *David* ‖ foretelling the Resurrection of *Christ*, together with St. *Peter*'s Comment upon them, I shall insert intire as

 they

* Mat. xxvii. 57. Mark xv. 43. † John xix. 39, 40.
‡ Isa. liii. 9. ‖ Psal. xvi. 8, &c.

they ſtand in the Second Chapter of the *Acts*, the 25th and following Verſes.

*FOR* David *ſpeaketh concerning him, I foreſaw the Lord always before my Face; for he is on my Right-hand, that I ſhould not be moved: Therefore did my Heart rejoice, and my Tongue was glad; moreover alſo my Fleſh ſhall reſt in Hope, becauſe thou wilt not leave my Soul in Hell, neither wilt thou ſuffer thy Holy One to ſee Corruption. Thou haſt made known to me the Ways of Life. Thou haſt made me full of Joy with thy Countenance. Men and Brethren, let me freely ſpeak to you of the Patriarch* David, *that he is both dead and buried, and his Sepulchre is with us to this Day; therefore being a Prophet, and knowing that God had ſworn with an Oath to him, that of the Fruit of his Loins, according to the Fleſh, he would raiſe up Chriſt to ſit upon his Throne; he ſeeing this before, ſpake of the Reſurrection of* Chriſt, *that his Soul was not left in Hell, neither his Fleſh did ſee Corruption.*

THE Apoſtle's Reaſoning was very well underſtood by the *Jews*, and ſo convincing, that

*three*

* *three thousand Souls were that Day added* to the Church, and baptized into the Faith of *Christ*. His Argument stands thus. You acknowledge *David* to be a Prophet, who under his own Person often spake of the Messiah. To the Messiah therefore belong these Words; *Thou shalt not leave my Soul* [Life] *in Hell* [Hades, the Grave;] *neither shalt* † *thou suffer thy Holy One to see Corruption*; because they are by no means applicable to *David*, who it is not pretended ever rose from the Dead; on the contrary, he was buried, and his Body remained and putrified in his Sepulchre, which *is with us even to this Day*. But by Divine Illumination he foresaw that the Messiah, or *Christ*, who *according to the Flesh* was to descend from him, should be raised up from the Dead to *sit upon his Throne*, i. e. to reign like him over the People of God; and therefore he foretold the Resurrection of *Christ* in Words most exactly fulfilled in *Jesus*, who rose alive out of the Grave in so short a Time after his Death, that *he saw no Corruption*, whereof, adds he, *we are Witnesses*.



* Acts ii. 41. † Psal. xvi. 11. See *Whitby* on this Passage.

Concerning these Words no other Question can be raised, than whether they relate to the Messiah; for to *David* most certainly they can never be applied. If they relate to the Messiah, then was *Jesus* the Messiah; for in his Resurrection were they accomplished; and doubtless the three thousand *Jews*, who were converted by the Preaching of *Peter*, acknowledged both the one and the other of these Propositions. And indeed, by the Manner in which these Words of the *Psalmist* were urged by St. *Peter*, and afterwards by * St. *Paul*, it seems to have been by them taken for granted, that as they were not applicable to *David*, they must be understood of the Messiah, whom therefore, according to *Moses*, the Prophets, and the *Psalmist*, it behoved to suffer, to die, to be buried, and to rise again from the Dead, as the several Passages above-cited clearly shew.

Besides the express Words of Prophecy, there were several Predictions of another Kind, of the Sufferings, Death, and Resurrection of *Christ*, held forth in Types and Figures; such as those two mentioned by our Saviour, and applied

* Acts xiii. 35.

applied to himself; * *As Moses*, says he, *lifted up the Serpent in the Wilderness, even so must the Son of Man be lifted up*: And again, *As Jonas was three Days and three Nights in the Whale's Belly, so shall the Son of Man be three Days and three Nights in the Heart of the Earth*: † The Paschal Lamb, alluded to by St. *Paul* in these Words, *Christ our Passover is slain*; the waved Sheaf alluded to in like manner by the same Apostle, 1 *Cor.* xv. 20, 23. *Rom.* xi. 16. and many others. I shall not here inquire how far, and in what Cases, an Argument from Types and Figures may be admitted, but shall content myself with quoting a Passage relating to this Point out of the incomparable Discourses of Bishop *Sherlock* ‖ upon Prophecy, as follows:

" ANOTHER Question, proper to be
" considered with respect to the State of Re-
" ligion under the *Jewish* Dispensation, is this:
" How far the Religion of the *Jews* was pre-
" paratory to that new Dispensation, which
" was in due Time to be revealed, in Accom-
" plishment of the Promise made to all Na-



" tions.

* John iii. 14. Numb. xxi. 9. Matt. xii. 48. Jonas i. 17. and ii. 10. 1 Cor. v. 7. † See *Lamy*'s Diss. de Pasch. and *Pearson* upon the Creed. ‖ Pag. 144.

" tions. Now if *Abraham* and his Posterity " were chosen, not merely for their own " Sakes, or out of any partial Views and " Regards towards them, but to be Instru- " ments in the Hand of God for bringing " about his great Designs in the World; if " the temporal Government was given for " the sake of the everlasting Covenant, and to " be subservient to the Introduction of it, 'tis " highly probable, that all the Parts of the " *Jewish* Dispensation were adapted to serve " the same End; and that the Law founded " on the temporal Covenant, was intended, " as the temporal Covenant itself was, to pre- " pare the Way to better Promises. If this, " upon the whole, appears to be a reasonable " Supposition, then have we a Foundation to " inquire into the Meaning of the Law, not " merely as it is a literal Command to the " *Jews*, but as containing the Figure and " Image of good Things to come. It can " hardly be supposed, that God, intending " finally to save the World by *Christ*, and the " Preaching of the Gospel, should give an in- " termediate Law, which had no Respect nor " Relation to the Covenant, which he intend-

" ed

" ed to establish for ever. And whoever will " be at the Pains to consider seriously the " whole Administration of Providence toge- " ther, from the Beginning to the End, may " see perhaps more Reason than he imagines, " to allow of Types and Figures in the " *Jewish* Law.

" To proceed then: The *Jewish* Dispen- " sation not conveying to *all Nations* the " Blessing promised through *Abraham's* Seed, " but being only the Administration of the " Hopes and Expectations, created by the " Promise of God; in this respect it stood " intirely upon the Word of Prophecy; for " future Hopes and Expectations from God " can have no other real Foundation. Inas- " much then as the *Jewish* Religion did vir- " tually contain the Hopes of the Gospel, the " Religion itself was a Prophecy, *&c.*"

THAT the *Jewish* Rabbins, and the Fathers of the Christian Church, as well as our Saviour and his Apostles, understood many Things in the Law of *Moses*, in the historical Books of the Old Testament, in the Prophets and the *Psalms*, to be Types and Shadows of

Things

Things to come, is very certain; and if the two former carried their Conceits upon this Head farther than Reaſon or Senſe could allow them to do, Types and Figures are not upon that Pretence to be wholly rejected; eſpecially as many Precepts and Ceremonies in the *Moſaic* Inſtitution, may very well be accounted for by ſuppoſing them intended as Images and Shadows of Things to come, and can but ill be reconciled to the Wiſdom of the Lawgiver without ſuch a Solution. And if ſuch Types be once admitted, it will be no difficult Matter to ſhew that they were fulfilled in *Chriſt Jeſus*, as the great Antitype to which they all referred.

§. 9. Whoever takes an attentive View of the Predictions relating to the Meſſiah *, contained in the Writings of *Moſes*, the *Prophets*, and the *Pſalmiſt*, will perceive the great Scheme of Providence in the Deliverance of Mankind from the Power of Sin and Death, opening by Degrees, in a Succeſſion of Prophecies thro' the ſeveral Ages of the World; each of which, in proportion as the Accompliſhment of the wonderful

* See Bp. *Sherlock*'s Diſc. on the Uſe and Intent of Prophecy, *&c.*

wonderful and gracious Purpose of God advanced, grew more explicit and particular; till they came at last to point out the very Times and Person of the expected Deliverer. Thus the Promise of Redemption to Mankind, which was given to our first Parents in very general and obscure Words, * *The Seed of the Woman shall bruise the Serpent's Head*; importing, that some of their Descendants should vanquish their great Enemy, was renewed to *Abraham* in clearer Terms, and limited to his Descendants thro' *Isaac*, † *In thy Seed shall all the Nations of the Earth be blessed*; then to *Jacob* the younger of the two Sons of *Isaac*; and afterwards to *Judah* and his Children; and lastly to the Family of ‖ *David*, who was of the Tribe of *Judah*. The particular Stock, from which this Branch of Righteousness and Immortality was to proceed, being thus limited and settled, God was pleased in the next Place, to bring into a nearer and more distinct View, the long-promised Seed; declaring by his Prophets the precise Time of his Coming, the Place, and miraculous Manner of his Birth, and so many wonderful Particulars of his Life, his Sufferings,

* Gen. iii. 15. † Gen. xxii. 18. Ib. xxvii. 29. xlix. 1. ‖ 2 Sam. i. 12.

ings, and his Death; that by such characteristical Marks and Notices, he might, when he should come, be readily and plainly known. These Prophecies, some of them at least, were not only at the Time of their Delivery, but even to that of their Accomplishment, very dark and obscure; but that Obscurity proceeded not so much from the Terms in which they were expressed, as from the Things foretold; which were so seemingly inconsistent, that no human Wisdom could reconcile them with each other. For as they sometimes represented the Messiah under the Character of a *Deliverer*, a *Prince whose Throne should endure for ever*, the *Desire of all Nations*, *the Holy One*, &c. so at other times they spake of him as *a Man of Sorrows, and acquainted with Griefs*, as *despised and rejected of Men*; as *afflicted, smitten, wounded, bruised and scourged*; *numbered with the Transgressors*, *cut off out of the Land of the Living*, *and making his Grave with the Wicked*, and yet, *with the Rich in his Death*. So much however of these Prophecies was at all Times clear, that from them the *Jews*, to whom they were delivered, were encouraged to expect a Redeemer to come at a certain limited Time; and so exactly were they able to compute

pute the Period prefixed by the Prophet *Daniel*, that at the Birth of *Christ* there was a general Expectation among the *Jews*, which from them ſpread into other Nations, of a great King being about that Time to be born in *Judea*. The Place alſo of his Birth, and the Stock from which he was to ſpring, were as clearly underſtood: But the *Jews*, too much attached to the temporal Covenant, proud of being the choſen and peculiar People of God, and, from that Pride, not comprehending the full Extent of the Promiſe made to *Abraham*, that *in his Seed all the Nations of the Earth ſhould be bleſſed*, expected a temporal Deliverer, a King of the *Jews* only, conſidered ſtill as a ſeparate and diſtinct Nation. The *Jews*, they imagined, were alone to be redeemed, and that from their temporal Enemies, and under their Meſſiah were to reign for ever over the other Kings and Nations of the Earth: And from this Imagination, than which nothing could be more contrary to the expreſs Promiſes made to *Abraham*, nor more injurious to the Character of that God, *whoſe Mercy is* univerſally *over all his Works*, proceeded their Blindneſs and Backwardneſs in ſeeing and believing *all* that the Prophets had ſpoken, and their Indignation againſt *Jeſus*, for aſſuming the Title, without aſſerting, what they eſteemed to be, the Kingdom of the Meſſiah, the Throne of *David*. With the ſame Prejudices were the Diſciples and Apoſtles themſelves ſo ſtrongly prepoſſeſſed, that when he told them of his Sufferings and Death, * *Peter rebuked him, ſaying, Be it far from thee Lord, this ſhall not be unto Thee*. *Jeſus* however ſuffered and died, and roſe again from the Dead, as he had foretold; and notwithſtanding his Sufferings, ſtill claimed to be the Meſſiah, nay, and even founded his Claim upon thoſe very Sufferings, aſſerting, that according to the Prophets, *thus it behoved the Meſſiah to ſuffer*. To the Prophets he therefore ſends them for their Conviction, and for the removing thoſe Prejudices, which, as long as they ſubſiſted, muſt have kept them effectually from ever acknowledging his Claim, unleſs they would renounce thoſe Scriptures upon whoſe Authority alone their Expectations of a Meſſiah were grounded. For if the Prophets ſpake only of a victorious triumphant Redeemer of *Iſrael*, a King who ſhould

* Matt. xvi. 22.

should never die, it is certain *Jesus* could not be that Redeemer; for he was oppressed and afflicted, and instead of delivering the *Jews*, was himself delivered up to their Enemies, and by them put to Death. What the Prophets have written about the Sufferings, &c. of the Messiah, we have just now seen; and cannot, I think, but acknowledge their Predictions to be very clear and express, and to have been most circumstantially accomplished in *Christ Jesus*; and perhaps to us, who are not blinded with the vain Imaginations of the *Jews*, it may seem Matter of Wonder that the Apostles should so long and so obstinately shut their Eyes against so strong a Light. The Truth is, they were unwilling to give up the pleasing and flattering Expectations of a temporal Kingdom, which they understood to be plainly spoken of by the Prophets, and knew to be incompatible with a suffering, dying Messiah. By *expounding* therefore *in Moses and all the Prophets the Things concerning Himself*, and *by opening their Understandings, that they might ununderstand the Scripture*, *Jesus* at length brought them to perceive that the Kingdom of the Messiah was not a temporal, but a spiritual and eternal

eternal Kingdom; that the Redemption promised to *Adam* and the Patriarchs, was not the Redemption of the Children of *Israel* only from their carnal Enemies and Oppressors, (an Event in which the First Father of the World, and even the Patriarchs themselves, could have little or no Interest) but the Redemption of all Mankind from the Power and Penalty of Sin; to be effected on the one hand by *Christ's fulfilling all Righteousness*, the original Covenant, upon which Happiness and Immortality was stipulated to *Adam*; and on the other, by his *offering up his Soul a Sacrifice for Sin*, i. e. paying the Penalty of Death, which all Sinners, all Mankind had incurred; paying it not as a Debtor, *for he was without Sin*, but as a *Surety*, who willingly and freely took upon himself to make good the Failings, and discharge the Obligations of others. Of this Plan the Death of *Christ* was a necessary Part, and so was his Resurrection from the Dead; by which, having vanquish'd that Enemy, who brought Death and Sin into the World, he was put into Possession of that Throne, which was *to endure for ever*; and was, like *David*, appointed by God to reign, not

over

over the *Jewish* Nation exclusive of the rest of Mankind, but over all those of every Nation of the World, who should, like the *Jews*, make themselves the People of God, by entering into a Covenant with him to keep his Commandments; the sole Tenure by which the Children of *Israel* became originally the People of God; over whom, as such, God, their legal, their constitutional King, if I may so speak, set *David* as a Ruler under him, and promised to continue that delegated vicarial Sceptre of Righteousness in his Posterity for ever. Of all these Points there are frequent Intimations in the Books of *Moses*, in the *Prophets*, and in the *Psalms*: By a fair and unprejudiced Examination of which, the Disciples and Apostles might be certainly convinced, that according to the Scheme of the Redemption of Mankind promised to *Adam* and the Patriarchs, as well as by the express Words of Prophecy, the Messiah was to die and rise again from the Dead. And as on the one Part, had the Scriptures been silent upon the latter of these two Articles, they had, from the Testimony of their own Senses, &c. sufficient Proofs of *Christ*'s being risen from the Dead; so on the other, from the exact Accomplishment of all the Predictions relating to his Life, his Sufferings, his Death and Burial, they might, without any farther Evidence, than that of his Body's being no where to be found, have infallibly collected from the Scriptures only, that he was risen from the Dead. And therefore, when all these Testimonies concurred to prove the Resurrection, how was it possible for them to with-hold their Assent?

The Prophecies of *Jesus* himself concerning his rising from the Dead on the third Day, were another Proof of the same Kind, upon which they might as reasonably and as certainly depend, as upon that grounded on the Predictions of *Moses* and the Prophets. *Moses* had foretold that the Messiah should be a *Prophet*, and they had been convinced that *Jesus* was one in the largest Sense of that Word, by many Instances, which had fallen under their own Observation, those particularly relating to his Passion and Crucifixion, most of the minute and extraordinary Circumstances of which he had acquainted them with before they came to pass. Such as the Treachery of *Judas*, the

Desertion of his Disciples, *Peter*'s disowning him thrice, the Insults and Abuses he underwent from the Chief Priests and Elders, and the cruel Mockery of the *Roman* Soldiers. The exact Correspondence of each of these Events with their several Predictions, afforded the strongest Presumption imaginable in favour of the Resurrection, as it was in like manner foretold by him, of whose Prescience they had just then received so many convincing Proofs; especially as some of the predicted Events were of such a Nature as not to be foreseen, but by that Eye, which penetrates into the inmost Recesses of the Heart of Man, and spieth out all his Thoughts even before they are conceived. For although the Chief Priests and Pharisees had for some time *sought how they might put him to Death* *, yet they had resolved against doing it on the *Feast-day for Fear of the People* †, who but a very few Days before had in a sort of triumphal Procession attended his Entry into *Jerusalem*, *cutting down Branches of Palm*, *strewing them before him*, *spreading their Garments in the Way*, *and crying*



* Matt. xxvi. † Mark xi. 8, 9.

*Hosannah, blessed is he that cometh in the Name of the Lord.* Yet on the *Feast-day* was he put to Death, at the Instance of the Chief Priests and Pharisees; and by the Clamours of this very People, against the Inclination and Endeavours of *Pilate*, in whom the Power of Life and Death resided; and who, as his Judge, declared him innocent, again and again; and when he gave him up to be crucified, * *took Water and washed his Hands before the Multitude, saying, I am innocent of the Blood of this just Person; see ye to it.* This sudden Change in the Counsels of the Chief Priests, in the Hearts of the Multitude, and in the Manners of *Pontius Pilate*, † who was a Man of a haughty, rough, untractable, and implacable Spirit, who so far from having any Complaisance for the *Jewish* Nation, or Regard for their Customs or Religion, had all along treated them with the most cruel and tyrannical Insolence, and who more than once had contemptuously acted in direct Opposition to their most just and reasonable Demands; a Change, I say, so sudden, from one Extreme to

* Mat. xxvii. 24.

† *Pearson* on the Creed, p. 196.

to another, could not with any Certainty be previously deduced from the Consideration of the Instability of human Counsels, and the Fickleness of the Mind of Man. The same Thing may be said concerning the Desertion of his Disciples, and *Peter*'s disowning him thrice, each of which Events came to pass within a few Hours after they were foretold, and within the very Time prefixed; contrary to their express and confident Declarations, that tho' they * *should die with him, they would never deny* [*renounce*] *him*, made at the Time and upon the Occasion of this very Prophecy. Add to this the inhuman Abuses, Insults, and Mockery he endured from the Chief Priests, and from the *Roman* Soldiers; for these surely, were no usual Part of the Punishment inflicted upon Criminals; the most flagitious of whom are seldom treated with more Severity than their Sentence requires; especially when that Sentence extends to taking away their Lives by a lingering and painful Death. And our Saviour's Case undoubtedly deserved more than ordinary Compassion, especially from the *Roman* Soldiers, as he had been pro-

 nounced

* Matt. xxvi. 33.

nounced innocent by the *Roman* Governor himſelf, and was known to be ſacrificed only to the Envy and Malice of the *Jews*. Therefore that *Jeſus*, who foretold all theſe extraordinary Particulars, was endued with the all-preſcient Spirit of God, the Diſciples could have no Reaſon to doubt; and conſequently could have as little Cauſe to call his Reſurrection in Queſtion, which he had foreſeen and foretold by the ſame divine Spirit, from whom no Event, how remote or uncommon ſoever, can be concealed, and who can never deceive or lye. And therefore the Apoſtles, even without the Teſtimony of thoſe who had ſeen him after he was riſen, without the Authority of the Scriptures foretelling his Reſurrection, and without the infallible Proofs of his being alive after his Paſſion, which they themſelves received from ſeeing him, handling him, and converſing with him, might and ought to have believed that he was riſen from the Dead, upon the ſingle Evidence of his having predicted it, joined to that of his Body's being no where to be found; as St. *John* in Fact did, and was therefore pronounced bleſſed by our Saviour himſelf, in

theſe

these Words spoken to St. *Thomas* upon the Occasion of his refusing to believe without the Attestation of his Senses; *Thomas, because thou hast seen me, thou hast believed; blessed are they who have not seen, and yet have believed.* Upon which more hereafter.

I SHALL here rest the Cause, and close the Evidence of the Resurrection of *Jesus*; since it is manifest that the Apostles, who were to be Witnesses of this great Event, and Preachers of the Gospel to all the World, had no Doubt or Scruple left concerning his being really (*i. e.* bodily) risen from the Dead, after his appearing to St. *Thomas*; * for they went into *Galilee, to a Mountain where Jesus had appointed them*, in Obedience to his Command, and in Expectation of meeting him there according to his Promise, *where when they saw him they worshiped him*; from thence they returned again to *Jerusalem*, and continued in that City in Obedience to another † Command, *waiting for the Promise of the Father*, which within a few Days after was made good to them by the coming of the Holy Ghost. Upon



* Matth. xxviii. 16, 17. † Acts i. 4. ii. 4.

on these two Points I beg Leave to say a few Words, for the better understanding some Passages relating to them in St. *Matthew*, St. *Luke*, and the *Acts* of the Apostles.

§. 20. All the Males among the *Jews* were by the Law of *Moses* *, commanded to repair thrice every Year to *Jerusalem*, *to appear*, as it is expressed, *before the Lord*; *viz.* at the three great Feasts; the Passover, called also the Feast of unleavened Bread, the Feast of Weeks, named Pentecost, and the Feast of Tabernacles. Each of these Solemnities lasted a whole Week. The Apostles therefore, and Disciples, who had come up to *Jerusalem* from *Galilee*, their native Country, not merely to attend upon their Master, but in Obedience to the above-cited Law of *Moses*, to keep the Passover, continued, as they were obliged to do, at *Jerusalem*, till the End of that Festival. And there *Jesus* appeared to them a second Time, (eight Days after his first Appearance,) † St. *Thomas* being with them. The next Appearance of *Christ* to any Number of his Disciples

* Exod. xxiii. 17. Deut. xvi. 16. † John xx. 26.

ciples together, was at the Sea of *Tiberias*, called also the Sea of *Galilee*; and this is expressly said, by St. *John, to be the third Time that Jesus shewed himself to his Disciples, after that he was risen from the Dead* ‡; from whence it is evident, that the Appearance on a Mountain in *Galilee* mentioned by St. *Matthew*, was subsequent to this spoken of by St. *John*, and was also in a different Place, on a Mountain, whereas the latter was by the Sea of *Tiberias*. Three Reasons may be assign'd for our Saviour's meeting his Disciples in *Galilee*. *Galilee* was the Country in which he had resided above thirty Years, from his Infancy to the Time when he first began to preach the Kingdom of God: There did he first begin to declare and evidence his Mission by Miracles, and in the Cities of that Region did he perform the greatest Part of his mighty Works; so that he must necessarily have been more known, and have had more Followers in that Country, than in any other Region of *Judea*. And therefore, one Reason for his shewing himself in *Galilee* after he was risen from the Dead seems to have been, that, where he was personally known to so many People, he might have

‡ John xxi. 14.

have the greater Number of competent Witnesses to his Resurrection. Accordingly, St. *Paul* tells us he was seen of above five hundred Brethren at once, which therefore in all Probability happened at the Mountain in *Galilee*, where St. *Matthew* says, *Jesus* appointed his Disciples to meet him, as I have observed once before. 2dly, *Galilee* was also the native Country of the greatest Part, if not of all the Apostles and Disciples. There they dwelt and supported themselves and Families, some of them at least, by mean and laborious Occupations. So strait and so necessitous a Condition of Life must needs have render'd a long Absence from their own Homes highly inconvenient to them at that Time especially, when the Barley-Harvest, which always fell out about the Time of the Passover, was either begun, or upon the Point of beginning. As soon therefore as the Paschal Solemnity was over, which detained them necessarily at *Jerusalem* for a whole Week, it was natural to suppose that they would return into *Galilee*. Upon which Supposition our Saviour, before his Death, promised, after he was risen, *he would go before them into Galilee*; which remarkable

markable Expression was again made * use of by the Angel after his Resurrection; who bade the Women tell his Disciples, that he [*Jesus*] *would go before them into Galilee*, *i. e.* would be in *Galilee* before them, and would meet them there. *Christ* indeed, afterwards, commands them by the same Women to go into *Galilee*, adding a Promise, that they should see him. But this Command must not be understood to imply a Suspicion, that without these peremptory Orders of their Master, they would have continued at *Jerusalem*, where, after the Festival was over, they had nothing to do. It ought rather to be taken as a Confirmation of his Promise of meeting them in *Galilee*, and a strong Encouragement to them to depend upon the Performance of it in the due Place and Season. The Time of their entering upon the Apostolical Office, of preaching the Gospel to all the World, was not yet come; neither were they yet fully prepared or qualified for that important Work; which, after they had once undertaken it, was to be not only the sole Employment of their Lives, but the Occasion of their leaving their Fathers, their

* Matt. xvi. 7.

their Children, their Country, and their Friends, to travel up and down the World, exposed to Hardships, Dangers, Persecution, and Death, in unknown and remote Corners of the Earth. Of all which their Master had frequently forewarned them before his Death, and particularly in that affectionate Discourse he held to them the Night in which he was betrayed. To prepare them therefore by Degrees for a State of so much Affliction and Mortification, and to give them an Opportunity of seeing and providing in the best Manner they were able, for their Relations and Families, to whom they were soon to bid Adieu for ever; their gracious Lord, who knew how to indulge, because he had himself felt, the Affections and Infirmities of human Nature; and who, * by recommending his Mother, even from the Cross, to the Care of his beloved Disciple, had taught them what Regards were due to those tender Ties of Nature, not only permitted them to return into *Galilee*, but promised to meet them there, and did in fact meet them there, not only once, but several times; as may be inferred from what

* John xix, 26, 27.

what St. *Luke* ſays of his having ſhewn himſelf to them * *for forty Days after his Paſſion*, compared with what St. *John* ſays of his Appearance by the Lake of *Tiberias*, which he expreſly calls the *third Time* that *Chriſt* ſhewed himſelf to his Diſciples after his Reſurrection. After this St. *Matthew* ſpeaks of another Appearance in *Galilee*, on *a Mountain*, where, adds he, *Jeſus had appointed his Diſciples*. When this Appointment was made, there is no Intimation given in any of the Evangeliſts. If it was not at the Appearance at the Lake of *Tiberias*, which there is no Reaſon to imagine it was, St. *John* ſaying nothing of any ſuch Matter, it was probably at ſome other Appearance in *Galilee*, between this laſt and that mentioned by St. *Matthew*. And as there was a great Number of Brethren preſent upon that Occaſion, it is rational to conclude, that timely Notice was given, as well of the Day, as of the Place of Meeting. But however this might have been, I am perſuaded that the greateſt Part of the Appearances of *Chriſt for the forty Days after his* Paſſion were in *Galilee*, ſince the Reaſons that required the Apoſtles to

* Acts i.

to return thither, were as ſtrong for their continuing there, till the Approach of the Feaſt of Weeks or *Pentecoſt* ſhould call them back to *Jeruſalem*.

ANOTHER Reaſon for meeting his Diſciples in *Galilee*, and for concluding that the Appearances mentioned in the *Acts* were chiefly in that Country, and that there were many of them, may be deduced from what * St. *Luke* tells us of the Subjects upon which our Saviour ſpoke to his Diſciples on theſe Occaſions, *viz. Of Things pertaining to the Kingdom of God.* Before they ſet out upon the great Work of preaching the Kingdom of God to all the World, it was neceſſary that they ſhould be fully inſtructed in the Doctrines they were to preach, and in the ſeveral Functions of the Apoſtolical Office: That they ſhould thoroughly underſtand the Intentions of their Maſter, and have ſome View of the Means and Aſſiſtances by which they ſhould be enabled to perform a Taſk ſo apparently above their Abilities, and ſome Hopes and Encouragement to ſupport them under the Proſpect

* Acts. Chap. i. 3.

Proſpect of thoſe Difficulties and Dangers they were given to expect in propagating the Goſpel. In order to all this, many inveterate Prejudices relating to the Law of *Moſes* and the *Jewiſh* Nation were to be rooted out; the Scheme of God in the univerſal Redemption of Mankind was to be laid open to them; many human Affections, Reluctances, and Terrors, were to be ſubdued, and their Hearts to be fortified with Courage and Conſtancy, a Diſregard and Contempt of Hardſhips, Perils, Pain and Death. To theſe ſeveral Purpoſes nothing could more conduce than frequent Viſits from their Lord; whoſe *Reſurrection* (of which every Appearance was a freſh Proof) was an unqueſtionable Evidence of his Power; whoſe every Appearance was an Inſtance of his Affection and Condeſcenſion to them, and of his Fidelity in performing the Promiſe he had made before his Paſſion of coming to them again after his Death, and being with them for a *little while before he went to his Father*, and whoſe Fidelity and Exactneſs in thus performing his Promiſe, was an infallible Earneſt and Security for the Coming of that Comforter who was to

 ſupply

ſupply his Place, *to guide them into all Truth, to bring to their Remembrance whatever he had ſpoken to them, to enable them to do greater Works than he had done*, and to fill their Hearts *with that Joy, which it ſhould not be in the Power of Man to take from them.* Add to this the Weight and Authority derived to his Precepts and Inſtructions from their being delivered by himſelf in Perſon; and the great Meaſure of Strength accruing to their Faith from their having frequently before their Eyes the *Captain of their Salvation*, who after having fought with the Powers of Darkneſs, and triumphed over Sin and Death, was to *ſit down thenceforth at the Right-hand of God*, inveſted with the Power of aſſiſting thoſe, who ſhould fight under his Banner, and rewarding their Toils, their Sufferings, and their Death, with a Crown of immortal Life. And if nothing could more effectually bring about all theſe great Effects than *Chriſt*'s frequently meeting his Apoſtles, it will evidently appear that no Place could be more proper for thoſe Meetings than *Galilee*; if we conſider, that the Apoſtles having their Habitations in that Country, might reſide there without any Suſpicion,

picion; and assemble without any Fear of the Persecutors and Murderers of their Master, the Chief Priests and the *Roman* Governor: * For *Galilee* was under the Jurisdiction of *Herod.* Whereas had they remained in *Jerusalem*, and continued to assemble frequently together, while the Report of their Master's being risen from the Dead was fresh and in every Body's Mouth, the Chief Priests and Elders, whose Hatred or Apprehensions of *Jesus Christ* were not extinguished by his Blood, as appears by their persecuting and murdering his Followers long after; these Rulers of the *Jews*, I say, would undoubtedly have given such Interruptions to those Meetings, and thrown such Obstacles in the Way, as must have necessitated our Lord to interpose his miraculous Power to prevent or remove them. Now as all these Inconveniences might be avoided by our Saviour's meeting his Disciples in *Galilee*, it is more agreeable to the Wisdom of God, (*which* as † Mr. *Lock* observes, *is not usually at the Expence of Miracles, but only in Cases that require them*) to suppose these frequent Meet-



* Luke xxiii. 7.    † Reas. of Christ. p. 508. Fol. Edit.

ings to have been in *Galilee* rather than in *Jerusalem*, and more analogous to the Proceeding of our Lord himself, who being in Danger from the Scribes and Pharisees, refrained from appearing publickly in *Jerusalem* for some Time before the Hour appointed for his Sufferings and Death was come, and *walked in Galilee*, as St. *John* * tells us, *for he would not walk in* Jewry, *because the* Jews *sought to kill him*. From these Considerations I think it clear, that all the Appearances of *Christ* to his Disciples, from that to St. *Thomas* mentioned in St. *John*, to that last in *Jerusalem*, on the Day of his Ascending, mentioned by St. *Luke* both in his Gospel and in the *Acts*, were in *Galilee*: From whence when the Apostles returned afterwards to *Jerusalem*, they were covered from the Apprehension of giving any Umbrage by residing there, for the short Space to come between their Return and the Time of their entering upon their Apostolical Office, by the Obligation they were under, in common with the rest of their Brethren the *Jews*, to repair to that City for the Celebration of the Feast of † Weeks, called also Pentecost: Upon

* John vii. 1. † Acts ii. 1, &c.

Upon the most solemn Day of which Festival they were, according to the Promise of their Master, filled with the Holy Ghost, and endued with Power from above to defy all Danger, and surmount all Opposition in preaching the Gospel of *Christ*.

AND hence we learn, that all the latter Part of the 24th Chapter of St. *Luke*'s Gospel, from the 49th Verse to the End inclusive, relates to what happened at *Jerusalem*, *&c.* after the Return of the Apostles from *Galilee*: Of whose Departure into *Galilee* after the Resurrection of *Christ*, or of his Promise of going thither before them, this Evangelist having not thought it to his Purpose to make any mention, thought it as needless to say any thing of their leaving *Jerusalem*; since the Scene of their last Appearance, as well as of the former related by him, was in that City; and since to those, who by any other Means should come to be acquainted with the whole History of our Saviour, there would be no Danger of confounding those two Appearances. As to those who should happen to meet with no other Account but his Gospel, (if such a Thing could be supposed)

 no

no great Damage could arise from their mistaking them to be one and the same.

§. 21. By this long and ſcrupulous Examination of the ſeveral Particulars, which conſtitute the Evidences of the Reſurrection, I have endeavoured to ſhew, that *never were there any Facts that could better abide the Teſt*. And if I have in any Degree ſucceeded in my Endeavours, I ſhall neither repent my own Labour, nor apologize to the Reader for having dwelt ſo long upon this Subject: Since the Concluſion that will inevitably follow from this Propoſition is, that *never was there a Fact more fully proved than the Reſurrection of Jeſus Chriſt*. For beſides the Teſtimony of ſome, who may be ſuppoſed to have had no Prejudices either for, or againſt the Reſurrection, I mean the *Roman* Soldiers, who reported that his Sepulchre was miraculouſly opened by an Angel, or a Divinity, (for ſo they muſt have ſtiled that Cœleſtial Apparition:) And beſides the Teſtimony of others, who were apparently prepoſſeſſed with Notions contrary to the Belief *Chriſt*'s being riſen from the Dead, and yet affirmed that they were not only told by

Angels

Angels that he was risen, but that they themselves had seen him, talked with him, and handled him: Besides this human Testimony, I say, which considering all the Circumstances attending it, must be allowed to have been sufficient to prove any Event, that was not either impossible or improbable in the highest Degree, there were (as it was reasonable to expect there should be) other Evidences as extraordinary and miraculous as the Resurrection itself. Of this Kind are the Predictions contained in the Writings of *Moses*, the *Prophets*, and the *Psalmist*, setting forth the Design and Purpose of God to redeem Mankind by the Righteousness, Sufferings, Death and Resurrection of the *Seed of the Woman*. Without the Resurrection, this great Scheme of Divine Mercy had been uncomplete; by That it was perfected, and the Triumph over Death added to That over Sin; the Messiah thereby accomplishing all that the Scriptures foretold of his Glory and Power. When therefore one Part of the Promises relating to *Jesus* had been so exactly made good in his Life and Death, it is reasonable to conclude, that God did not fail to fulfil the others in his Resurrection.

In the ſame Claſs of Evidence may alſo be ranked the Prophecies of *Jeſus* himſelf, relating to his riſing from the Dead, which coming from one, whoſe other Predictions (of which there had been many) had been always accompliſh'd, deſerved to be credited no leſs than the others, and were not only verified by the Event itſelf, but confirmed by other ſubſequent Events, foretold likewiſe by him before his Paſſion, and linked with and depending upon that great Proof of his Divine Power. Such, for Inſtance, were his meeting his Diſciples in *Galilee*, his being with them a little while before he went to his Father, his Aſcenſion into Heaven, and his ſending to them the promiſed Comforter, with all the glorious Faculties and Powers they receiv-ed upon his Coming. With ſo various, ſo aſtoniſhing, ſo well-connected and irrefragable a Chain of Evidence, is this important Article of the Reſurrection bound up and fortified.

But all theſe Proofs were not exhibited to all the *Jews*, for *not to all the People was* Jeſus *ſhewn* alive after his Paſſion, but *to Wit-*

*nesses chosen before of God*; *to Us* (saith St. *Peter*) *who did eat and drink with him after that he arose from the Dead* *. That *Christ* made Choice of a select Number of Disciples, and particularly of Twelve, (who were called Apostles) to be Witnesses of the great Actions of his Life, and especially of his Resurrection, and Preachers of his Gospel to all the World, is a Thing too well known to need any Proof. To qualify them for this double Office, he not only, upon many Occasions both before and after his Crucifixion, discoursed to them in particular *of the Things pertaining to the Kingdom of God*, and poured upon them all the various Gifts of the Holy Spirit, but gave them every kind of Evidence of his being risen from the Dead, which the most Scrupulous and Sceptical could imagine or require; *shewing himself alive* to them *by many infallible Proofs*, such as eating and drinking with them, *&c.* *for forty Days after his Passion*. And indeed, it is highly expedient that Those, upon whose Testimony and Credit the Truth of any Fact is to be established, should have the fullest and most unexceptionable Evidence of it, that can

 be

* Acts x. 41.

be had; because their having had all possible Means of Information, must needs add great Weight and Authority to their Depositions. Hence then we may learn the Reason of our Saviour's appearing so often to his Disciples after his Resurrection, of his requiring them to handle him, and see that it was he himself, of his eating and drinking with them, of his referring them to the Scriptures, to his own Predictions, and to the Testimony of those to whom he had appeared, before he came to them; and lastly, of his satisfying the unreasonable Scruples of St. *Thomas*; who being one of the chosen Witnesses, (one of the Twelve) it was proper he should have an equal Knowledge of the Fact he was to attest with his other Brethren the Apostles. That this perfect Knowledge of the Things they were to give Testimony to, was necessary for those, who were ordained to be Apostles, is farther evident from the following Words of St* *Peter*; who after the Ascension of our Lord, proposing to the rest of the Disciples to fill up the Vacancy made by the Transgression and Death of *Judas*, by electing one to take

Par

* Acts i. 15—26.

Part with them in their *Ministry* and *Apostleship*, describes the Qualifications requisite in an Apostle, by limititng their Choice in these Words: *Wherefore of these Men, that have accompanied with us all the Time that the Lord* Jesus *went in and out amongst us, beginning from the Baptism of* John, *unto that same Day that he was taken up from us, must one be ordained to be Witness with Us of his Resurrection.* Hence also it is plain, that all these infallible Proofs were not vouchsafed by *Christ* to his Disciples, merely out of a particular Favour and Regard to them, that they might believe and be saved; but with a farther View, that others also through their Testimony founded on the compleatest and exactest Information, might likewise believe and be saved. The Reproof of *Christ* to St. *Thomas*, for not believing without the Attestation of his Senses, implied in the Blessing pronounced by him on Those, *who having not seen had yet believed*, is a clear Argument, that our Saviour thought his Disciples had sufficient Cause to believe he was risen from the Dead, even before he shewed himself to them. And that they had so in fact, I have above endeavoured to prove: and

that

that St. *John* did believe, before he saw his Master, he himself assures us. Had *Christ* therefore intended nothing more, than to bring his Disciples to a Belief of his Resurrection, he might have left them to the Testimony of the *Roman* Soldiers; to that of the Women; to the Writings of *Moses* and the Prophets; to his own Predictions; to the State of the Sepulchre, and that wonderful Circumstance of his Body's being no where to be found; to all this Evidence he might, I say, have left them, without appearing to them himself, and left them without Excuse, had they still continued faithless and unbelieving. But though the Apostles had upon this Evidence believed their Master to be risen from the Dead; yet, without those other infallible Proofs mentioned by St. *Luke*, they would certainly have not been so well qualified for Witnesses of the Resurrection to all the World; that is to say, the Reasons upon which they believed, would not have appeared so convincing. The Heathens would not have admitted the Testimony of *Moses* and the *Prophets*; of whose Writings they knew nothing, and of whose Divine Authority they had no Proof. And as to the Depositions of the Women; besides that they were Strangers to their Characters, they might, from *Christ*'s appearing to *them*, with some Colour have demanded why he did not appear likewise to those, whom he commissioned to preach his Gospel, and to be Witnesses of his Resurrection. But when, on the contrary, the Apostles could tell them that they themselves had seen *Christ*, had handled him, eat and drank with him, and conversed with him for forty Days after that he was risen from the Dead, they could not but allow them to have had the fullest Evidence of the Resurrection, supposing what they told them to be true; and of this, the Purity of their Doctrine, the Holiness of their Lives, their Courage and Constancy in defying and undergoing all Kinds of Hardships, Dangers, Pain and Death, in advancing a Cause, which every worldly Interest obliged them to desert, joined to the Attestation of the Holy Spirit, *working with them, and confirming the Word with Signs following*, were such Assurances as no other Man could give of his Veracity.

FROM

FROM what has been said, it may appear, how little Ground there is for the Cavils that have been raised upon our Lord's forbidding *Mary Magdalene* to *touch him*; and upon his not shewing himself after he was risen to the *Jews*, to the Chief Priests and Elders, to the Scribes and Pharisees: The one of which has been interpreted as a Refusal to *Mary Magdalene*, of the necessary Evidence of his being risen from the Dead; and the other as a Breach of the Promise, implied in these Words,* *An evil and adulterous Generation seeketh after a Sign, and there shall be no Sign given to it, but the Sign of the Prophet* Jonas; *for as* Jonas *was three Days and three Nights in the Whale's Belly, so shall the Son of Man*, &c. In which (it is said) *Christ* promised to appear, after he was risen, to that *evil and adulterous Generation*, that is, to the *Jews*, &c. as contra-distinguished from his Disciples and Apostles. That *Christ* promised by these Words to give that *evil Generation* sufficient Proof of his rising from the Grave after having lain in it three Days, I readily allow; but that he promised to *appear* to

* Matt. xii. 39, 40.

to them, I absolutely deny, and think it impossible to prove he did, from the above-cited Passage. Of his rising again from the Grave on the third Day, the *Jews* had the Testimony of the Prophets, of the Predictions of *Christ* himself, the Evidence of the *Roman* Soldiers, of his Body's being no where to be found, of the Women and Disciples, and Apostles, to whom he had appeared; and who, before the *Sanhedrim*, bore Witness to his Resurrection, and having just before wrought a Miracle upon a * lame Man, declared that they had done it in the Name of *Jesus of* Nazareth, *whom*, say they, *ye crucified, whom God raised from the Dead.* This surely was Evidence sufficient to convince any reasonable and unprejudiced Person; and consequently, to acquit our Lord of the Promise of giving that *evil Generation* satisfactory Proofs of his being risen from the Dead. To the Evidence vouchsafed by *Christ*, either out of Favour to those, *who had forsaken all and followed him*; or to those, whom he had chosen to be *Witnesses of him to all the World*, they certainly could have no just Pretensions; who, instead of being his Disciples, had re-

jected

* Acts iv. 10.

jected his Doctrine, and put him to Death as an Impostor and Blasphemer; and instead of shewing any Disposition to embrace or propagate his Gospel, opposed it with all their Power; and by Threats and Punishments, forbade his Apostles to preach any more in his Name. That *Mary Magdalene* was convinced that it was *Jesus* who appeared to her, I have already shewn very fully; and that was all that was necessary for her single self; supposing therefore that she never had afterwards the Permission of touching or embracing her Master; (which by the way cannot be proved) neither had she, nor any one else Reason to complain or cavil, since neither her own Faith, nor that of any other Person, depended upon her having that Proof of the Resurrection of *Christ*; for she was not an *Apostle*, not one of the *chosen Witnesses*. And it is very remarkable, that none of the Apostles, either in preaching to the unconverted *Jews* or *Gentiles*, or in their Epistles to the Church, ever make any Mention of the Appearances of *Christ* to the Women: And the Evangelists seem to have related them only upon account of their being connected with other more important Parts of

the

the Hiſtory of the Reſurrection. The Truth is, the Teſtimony of the Women, though of great Weight with the Apoſtles, and with thoſe who received it from their own Mouths, was but ſecond-hand Hear-ſay Evidence to thoſe, who had it only from the Apoſtles Report; who, for that Reaſon, inſiſted always upon their having themſelves ſeen their Maſter, *after that he was riſen from the Dead*; a Circumſtance, as far as I can recollect, not omitted by any of them, in their Arguments upon the Reſurrection of *Jeſus*; as may be ſeen in the Paſſages of Scripture that give any particular Account of thoſe Diſcourſes. And thus * St. *Paul* in his Epiſtle to the *Corinthians*, after enumerating many Appearances of *Chriſt* to the Twelve Apoſtles, and others, cloſes all with ſaying, *And laſt of all he was ſeen of me alſo.* So much Care did they take to give reaſonable Evidence for the reaſonable Faith they required.

§. 22. All that has hitherto been ſaid relates chiefly to the Proofs of the Reſurrection of

*Jeſus*

* 1 Cor. xv. 8.

*Jesus Christ*, as they were laid before the Apostles, those *chosen Witnesses* of that great and astonishing Event. And I hope, upon a serious and attentive View of the fair and unimposing Manner in which those Proofs were offered to their Consideration, and of the Number and Certainty of the Facts upon which they were grounded, every judicious and candid Inquirer after Truth will allow, that, to the Apostles at least, the Resurrection of *Jesus* was most fully and most unexceptionably proved. I shall now proceed to lay before the Reader some Arguments (for I cannot enter into all) that may induce us, who live at so remote a Distance of Time from that Age of Evidence and Miracles, to believe that *Christ* rose from the Dead.

The first and principal Argument, is the Testimony of those chosen Witnesses, transmitted down in Writings, either penn'd by themselves, or authorised by their Inspection and Approbation.

The second, is the Existence of the Christian Religion.

BEFORE we admit the Testimony of these *chosen Witnesses* contained in the *Gospels*, the *Acts*, the *Epistles*, and the *Revelations*, it may be proper to consider, in the first Place, what Reasons there are for our believing this Testimony to be genuine; or in other Words, believing *them* to be the Authors of those Books, which are now received under their Names: And in the next Place, what Arguments can be offered to induce us to give Credit to this Testimony, supposing it genuine.

To prove the Apostles * and Evangelists to be the Authors of those Scriptures, which are now received under their Names, we have the concurrent Attestation of all the earliest Writers



* I use these two Words *Apostles* and *Evangelists* in this Place, to denote and distinguish the Authors of the four Gospels, the Acts, and the Epistles, &c. though they might all have been comprehended under the general Term *Apostles*, by which Title not only the Twelve, so called by *Christ* himself, but *Mathias* afterwards and *Paul*, and all the seventy or seventy-two Disciples, are mentioned by some of the Fathers. Of this last Number were the Evangelists *Mark* and *Luke* (as Dr. *Whitby* has shewn from *Origen* and *Epiphanius*) and as such were qualified by their own personal Knowledge of most of the Facts, and by the Inspiration of the Holy Ghost, to write their Gospels, without the Inspection of the two great Apostles *Peter* and *Paul*, which yet (as we are told by some of the Fathers) was a farther Authority given to them, and such as would have sufficed tho' they had not been themselves particularly inspired.

ters of the Church, deduced by an uninterrupted and uncontrolled Tradition, from the very Times of the Apostles. Which is such an Authentication of these sacred Records, as is not to be overturned by bare Presumptions, and a surmised and unproved Charge of Forgery. But for the Proofs of this Proposition, I shall refer the Reader to the * Discourses of those learned Men, who have treated more particularly upon this Subject, and shall content myself with offering in Support of those Proofs the following Considerations; in which I shall endeavour to shew, 1st, the Probability of the Apostles having left in Writing the Evidences and Doctrines of the Religion they preached, and of their Disciples having preserved and transmitted those Writings to Posterity: 2dly, The Improbability of any Books forged in the Names of the Apostles escaping Detection.

*First*, If the Precepts and Examples of *Jesus Christ* and his Apostles were to be the Rules, by which all those, who in succeeding Ages should believe in him, were required to govern themselves, it seems most consonant

* See Dr. *Whitby*'s Prefatory Discourses to his Annotations upon the Gospels, Acts, *&c.* See also *L'Abadie de la Religion Chrétienne*, Tom. II.

nant to the Wiſdom of God, becauſe agreeable to what he himſelf practis'd when he gave the *Law* to the *Iſraelites*, to commit thoſe *Rules of Salvation* to Writing, rather than to the unſure and treacherous Conveyance of *oral Tradition*; which cannot with any Safety be depended upon for ſcarce ſo much as one or two Generations. It is therefore highly reaſonable to ſuppoſe that the ſame Spirit, which incited and enabled the Apoſtles to preach the Goſpel, and bear Witneſs to the Reſurrection of *Jeſus Chriſt* in every Nation of the known World, ſhould likewiſe incite and enable them to deliver down to Poſterity, in a Method the leaſt liable to Uncertainty and Error, that Teſtimony, and thoſe Precepts, upon which the Faith and Practice of After-Times were to be eſtabliſhed, eſpecially when it is (in the ſecond Place) conſidered, that all Revelation (Revelation I mean of the Doctrines and Syſtem of the Goſpel) was confined to the Apoſtles, and conſequently ended with them. The Power of working Miracles, ſpeaking with other Tongues, caſting out unclean Spirits, *&c.* was frequently, if not univerſally given to the firſt Converts to Chriſtianity; and ſome of theſe Gifts were continued for many Generations in the

 Church.

Church. But to the Apostles only was our Saviour pleased to reveal his Will. Accordingly in the Epistles of * St. *Paul* we see that those Christians, who were endowed with many and various Gifts of the Holy Spirit, stood however in need of the Instructions and Directions of that Apostle, in many Points both of Faith and Practice; and the earliest Writers after the Apostles, tho' possessed themselves of many of those miraculous Powers, instead of pretending to immediate Revelation, have upon all Occasions recourse to the holy Scriptures, which they acknowledge to have been written by the Assistance of the divine Spirit, as to that Fountain, from whence alone they could derive the Waters of Life: Both which Appeals, as well that made to the Apostles by their Cotemporaries, as those made by succeeding Christians to the Scriptures, would have been unnecessary, had they, like the Apostles, been taught all Things by Revelation, and been guided into all Truth by the Holy Spirit.

THIS being the Case with those Christians who were converted to the Faith by the Preaching

* See particularly the Epistles to the *Corinthians*.

Preaching of the Apoſtles themſelves; and who were to tranſmit to ſucceeding Ages that Goſpel, upon which, according to their Belief, the Salvation of Mankind depended; is it not natural to imagine they would take the moſt effectual Means to ſupply thoſe Defects, which they were ſenſible of in themſelves; and to guard againſt thoſe Errors, which through the Imbecillity of the human Mind they had fallen into, even while the Voices of the Apoſtles ſtill ſounded in their Ears, and to which their Poſterity muſt of neceſſity be ſtill more liable? And what more effectual Means could they purſue, than either to obtain in Writing from the Apoſtles themſelves, the Evidence and Doctrines of the Chriſtian Faith; or, which amounted to much the ſame Thing, to write them down from their Mouths, or under their Inſpection and Approbation; or laſtly, to tranſcribe from their own Memories what they could recollect of the Doctrines and Inſtructions of the Apoſtles? Of theſe three Methods, the two firſt were unqueſtionably the beſt; the laſt was ſubject to many Imperfections and Miſtakes: For tho' our Saviour promiſed to enable his Apoſtles by the Holy Spirit, *to call to Mind whatever he had said unto them*, I do not find, that the Memories of those who heard the Apostles, were ever assisted in the like miraculous Manner. If the Apostles therefore had not, either from their Care for the *Houshold of Faith*, or from the Suggestions of the Holy Spirit, transmitted the Proofs and Doctrines of the Gospel to Posterity in one of the two first-mentioned Ways, it is to be presumed they would have been called upon to do it by those, who looked upon *them* as Teachers commissioned and inspired by the Spirit of Truth, and *who alone had the Words of eternal Life*. And if neither of those two desirable Things could have been obtained, Recourse would undoubtedly have been had to the last. And indeed it is evident, from St. *Luke*'s Preface to his Gospel, that many Writings of this Kind were current among the Christians of those Times: None of which, that I know of, having come down to us, it is to be presumed they were superseded by Writings of greater Authority; that is to say, Writings either pen'd by the Apostles themselves, or authorised by their Inspection and Approbation; because this seems to be the best Account that can be given for the different Fate that

that hath attended these several Writings; the former having disappeared and died soon after their Birth; and the latter having survived now almost seventeen Centuries, in the same Degree of Esteem and Veneration, with which they were at first received by the Converts of the Apostolick Age: For that the Difference between these Writings was made in that Age is very probable; 1st, Because those very Cotemporaries of the Apostles stood themselves in need of their Instructions, Admonitions, and Exhortations for their own Direction and Encouragement: And 2dly, for the Conviction of the next Age, who were to receive the Gospel from their Hands, they wanted the Testimony and Authority of those Persons, to whom the Facts upon which their Faith depended, were the most compleatly proved; and who alone, in Matters of Doctrine, were *guided into all Truth* by the infallible *Spirit of God*. For by their own Evidence, they could prove no more than what fell within the Compass of their own Knowledge, which could extend no farther than to what they had themselves seen of the Apostles, or heard from their Mouths: And this Evidence of theirs could acquire no farther Authority by having been committed to Writing. The *Apostles alone* could prove, what *they only* knew, and were the only authentick Preachers of those Doctrines, which they alone received from *Christ*, or after his Ascension from the Holy Spirit. Their Successors, besides bearing Testimony to their Characters, and giving Evidence perhaps of some collateral Facts which had fallen under their own Observations, could do no more than *witness their Depositions*; that is, that these and these were the *Facts*, and these and these were the *Doctrines* delivered by the Apostles. If the Apostles therefore, either from the secret Instigation of the *Holy Ghost*, or from their paternal Care and Affection for *the Houshold of Faith*, or at the Request of their *Children in Christ Jesus*, did commit to Writing the Proofs and Doctrines of the Christian Religion (as it is reasonable to suppose they did) it is as reasonable to conclude, that, what they either writ or approved, must necessarily have been preferred to all other Writings whatever.

And as the Writings of the Apostles must, for the Reasons above-mentioned, have been of great Weight and Importance to the Christians of their Times; and of ſtill greater to thoſe of the ſucceeding Ages, who could not like their Predeceſſors, upon any Occaſion, have recourſe to the living and infallible Oracles of God; it is natural to imagine that the Perſons, in whoſe Hands thoſe ſacred and invaluable Treaſures were depoſited, would preſerve and guard them with the utmoſt Fidelity and Care; would impart Copies of them to ſuch of their Brethren, who could not have Acceſs to the Originals; and would, from the ſame Principle of Chriſtian Benevolence and Fidelity, ſee that thoſe Copies were tranſcribed with all that Exactneſs, which human Nature, ever liable to Slips and Errors, was capable of. The ſame Care under the ſame Allowances, it is to be ſuppoſed would be alſo taken by thoſe who ſhould tranſlate them into the ſeveral Languages ſpoken by Chriſtians of different Nations, who did not underſtand *that* in which the Apoſtles wrote.

THESE ſeveral Steps appear to me ſo natural and obvious, that I cannot but think any Set of reaſonable and honeſt Men could not fail of making them, under the ſame Circumſtances,

ſtances, as attended the firſt Preachers and Converts of Chriſtianity. And from hence ariſes a ſtrong Preſumption in favour of thoſe Accounts which inform us,—That the Apoſtles and Evangeliſts were the genuine Authors of thoſe Writings, which are now received under their Names.—That altho' *many*, even in the Apoſtles Times, *had taken in Hand*, as St. *Luke* expreſſes it, *to ſet forth in order a Declaration of thoſe Things which were moſt ſurely believed amongſt* Chriſtians, *even as they delivered them, who were Eye-witneſſes and Miniſters of the Word*; and although ſome Years after the Deaths of the Apoſtles, many Goſpels, Epiſtles, &c. appeared, which were aſcribed to *Them*, to the *Virgin Mary*, and even to *Jeſus Chriſt* himſelf; yet thoſe only, which we now account Canonical, were admitted as ſuch, from the very earlieſt Ages of Chriſtianity.----That theſe Canonical Books were preſerved and kept, with the moſt ſcrupulous and religious Care, by the ſeveral Churches or Societies of Chriſtians; who did not, and indeed upon their Principles could not, preſume to add to them, or to take from them the leaſt Tittle.---That Copies of them were immediately diſperſed throughout the whole Chriſtian

Christian World; *the Apostles* (saith *Irenæus*, Lib. 3. l. 1.) *first preaching the Gospel, and afterwards, by the Will of God, delivering it to us in the Scriptures, to be thenceforward the Pillar and Foundation of our Faith. And the first Successors of the Apostles,* (as *Eusebius* informs us, Hist. Eccles. Lib. iii. C. 37.) *leaving their Countries, preached to them who had not heard of the Christian Faith, and then delivered to them, as the Foundation of their Faith, the Writings of the Holy Evangelists.*---That the Originals of the Epistles were still preserved in the respective Churches to which they were directed in the Time of *Tertullian*, who writing to the Hereticks of his Age, *viz.* of the third Century, bids them *go to the Apostolical Churches, where the authentick Epistles of the Apostles*(saith he) *are still recited.*—That lastly, Translations of these Scriptures were made so early as to precede the general Admission of some Parts of them, which were afterwards received as genuine; the *Syriac* Version for Instance being so ancient, that it leaves out the second Epistle of *Peter*, the second and third Epistles of *John*, and the *Revelations*, as being for a Time controverted in some of the Eastern Churches; which by the way ſhews how ſcrupulous the firſt Chriſtians were about admitting into the Canon of Scripture, Writings which, though bearing the Names of the Apoſtles, and received by ſome Churches as genuine, were yet queſtioned and ſuſpected by others. To all which we may add ſtill farther, that theſe ſeveral Accounts relating merely to Facts, tend only to eſtabliſh another Fact, *viz.* That the Apoſtles and Evangeliſts did compoſe the Goſpels, Epiſtles, *&c.* aſcribed to them, which Fact is capable of being proved by the ſame kind of Evidence as any other Fact of the ſame Nature.---That the Evidences of this Fact cannot be overturned, but upon ſuch Principles as will equally ſubvert the Proofs of all Facts, that exiſted at any great Diſtance of Time from the preſent.----That we ought *therefore* either to admit this Fact, or reject all thoſe without Diſtinction, which ſtand only upon the Credit of Hiſtories and Records; of the Truth of any of which, we can have no ſtronger Aſſurances than we have of the Authenticity of theſe Holy Writings.

§. 23.

* The Reader who is inclined to ſee the *Authorities*, upon which theſe ſeveral Articles were founded, may conſult *Whitby*'s Preface to the Goſpels, *&c.*

§. 23. The next Point to be confidered is, the Improbability of any Books forged in the Names of the Apoftles efcaping Detection.

The Reafons given under the foregoing Article, to fhew the Probability of the Apoftles having left in Writing the Evidences and Doctrines of Chriftianity, and of their Difciples having preferved and tranfmitted thofe Writings to their Succeffors, will lead us to difcover the Improbability of any Books forged in the Names of the Apoftles efcaping Detection. For if it was neceffary for the Chriftians, even of the Apoftolick Age, to have in Writing the Directions and Inftructions of the Apoftles in many Points both of Faith and Practice, as is evident it was from almoft all the Epiftles, it was as neceffary for them to be affured, that what was delivered to them in the Name of an Apoftle, was certainly of his inditing. And this was to be known many Ways; for furely we may have undoubted Proofs of fuch a one's being the Author of fuch a Book or Letter, without having feen him write it with his own Hand, or having heard from his own Mouth that he

wrote

wrote it. *The Apostles* (saith *Irenæus*) *having first preached the Gospel, delivered it afterwards to us in the Scriptures.* Now, as we have no Reason to believe, from any Accounts that can be depended upon, that any of those stiled Apostles, besides the * six whose Works we now have, left any thing in Writing, if these Words of *Iræneus* be taken to relate to the whole Number of the Apostles, it will follow from them that even those Apostles, who wrote nothing themselves, did yet deliver to their *Children in Christ* such Parts of the Scriptures, as had come to their Hands. In which Case those Scriptures, thus delivered and recommended by an Apostle, must have been allowed to have the same Authority, as if they had been written by that Apostle himself; since He, as well as his Brethren who wrote them, was under the Inspiration and Guidance of that Holy Spirit, who, according to the Promise of *Christ*, was to *lead them into all Truth*; and therefore could not be ignorant whether the Matters contained in those Scriptures were true or false. But if the general Term *Apostles*

* These six are *Matthew*, *John*, *Peter*, *Paul*, *James*, and *Jude*. *Mark* and *Luke*, though supposed with good Reason to be of the Number of the seventy-two Disciples, were not Apostles, in the strict and limited Sense of that Word.

*ſtles* be limited to ſuch of them only, as compoſed the Writings, called by *Irenæus the Scriptures*; the Meaning of his Words will be, that the Apoſtles, when they had preached the Goſpel, (*i. e.* the whole Syſtem of Facts and Doctrines, which it was neceſſary for Chriſtians to know and believe) committed it to Writing for the Uſe of the Churches, to ſerve thenceforward, as he expreſſes it, for the *Pillar and Foundation* of their Faith in *Chriſt Jeſus.* Thoſe Churches therefore were the proper Evidences to prove the Apoſtles to be the Authors of thoſe Writings, which they received from them. And the Teſtimony they gave to that Matter of Fact, as, on the one hand, it does not appear to have been liable to any Suſpicion of Fraud; ſo, on the other, it ſeems equally free from any Probability of Error, or Miſinformation. For they muſt have had certain Knowledge of the Character and Credit of the Perſons who delivered thoſe Writings to them in the Name of any of the Apoſtles *, and many other indubitable Proofs,

* Thus *Tychicus*, mentioned by St. *Paul* in his Epiſtle to the *Epheſians*, as ſent by him, and moſt probably the Bearer of that Epiſtle, and of that to the *Coloſſians*†, where he is alſo mentioned as ſent to them by that Apoſtle, together

† Chap. iv. 7, 8, 9.

Proofs, both *external* and *internal*, to convince them of their being genuine, or to discover the Falshood, if they were not. Allowing, for Instance, the Epistles which now pass under the Name of St. *Paul*, to have been received during his Life by the Churches to which they were directed; there are in all of them many Circumstances, by which they might certainly have known him to be the Author. These Circumstances the Reader, if he has either received or wrote any Letters of Business to or from his Acquaintance and Friends, may easily suggest to himself, and may as easily discover them upon perusing those Epistles. But it will, nay it must be said by those, who deny these Scriptures to have been written by the Apostles, whose Names they bear, that they were forged after their Deaths, and consequently could not have been received by the Churches during their Lives. This, doubtless, Infidels will say, (for what else can they pretend?) But I am at a Loss to think how they can support their Assertion, since not only the Testi-

ther with *Onesimus*; *Tychicus*, I say, and *Onesimus* were doubtless able to give such Proofs of St. *Paul*'s being the Author of those two Epistles, as the Christians of these Nations must have been satisfied with, could it be supposed that they wanted other Reasons to convince them of it; but this Supposition, I believe, no one will think it reasonable to make.

Testimony of all the earliest Writers of the Church, but common Sense itself is against them. For can it be imagined that the *Corinthians*, for Example, would have received as genuine an Epistle, not deliver'd to them till after the Death of the Apostle whose Name it bore; and yet appearing from many Circumstances therein mentioned, to have been written several Years before; unless such an extraordinary Delay was very satisfactorily accounted for? Is it not to be presumed, that in a Matter of such Importance, not only to themselves, but to all Christians, they would have demanded of the Person, who first produced it, How he came by it? How he knew it was written by St. *Paul*, and address'd to Them? Why it was not sent at the Time it was written, especially as it was evident, upon the Face of the Epistle itself, that it was written upon Occasion of some Disturbances and Irregularities crept into that Church, and in answer to some Questions proposed to that Apostle, which required a speedy Reformation and Reply? These Questions and many more, which the Particulars referred to in the Epistle must have suggested, the *Corinthians* would in common Prudence have asked; and if the Impostor could not (as it is most reasonable to conclude he could not) return a satisfactory Answer to those Questions; can we believe the *Corinthians* would have admitted, upon his bare Word, or even upon probable Presumptions, an Epistle, which, if they acknowledged it to have been written by St. *Paul*, they must thenceforward have regarded as the infallible Rule of their Faith and Practice? This is supposing that the first Christians (as their candid Adversaries are indeed apt to suppose) acted with much less Wisdom and Circumspection, than any Men would now act upon any momentous Affair in ordinary Life. And let it not be forgotten that Christianity, at its first Appearance in the World, *very deeply* affected the Temporal Concerns of its Professors. The Profession of Christianity did not, then, as it does now in some Parts of the World, entitle Men to, and *qualify* them for Honour and Preferments. Christians, upon barely confessing themselves such, were many Times, without any Crime alledged, put immediately to Death; all the Advantages they reapt from a Life of Faith and Virtue, were

the

the Peace of a quiet Conscience here, and the Hopes of a blessed Immortality hereafter. The professing Christianity therefore was a Matter of Temporal Deliberation. And why is it more reasonable to imagine that the People of those Ages would give up all their worldly Views and Interests, without being convinced that it was worth their while to do it, than it is to imagine that a Man in his Senses, either of this or any past Age, would without a valuable Consideration surrender his Estate to a Stranger, and leave himself a Beggar? I say this to those People, who seem to consider all the Primitive Christians, either as Fools or Knaves, Enthusiasts or Impostors; without being able to assign any Reason for their Opinion, but that there have been Fools and Knaves, Enthusiasts and Impostors, among the Professors of all Religions whatsoever. But in order to prove a Man a Fool, or an Enthusiast for embracing this or that Religion, it will be necessary to shew in the first Place, that he took up his Faith without duly examining the Principles or Facts, upon which it is founded, that his Faith was not properly deducible from those Facts or Principles, or that those Principles and Facts were in themselves absurd and false. These Points, I say, are not to be *presumed*, but *proved*. And with regard to the Question now under Consideration, unless it is proved by positive and undeniable Evidence, that the Scriptures upon which the Christians, who lived immediately after the Times of the Apostles, built their Faith, were either forged or falsified (that is, forged in part) it cannot, I apprehend, be fairly concluded, that they acted like Fools or Madmen, in *forsaking all*, and *taking up the Cross of Christ*. Let this Point be once *proved*, and it will readily be allowed that they took up their Faith without due Examination; since it must be owned that if we, at this Distance, are able to discover the Forgery, they, who *lived* at the very Time when those Writings first appeared, could not have wanted the Means of detecting it, had they thought proper to make Use of them. For as it is evident from the Testimonies of the oldest Christian Writers, some of whom lived very near the Times of the Apostles themselves, that these Scriptures were cited, read, and generally received, as genuine by the Christians of their Age, and

even

even before, they must have been forged, either in the Life-time of the Apostles, or very soon after their Deaths. That they were forged and generally received as authentick, while the Apostles were yet living; no body, I imagine, will venture to assert, who considers the many Circumstances and Facts therein related, concerning the Apostles themselves, and numberless other People then living; any one of which being falsified, must have utterly destroyed the Pretence of their having been composed by an Apostle, whom some of those Scriptures affirmed to have been under the Guidance and Inspiration of the Spirit of Truth. If they were forged and published soon after the Deaths of the Apostles, there was still great Danger of the Fraud's being detected, if not by many living Witnesses, yet by such a Tradition of Facts and Doctrines, whether oral or written, as, if it had been found to clash with that supposed Gospel or Epistle, must have rendered its Authenticity suspected, unless supported by better Evidence than the bare Name of an Apostle prefixed to it. And if it could be supposed that the bare Name of an Apostle was, in those Times, of Weight sufficient to establish the Authority of any Writing, though otherwise liable to Suspicion; how came it to pass that those cunning Impostors, who wrote the Gospels of *Mark* and *Luke*, did not publish them under the venerable and all-sanctifying Names of the Apostles? If these Scriptures therefore were forged and published in either of the above-mentioned Periods (and for the Reasons before given, the Forgery could not have been of a later Date) it is highly improbable, that the Imposture should have escaped Detection; and had it been detected, it is equally improbable, that Christians, who staked their All upon the Truth of the Gospel, should receive as genuine, and acknowledge as divinely inspired, Writings which were known or even suspected to be forged. But it will perhaps be urged, that the Cheat was discovered and known only by a few of the wiser Sort; who for the Advancement of a good Cause, thinking it at least a venial Sin, a Fraud, which might even be stiled *pious*, to impose upon their weaker Brethren, recommended to them, under the Name of an Apostle, a religious Treatise, which tended only to improve their Piety, and strengthen

their

their Faith. But this Suspicion will appear as groundless and improbable as any of the former, if it be considered, that the Abettors, as well as the Authors of the Forgery, must have been Christians; (Christians I mean, as contradistinguished from *Jews*, Heathens and Hereticks,) and Men of Capacities and Knowledge superior to the Vulgar. As Christians they could not, in those Ages of Persecution, have any worldly Interest in promoting the Cause of Christianity, and therefore could have no Motive to induce them to impose upon their Brethren, but a Persuasion that it was lawful at least to *do Evil, that Good might come on it*: A Principle, which as Men of Parts and Knowledge, they could not but be sensible was unworthy of a Disciple of the Lord of Truth and Righteousness; and which is expresly condemned in the Epistle to the *Romans* *; which Epistle therefore cannot be supposed to have been forged by Men, who acknowledged that Principle, and proceeded upon it. Besides, as far the greater Number of the Books of Scripture contain Facts, as well as Precepts and Doctrines, these Impostors, however well-



* Rom. iii. 8.

intentioned, could not be assured that their Imposture would not turn more to the Prejudice, than Advantage of Christianity; since though they might think themselves secure in the Acquiescence of their weaker Brethren, and the Fidelity of their Partners in the Fraud, they had Reason to apprehend the Zeal and Abilities of their open and avow'd Enemies, Heathens, *Jews* and Hereticks; who wanting neither the Means nor Inclination to examine the Principles of a Religion, which with their utmost Power they endeavoured to subvert, might very probably discover their Imposture, and would certainly take every Advantage, which such a Discovery could furnish them with, of decrying a Religion, which they might then with some Colour have suggested, could not be maintained without *Fraud*. This Danger, which with the same Penetration that enabled them to discover a Cheat that had passed upon the Vulgar, they must undoubtedly have foreseen, would, it may be supposed, have checked their Zeal, and rendered them cautious, how they ventured upon an Imposture, the Success of which was so very precarious.

Since therefore no Motive can be assigned of Force sufficient to induce any Christians of those Times, either to contrive or support a Forgery of this Kind; since had any of those Scriptures attributed to the Apostles, and especially the Epistles of St. *Paul*, been forged and published so early, as the Writings of the most ancient Fathers shew them to have been known and received, it is next to impossible that the Fraud should have escaped Detection; and since the Christians of those Ages must, in Consequence of such a Detection, have necessarily disowned and rejected those Scriptures as spurious, may we not from their having acknowledged them as authentick, conclude for the several Reasons above given, that the Apostles and Evangelists were the undoubted Authors of the Writings now received under their Names?

But allowing the Christians of those early Ages to have been able to discover the genuine Works of the Apostles, from any spurious Writings forged in their Names; and allowing those Books, now received into the

Canon

Canon of the Holy Scriptures, to have been written by those Authors, whose Names they bear; it may be demanded how we at this Time can be assured, that, among the great Number which have since been ascribed to them, they wrote only these? or that in such a Succession of Ages these are come down to us pure and uncorrupted? To the first of these Questions I answer, that as the Christians of those early Ages must be acknowledged for competent Judges of the Authority of any Books or Writings ascribed to the Apostles; such Book or Writing as they allowed to be genuine, hath an indisputable Title to that Character. But to this Title no other Writings ascribed to the Apostles, besides those now received into the Canon of Scripture, can pretend; since of most of them, especially the false Gospels, we find no mention till the fourth Century.

For an Answer to the second Question, I shall refer the learned Reader to Dr. Whitby's *Examen Variantium Lectionum Dr. Millii*, published at the End of his second Volume of

Anno-

* See *Whitby*'s Prefatory Discourse to the four Gospels.

Annotations on the New Testament, where he will find that the various Readings, upon which the Adversaries of Christianity (among whom I reckon the Clergy of the Church of *Rome*) have laid so great a Stress, will be of little Service to their Cause; the greatest Part of them being absolutely insignificant, and none of them, saith that learned Writer, *either changing or corrupting any Article of Faith, or Rule of Life.*

And although considering the great Length of Time that is past since these Scriptures were written, and the Number of Copies and Translations that have been made of them, it is no Wonder that many Errors should have crept into them, either from the Ignorance or Inadvertency of Transcribers and Translators; all of which have helped to swell the Sum of various Readings; yet considering on the other hand the Number of Heresies, that have sprung up in every Age of Christianity, all of which pretended to derive their Opinions from the Scriptures; considering also the Watchfulness of the *Jews* and *Heathens*, those avowed Enemies of the Gospel, who, as appears from [illegible] their

their Writings, were no Strangers to the Scriptures, it would be a ſtill greater Wonder that any material Alteration ſhould have been made in them; ſince whoever had attempted any ſuch Alteration, whether Chriſtian, Heretick, *Jew*, or Heathen, could not but know it was impoſſible it ſhould eſcape the Obſervation of ſo many Eyes, as were continually prying, though with different Views, into theſe important Writings. And this ſeems to me the only Reaſon for their having paſſed uncorrupted through the treacherous Hands of the Church of *Rome*, who had them ſo long in her keeping. She was reſtrained from altering the Scriptures, by the Fear of being detected by the Eaſtern Churches, who diſowned her Authority; and yet there is little Queſtion to be made that ſhe would have done it, had ſhe not fallen upon that leſs dangerous, though more abſurd Expedient of locking them up from the Laity, and aſſuming to herſelf the ſole Right of expounding them: A Right which ſhe hath aſſerted and maintained with all the Artifices and Cruelty that Fraud and Tyranny could invent. This Expedient however, tho' it hath hitherto preſerved Popery, hath

hath ſaved the Scriptures, and with them Chriſtianity. For conſidering the Duration, Extent, and Abſoluteneſs of her Power in the Weſt, had ſhe altered the Text of Scripture, according to the Comments ſhe had made upon it, Chriſtians (could there have been any really ſuch at this Time, and in theſe Parts of the World) muſt have been reduced to contend with the Church of *Rome*, not *from* the Scriptures, but *for* the Scriptures themſelves. And what Advantages Infidelity and Scepticiſm would have had in the mean time, is eaſy to imagine; ſince they are bold enough to diſpute even now the Genuineneſs of thoſe Scriptures, which the very Perſons, whoſe Doctrines are the moſt oppoſite to them, have been neceſſitated to acknowledge and maintain.

§. 24. I AM now to conſider what Arguments can be offered to induce us to give Credit to the Teſtimony of the Apoſtles and Evangeliſts.

Two Qualities are requiſite to eſtabliſh the Credit of a Witneſs, *viz.* a perfect Knowledge

ledge of the Fact he gives Testimony to; and a fair and unblemished Character.

After what has been said in the preceding Parts of this Discourse concerning the Evidences of the Resurrection of *Jesus Christ*, it will, I hope, be granted that the Apostles were duly qualified to be Witnesses, in point of Knowledge of the Fact, which they are brought to give Testimony to. It remains then that we enquire into their Characters, which may very clearly be collected from the Tenor of their Lives and Conduct, as Preachers of the Gospel, and the Purity of the Doctrines they taught; not to insist in Favour of them upon the Conclusion, which may be drawn from their very Enemies not having been able to fix upon them any *Stain* or Blemish, which they themselves have not acknowledged and lamented.

Their Lives then, after they had embraced Christianity, were not only irreproachable, but holy; and their Conduct, as Preachers of the Gospel, disinterested, noble, and generous, in the most exalted Degree. For they not only quitted

quitted their Houses, their Lands, their Occupations, their Friends, Kindred, Parents, Wives and Children, but their Countries also, every Pursuit, and every Endearment of Life, in order to propagate, with infinite Labour, through innumerable Difficulties, and with the utmost Dangers, in every Corner of the known World, the Salvation of Mankind; certain of meeting, in every new Region, with new Enemies and Opposers; and yet requiring of those, who through their Preaching were become their Friends and Brethren, nothing but a bare Subsistence; and sometimes labouring with their own Hands, to save them even from that light and reasonable Burthen; disclaiming for themselves all Authority, Preeminence, and Power; and teaching those ignorant and superstitious People, who, taking them for Gods, would have worshiped them, and sacrificed to them, that they were Men like themselves, and Servants of that One God, to whom alone Worship was due. Would Impostors, who are most commonly interested, vain-glorious and ambitious, have acted in this Manner? No certainly; but it may be said, Enthusiasts would. Be it so.

But

But how can it be made appear that the Apostles were Enthusiasts? If *Christ* did not rise from the Dead, most assuredly he did not preach to them after his Crucifixion: Upon which Supposition, I apprehend it will be very difficult to account for their returning to their Faith in that Master, whom in his Distress they had abandoned and disowned. But if *Christ* did rise from the Dead, and did, after his Resurrection, converse with his Apostles, I suppose it will be easily granted, that they had sufficient Reason for believing in him, and for acting in Obedience to the Command given them by him, to preach the Gospel throughout the World, especially when they found themselves so well qualified for that important Commission, by the miraculous Powers conferred upon them by the Holy Ghost, and particularly the Gift of Tongues, so apparently and so wisely calculated to carry on that great, that universal Service. If this, I say, was the Case, then surely the Apostles were no Enthusiasts, since they neither believed themselves without reasonable Proof, nor pretended to Inspiration and a divine Commission, with-

out

out being able to give to others sufficient Evidences of both *.

Of all the admirably pure and truly divine Doctrines taught by the Apostles, I shall consider only two, as more peculiarly relative to the present Argument; and they are, the Belief of a Judgment to come, and the Obligation of speaking Truth. That God will judge the World by *Jesus Christ*, is a necessary Article of the Christian Faith; and as such, is strongly and frequently inculcated in the Writings of the Apostles and Evangelists, of which it is needless to procure Instances. And that Christians were required by these Preachers of Holiness to speak Truth upon all Occasions, the following Texts will clearly evince. In *Ephes.* iv. 25. the Apostle commands that, *putting away Lying, they speak every man Truth with his Neighbour*. And again, *Coloss.* iii. 9. *Lye not one to another.* Nay, that even the Man who lyes through Zeal for the Glory of God, is, according to their Estimation, to be accounted a Sinner, may be inferred from these Words in *Rom.* iii. 7, 8.—— *If the Truth*

 of

* See Mr. *Locke*'s Chap. on Enthusiasm.

*of God hath more abounded through my Lye unto his Glory, why yet am I also judged as a Sinner? And not rather as we be slanderously reported, and as some affirm that we say, Let us do Evil that Good may come? Whose Damnation is just.* That the Apostles themselves were fully persuaded of the Truth of those two Propositions, no body can deny, who will call to mind that they chose to suffer Persecution and Death itself, rather than not *speak the Things which* they *had seen and heard*; and that, *if in this Life only they had Hope, they were of all Men the most miserable.* Now, that any Men, who firmly believed that God would punish them for speaking an Untruth, though for the Advancement of a good Cause, should, at the Hazard of their Lives, and without any Prospect of Gain, or Advantage, assert Facts, which at the same time they knew to be false; should, for Instance, affirm, that they saw and conversed with *Jesus Christ* after his Resurrection, knowing or believing that he was not risen from the Dead, and yet expect to be judged hereafter by that very same *Jesus*, is too improbable to gain Credit with any, but those great Believers of Absurdities the Infidels and Scepticks.

§. 25. But besides the many infallible Tokens and Evidences of the Integrity of the Apostles and Evangelists, that may be collected from their Lives and Doctrines, there are also in their Writings several internal Marks of their Veracity: Some of which I shall now endeavour to point out, confining myself to such Parts of their Writings as belong to the present Subject.

The Contradictions and Inconsistencies which some imagine they have discovered in the Evangelical Accounts of the Resurrection, have been urged as Arguments for setting aside the Authority, and rejecting the Evidence of the Gospels. But these supposed Contradictions having been considered in the foregoing Parts of this Discourse; and having, upon a close Inspection, and comparing the several Narratives with each other, been shewn to be shadowy and imaginary, and to lie no deeper than the Superficies and Surface of the Words: We need not be afraid of admitting these *Appearances of Inconsistency*; since from them it may be inferred, to the Advantage of the

Evangelists, *that they did not write in Concert.* For had they agreed together upon giving an Account of the Resurrection of *Christ*; and each of them taken, by Allotment, his several Portion of that History, it is probable they would somewhere or other have dropt some Intimations, that the Particulars omitted by them were supplied by others; and that such and such Parts of their Narrations were to be connected with such and such Facts, related by their Brethren; or they would have distinguished the several Incidents by such strong and visible Marks, and Circumstances of Time and Place, *&c.* as might have been sufficient at first sight, to discover their Order, and keep them from being confounded with each other: Some, or all of these Things, I say, they would probably have done, had they written in Concert. And doubtless they would, nay they must have written in Concert, had they endeavoured to impose upon the World a *cunningly-devised Fable*; and had they not trusted to the Truth and Notoriety of the Facts they related. Truth, like Honesty, oftentimes neglects Appearances: Hypocrisy and Imposture are always guarded.

And as from these seeming Discordances in their Accounts, we may conclude they did not write in Concert, so from their agreeing in the principal and most material Facts, we may infer that they wrote after the Truth. * In *Xiphilin* and *Theodosius*, the two Abbreviators of *Dio Cassius*, may be observed the like Agreement and Disagreement; the one taking notice of many Particulars, which the other passes over in Silence, and both of them relating the chief and most remarkable Events. And as from their both frequently making use of the very same Words and Expressions, when they speak of the same Thing, it is apparent that they both copied from the same Original; so I believe no body was ever absurd enough to imagine that the Particulars mentioned by the one, were not taken out of *Dio Cassius*, merely because they are omitted by the other. And still more absurd would it be to say, as some have lately done of the Evangelists, that the Facts related by *Theodosius* are contradicted by *Xiphilin*, because the latter says nothing of them. But against the Evangelists, it seems, all Kinds of Arguments may not only be employed but ap-

 plauded.

* Vide Dio Caf. Hist. edit. Leunclav. Fol. Hanov. 1606.

plauded. The Case however of the sacred Historians is exactly parallel to that of these two Abbreviators. The latter extracted the Particulars related in their several Abridgments from the History of *Dio Cassius*, as the former drew the Materials of their Gospels from the Life of *Jesus Christ*. The two last transcribed their Relations from a certain Collection of Facts contained in one and the same History; the four first from a certain Collection of Facts contained in the Life of one and the same Person, laid before them by that Spirit, which was to lead them into all Truth; and why the Fidelity of the four Transcribers should be called in Question for Reasons which hold equally strong against the two who are not suspected, I leave those to determine who lay such a Weight upon this Objection.

ANOTHER Mark of the Veracity of the Evangelists appears in their naming the Time, the Scene of Action the Actors, and the Witnesses, of most of the Facts mentioned by them; which I shall give a remarkable Instance of in one relating to the present Subject, the Resurrection; *viz.* the guarding the Sepulchre of *Christ*. The Time, was that of the

Celebra-

Celebration of the Paſſover, the moſt ſolemn Feſtival of the *Jews*; the Scene was in *Jeruſalem*, the Metropolis of *Judea*; and at that Time crouded with *Jews*, who came thither from all Parts of the Earth to keep the Paſſover: The Actors and Witneſſes were the Chief Prieſts and Elders, *Pontius Pilate* the *Roman* Governor, and the *Roman* Soldiers who guarded the Sepulchre. Now if the Story of guarding the Sepulchre had been falſe, it is not to be doubted but the Chief Prieſts and Elders, who are ſaid to have obtained the Guard, and ſealed the Door of the Sepulchre, would by ſome authentick Act have cleared themſelves of the Folly and Guilt imputed to them by the Evangeliſt, who charges the Chief Prieſts with having bribed the Soldiers to tell not only a Lye, but an abſurd Lye, that carried its own Confutation with it; the Soldiers, with confeſſing a Breach of Diſcipline, that by the military Law was puniſhable with Death; and the Governor, with the Suſpicion at leaſt of being capable of overlooking ſo heinous a Crime, at the Inſtigation of the Chief Prieſts, *&c.* All theſe ſeveral Charges upon the whole Government of *Judea*, might have been anſwered at once by an Atteſtation from the Chief Priests, setting forth that they never demanded a Guard to be set at the Sepulchre, confirmed by the Testimony of all the *Roman* Officers and Soldiers (many of whom were probably at *Jerusalem* when this Gospel was written) denying that they were ever upon that Guard. This not only the Reputation of the Chief Priests, but their avowed Malice to *Christ*, and Aversion to his Doctrine and Religion required; and this, even upon the Supposition of the Story of guarding the Sepulchre being true, they would probably have done, had they been at Liberty to propagate and invent what Lye they pleased: But that a Guard was set at the Sepulchre, was in all Likelihood, by the Dispersion and Flight of the Soldiers into the City, too well known in *Jerusalem* for them to venture at denying it; for which Reason, as I have before observed, they were obliged to invent a Lye consistent with that known Fact, however absurd and improbable it might appear when it came to be considered and examined. Now as the Report put into the Mouths of the *Roman* Soldiers by the Chief Priests and Elders, is no Proof of the Falsehood of this Fact, but rather of the contrary, so does the naming the Time, the Scene, the

Actors,

Actors, and the Witnesses, form a very strong Presumption of its being true, since no Forger of Lyes willingly and wittingly furnishes out the Means of his own Detection; especially when we consider that this Story is related by that Evangelist, who is said to have written nearest the Time, and to have composed his Gospel for those Christians who dwelt in *Judea*, many of whom then living were probably at *Jerusalem* when this Thing was done.

The strict Attachment and Regard to Truth, of all the Evangelists, is farther manifested in their relating of themselves and their Brethren many Things, that in the Opinion of the World could not but turn much to their Dishonour and Discredit. Such as their denying and deserting their Master in his Extremity, and their Dulness in not understanding his Predictions about his rising from the Dead, tho' expressed in the plainest and most intelligible Words. A Man's Confession against himself, or his Friends, is generally presumed to be true. If the Evangelists therefore be allowed to be the Authors of those Gospels which bear their Names, or if those

Writings

Writings are supposed to have been forged by some Friends of Christianity, they must in these Instances at least be acknowledged to relate the Truth, till some other good Reason, besides that of their Attachment to the Truth, can be assigned for their inserting such disgraceful and dishonourable Accounts of themselves and their Friends.

But there is nothing that sets the Veracity of the sacred Writers so much above all Question and Suspicion, as what they tell us about the low Condition, the Infirmities, the Sufferings, and the Death of the great Author and Finisher of their Faith, *Christ Jesus*. He hungered, they say, he was poor, so poor, as not to *have where to lay his Head*; he wept, hid himself for fear of the *Jews* who sought to kill him; and when his Hour drew nigh, he was dejected, sorrowful, *exceeding sorrowful, even unto Death*. He prayed, that the Cup of Affliction, which was then mixing for him, might, if possible, pass from him. And tho' he was *strengthened by an Angel from Heaven*, yet, *being in an Agony, he prayed more earnestly, and his Sweat was as it were great Drops of Blood*

*Blood falling down to the Ground.* After this, he was ſeized like a common Malefactor, abandoned by all his Followers and Friends; led bound, firſt to *Annas*, then to *Caiaphas*, then to *Pilate*, then to *Herod*, then back again to *Pilate*; and laſtly, after enduring a thouſand Inſults and Indignities, after having been buffeted, ſpit upon, and ſcourged, was carried to ſuffer upon the Croſs the infamous and painful Death of offending Slaves, and the vileſt Criminals. And yet this hungry, houſeleſs, ſuffering, dying *Jeſus*, is by the ſame Writers ſaid to have fed a Multitude of many Thouſands with five Loaves and two Fiſhes; to have commanded the Fiſh of the Sea to provide him Money to pay the Tribute; to have been miniſter'd unto by Angels; to have been obeyed by the Winds and Seas; to have had in himſelf, and to have imparted to his Diſciples, Authority over unclean Spirits, and the Power of healing all Manner of Diſeaſes; to have raiſed the Dead by a Touch, a Word; to have been able to have obtained from God, whom he called his Father, an Army of more than twelve Legions of Angels; a Force ſufficient not only to have reſcued him from

from the Sufferings and Death he deprecated, but to have acquired him the Empire of the World: And lastly, as an Instance of his being endued with a Power superior even to Destruction itself, he is said to have risen from the Dead; to have ascended into Heaven, and to sit down for ever at the Right-hand of God. From these Accounts it is plain, that the Character of *Jesus Christ*, as drawn up by the Evangelists, is a Mixture of such seeming Inconsistencies, so wonderful a Composition of Weakness and Power, Humiliation and Glory, Humanity and Divinity, that as no mere Mortal could pretend to come up to it, so the Wit of Man would never have conceived and proposed such a one for the Founder of any Sect or Religion. The Sufferings and Cross of *Christ* were, as St. *Paul* confesses, *to the* Jews *a Stumbling-block, and Foolishness to the* Greeks. The *Jews*, it is well known, expected a temporal Deliverer, an earthly Prince, a glorious conquering Messiah; and were therefore so scandalized at the low Condition and abject Fortunes of *Jesus*, so ill-proportioned, as they imagined, to the sublime Character of the Son of God, that upon Account of those

human

human Blemishes only, they rejected all the miraculous Evidences of his divine Mission, and put him to Death as a Blasphemer, for taking upon him the Name, without the temporal Splendor and Power of the Messiah. That the Disciples of *Jesus* were tainted with the like Prejudices with their unbelieving Brethren the *Jews*, is very natural to believe, and may certainly be collected from the Writings of the Evangelists, from whom we learn, that when convinced by his Miracles, his Doctrine, and his Life, they had acknowledged him to be the Messiah, they were so offended at what he told them of his Sufferings and Death, that they refused to believe him; * *and* Peter *took him, and began to rebuke him, saying, Be it far from thee, Lord, this shall not be unto thee.* The despicable Condition, the Sufferings and Death, of *Christ*, being admitted, I think it impossible to give one probable Reason for supposing that the Apostles and the Evangelists invented the other more than human Part of his Character. Had he wrought no Miracles, had he not risen from the Dead, their Religious Prejudices, as they were *Jews*, must

* Matt. xvi. 22.

must have with-held them for ever from acknowledging him for their Messiah; and yet it is notorious, that not only they themselves acknowledged him as such, but endeavoured to persuade their unbelieving Brethren, that *God had made that same* Jesus, *whom they had crucified, both Lord and Christ.* This was the great Article, the Foundation-Stone, upon which the whole Superstructure of Christianity was raised; and to prove this Article, they appealed to his Miracles, as so many Evidences of his divine Mission. But here *modern* Unbelievers (for *Celsus*, who lived nearest those Times, admits all the Miracles of *Christ*, but imputes them to his Skill in Magick) come in with their Suspicions, and pretend to call in Question the Accounts given us of these Miracles in the Evangelists, which, without any Proof, they are pleased to take for Forgeries: In Answer to which, (not to insist upon the Improbability that any Man, or any Set of Men in their Senses, should venture to appeal to their Enemies for the Truth of Facts, which they themselves knew to be false, especially when those Enemies had not only the Means of detecting them, but the Inclination and

Power

Power to punish them for their Impostures: Not to insist, I say, upon this Topick, nor upon that which I just now mentioned of its being impossible to assign any Motive that could induce them to be guilty of such a Forgery,) I shall only observe, that allowing them to have been so shameless and so wicked as to invent and propagate a Set of Lyes in order to get Credit to their Master and his Religion, it is strange they should not go one Step farther, and suppress at least, if not deny his Infirmities, his Sufferings, and his Crucifixion; and so remove that Stumbling-block, which they could not but know would be the greatest Obstacle to the Advancement of their Religion, as well among the *Gentiles* as the *Jews*. But it will be urged perhaps, that his Sufferings and Crucifixion were too publick to be denied; and so, say the Evangelists, were most of his Miracles: And this undoubtedly was the Reason why they were acknowledged by *Celsus*. To suppose therefore that the Evangelists, for Fear of being detected, would confess Truths, which manifestly prejudiced their great Design of propagating the Faith in *Christ Jesus*, and yet would not by the same

Fear

Fear of Detection be restrained from relating Untruths, because they might imagine them to be advantageous to their Cause, is no Mark of Equity and Candour, but of Partiality and Prejudice. But it will possibly be said (for what will not Infidels *say?* and I will add, how strange soever it may sound, what will they not *believe?*) that the Scriptures were forged long after the Events recorded in them, and consequently long after all the Evidences of their Truth or Falshood were extinct and lost. In Answer to this it may be again demanded, as in the Case of the Evangelists, how came these later Forgers to chuse the suffering crucified *Jesus* for the Author of their Religion? And why, since they were at Liberty to say what they pleased, without any Apprehension of being discovered, why, I say, did they relate such Things both of Him and his Disciples, as, in the Opinion of the World, could not fail of discrediting the Faith they preached in his Name, and by an Authority pretended to be derived from him and his Disciples? But without entering into these Considerations, it may be sufficient barely to deny this Charge, till they, who insist upon it, shall

be

be able to make it good, by shewing either from authentick Testimonies, or even probable and presumptive Arguments, when they were forged? by whom? and to what End? Till they are able to do this, (which I will venture to pronounce will never be) we have a Right to insist for the Reasons above given, that the Scriptures of the New Testament were written by those whose Names they bear, and that all the Facts related in them are most unquestionably true.

BEFORE I quit this Subject, I cannot forbear taking Notice of one other Mark of Integrity which appears in all the Compositions of the Sacred Writers, and particularly the Evangelists, and that is, the simple, unaffected, unornamental, and unostentatious Manner, in which they deliver Truths so important and sublime, and Facts so magnificent and wonderful, as are capable, one would think, of lighting up a Flame of Oratory, even in the dullest and coldest Breasts. The speak of an Angel descending from Heaven to foretell the miraculous Conception of *Jesus*, of another proclaiming his Birth, attended by *a Multi-*

*tude of the Heavenly Host praising God, and saying, Glory to God in the highest; and on Earth Peace, Good Will towards Men*: Of his Star appearing in the East; of Angels ministring to him in the Wilderness; of his Glory in the Mount; of a Voice twice heard from Heaven, saying *this is my beloved Son*; of innumerable Miracles perform'd by him, and by his Disciples in his Name; of his knowing the Thoughts of Men; of his foretelling future Events; of Prodigies and Wonders accompanying his Crucifixion and Death; of an Angel descending in Terrors, opening his Sepulchre, and frightning away the Soldiers, who were set to guard it; of his rising from the Dead, ascending into Heaven, and pouring down, according to his Promise, the various and miraculous Gifts of the Holy Spirit upon his Apostles and Disciples. All these amazing Incidents do these inspired Historians relate nakedly and plainly, without any of the Colourings and Heightnings of Rhetorick, or so much as a single Note of Admiration; without making any Comment or Remark upon them, or drawing from them any Conclusion in Honour either of their Master or themselves, or to the Advantage of the Religion they preached in his Name; but contenting themselves with relating the naked Truth, whether it seems to make for them or against them, without either magnifying on the one Hand, or palliating on the other; they leave their Cause to the unbiassed Judgment of Mankind; seeking, like genuine Apostles of the Lord of Truth, to convince rather than to persuade; and therefore *coming*, as St. *Paul* speaks of his own Preaching, *not with Excellency of Speech,— not with enticing Words of Man's Wisdom, but with Demonstration of the Spirit, and of Power; that*, adds he, *your Faith should not stand in the Wisdom of Men, but in the Power of* * *God.* And let it be remembered that he who speaks this, wanted not Learning, Art, or Eloquence, as is evident from his Speeches recorded in the Acts of the Apostles, and from the Testimony of that great Critick *Longinus*, who in reckoning up the *Grecian* Orators, places among them *Paul* of *Tarsus* †; and surely had they been left solely to the Suggestions and Guidance of human Wisdom, they would not have failed to lay hold on such Topicks, as the Wonders

 of

* 1 Cor. ii. 2. iv. 5. † Vide Long. Frag. Edit. Pearce.

of their Maſter's Life, and the tranſcendent Purity and Perfection of the noble, generous, benevolent Morality contained in his Precepts, furniſhed them with. Theſe Topicks, I ſay, greater than ever *Tully*, or *Demoſthenes*, or *Plato* were poſſeſſed of, mere human Wiſdom would doubtleſs have prompted them to make uſe of, in o der to recommend in the ſtrongeſt manner the Religion of *Chriſt Jeſus* to Mankind, by turning their Attention to the Divine Part of his Character, and hiding as it were in a Blaze of heavenly Light and Glory, his Infirmities, his Sufferings, and his Death. And had they upon ſuch Topicks as theſe, and in ſuch a Cauſe, called in to their Aſſiſtance all the Arts of Compoſition, Rhetorick and Logick, who would have blamed them for it? Not thoſe Perſons, I preſume, who dazzled and captivated with the glittering Ornaments of Human Wiſdom, make a Mock at the Simplicity of the Goſpel, and think it Wit to ridicule the Style and Language of the Holy Scriptures. But the all-wiſe Spirit of God, by whom theſe Sacred Writers were guided into all Truth, thought fit to direct or permit them to proceed in a different Method; a Method

thod however very analogous to that, in which he hath been pleaſed to reveal himſelf to us in the great Book of Nature, the ſtupendous Frame of the Univerſe; all whoſe Wonders he hath judged it ſufficient to lay before us in Silence, and expects from our Obſervations the proper Comments and Deductions, which, having endued us with Reaſon, he hath enabled us to make. And tho' a careleſs and ſuperficial Spectator may fancy he perceives even in this fair Volume many Inconſiſtencies, Defects and Superfluities; yet to a diligent, unprejudiced, and rational Inquirer, who will take the Pains to examine the Laws, conſider and compare the ſeveral Parts, and regard their Uſe and Tendency, with reference to the whole Deſign of this amazing Structure, as far as his ſhort Abilities can carry him, there will appear in thoſe Inſtances, which he is capable of knowing, ſuch evident Characters of Wiſdom, Goodneſs and Power, as will leave him no room to doubt of their Author, or to ſuſpect that in thoſe Particulars which he hath not examined, or to a thorough Knowledge of which he cannot perhaps attain, there is nothing but Folly, Weakneſs and Malignity.

 The

The ſame Thing made be ſaid of the *written Book*, the *ſecond Volume* (if I may ſo ſpeak) of the Revelation of God, the Holy Scriptures. For as in the Firſt, ſo alſo in this are there many Paſſages, that to a curſory unobſerving Reader appear idle, unconnected, unaccountable, and inconſiſtent with thoſe Marks of Truth, Wiſdom, Juſtice, Mercy and Benevolence, which in others are ſo viſible, that the moſt Careleſs and Inattentive cannot but diſcern them. And even Theſe, many of them at leaſt, will often be found, upon a cloſer and ſtricter Examination, to accord and coincide with the other more plain, and more intelligible Paſſages, and to be no heterogeneous Parts of one and the ſame wiſe and harmonious Compoſition. In both indeed, in the *Natural* as well as the *Moral Book of God*, there are, and ever will be many Difficulties, which the Wit of *Man* may never be able to reſolve; but will a wiſe Philoſopher, becauſe he cannot comprehend every thing he ſees, reject for that Reaſon all the Truths that lie within his Reach, and let a few inexplicable Difficulties over-balance the many plain and infallible Evidences of the Finger of God, which

which appear in all Parts, both of his *created* and *written Works*? Or will he presume so far upon his own Wisdom, as to say, God ought to have expressed himself more clearly? The Point and exact Degree of Clearness, which will equally suit the different Capacities of Men in different Ages and Countries, will, I believe, be found more difficult to fix than is imagined; since what is clear to one Man in a certain Situation of Mind, Time and Place, will inevitably be obscure to another, who views it in other Positions, and under other Circumstances. How various and even contradictory are the Readings and Comments, which several Men, in the several Ages and Climates of the World, have made upon Nature! And yet her Characters are equally legible, and her Laws equally intelligible in all Times and in all Places; *there is no Speech nor Language where* her *Voice is not heard*. Her *Sound is gone out through all the Earth, and* her *Words to the Ends of the World*. All these Misinterpretations therefore, and Misconstructions of her Works, are chargeable only upon Mankind, who have set themselves to study them with various Degrees of Capacity, Ap-

 plication,

plication, and Impartiality. The Question then should be, why hath God given Men such various Talents? And not, why hath not God expressed himself more clearly? And the Answer to this Question, as far as it concerns Man to know, is, that God will require of him according to what he hath, and not according to what he hath not. If what is necessary for all to know, is knowable by all; those Men, upon whom God hath been pleased to bestow Capacities and Faculties superior to the Vulgar, have certainly no just Reason to complain of his having left them Materials for the Exercise of those Talents, which, if all Things were equally plain to all Men, would be of no great Advantage to the Possessors. If therefore there are in the Sacred Writings, as well as in the Works of Nature, many Passages hard to be understood, it were to be wished that the Wise and Learned, instead of being offended at them, and teaching others to be so too, would be persuaded that both God and Man expect that they would set themselves to consider and examine them carefully and impartially, and with a sincere Desire of discovering and embracing the Truth, not

with

with an arrogant unphilosophical Conceit of their being already sufficiently wise and knowing. And then I doubt not but most of those Objections to Revelation, which are now urged with the greatest Confidence, would be cleared up and removed, like those formerly made to Creation, and the Being, and Providence of God, by those most ignorant, most absurd, and yet most self-sufficient Pretenders to Reason and Philosophy, the Atheists and Scepticks.

§. 26. To these internal Evidences of the Veracity (and may I not add Inspiration?) of the Apostles and Evangelists, I shall beg leave to subjoin two external Proofs of great Weight in an Inquiry into the Reasons we have for giving Credit to their Testimony, the one negative, the other positive.

The negative Proof is contained in this Proposition, *viz.* That out of the great Number of Facts related by the Sacred Writers, publick and extraordinary as they are said to have been, not one in the Course of now almost seventeen hundred Years, hath ever been disproved

disproved or falsified. Denied indeed many of them have been, and still are; but there is a great deal of Difference between *denying* and *disproving*. To prove a Fact to be false, it is necessary that the positive and probable Evidence brought against it should over-balance that produced in Support of it. In Opposition to the Testimony of the Disciples of *Jesus Christ*, asserting that he was risen from the Dead, the Chief Priests and Elders of the *Jews* affirmed, that his Disciples stole away his Body, and then gave out that he was risen; in Maintenance of which Charge they produced, as St. *Matthew* tells us *, the *Roman* Soldiers, who were set to guard the Sepulchre, who deposed that *his Disciples came by Night and stole him away while they slept.* Not to insist again upon the Absurdity of this Report, as it stands in the Evangelist, and taking it as it was afterwards prudently amended by the *Sanhedrim*, and propagated by an express Deputation from them to all the Synagogues of the † *Jews* throughout the World, in which, without making any mention of the *Roman* Guard, they say no more than that the Disciples

* Chap. xxviii. 13. † Justin. Martyr. Dial. cum Tryph. Jud.

ciples came by Night, and ſtole away the Body; taking it, I ſay, in the Manner, in which thoſe wiſe Counſellors were upon maturer Deliberation pleaſed to put it, it may be ſufficient to obſerve, that this Theft charged upon the Diſciples, was ſo far from being proved, that it was not ſo much as ever inquired into. And yet the Accuſers were the Chief Prieſts and Elders of the *Jews*; Men in high Reverence and Authority with the People, veſted with all the Power of the State, and conſequently furniſhed with all the Means of procuring Informations, and of gaining or extorting a Confeſſion. And what were the Accuſed? Men of low Birth, mean Fortunes, without Learning, without Credit, without Support; and who out of Puſillanimity and Fear had deſerted their Maſter, upon the firſt Occaſion offered of ſhewing their Fidelity and Attachment to him. And can it be imagined that the Chief Prieſts and Council would have made no Inquiry into a Fact, the Belief of which they took ſo much Pains to propagate, had they themſelves been perſuaded of the Truth of it? And had they inquired into it, can it be ſuppoſed that out of ſuch a Number of of mean Perſons as muſt have been privy to it, no one either from Honeſty or Religion, the Fear of Puniſhment or Hope of Reward, would have betrayed the Secret, and given them ſuch Intelligence, as might have enabled them to put the Queſtion of the Reſurrection out of all Diſpute? For had it been once proved that the Diſciples ſtole away the Body of *Jeſus*, their Words would hardly have been taken for his Reſurrection. But how did theſe poor Men act? Conſcious of no Fraud and Impoſture, they remained in *Jeruſalem* a Week or more, after the Report of their having ſtolen their Maſter's Body was ſpread over the City; and in about a Month returned thither again; not long after which they aſſerted boldly to the Face of their powerful Enemies and Accuſers, the Chief Prieſts and Elders, that *God had raiſed from the Dead that ſame* Jeſus, *whom they had crucified.* And what was the Behaviour of theſe learned *Rabbins*, theſe watchful Guardians of the *Jewiſh* Church and State? Why, they ſuffered the Diſciples of *Jeſus*, charged by their Order with an Impoſture tending to diſturb the Government, to con-

tinue

tinue unquestioned at *Jerusalem*, and to depart from thence unmolested: And when upon their Return thither they had caused them to be seized, and brought before them, for * *preaching through Jesus the Resurrection of the Dead*, what did they say to them? Did they charge them with having stolen away the Body of their Master? Nothing like it. On the contrary, not being able to gainsay the Testimony given by the Apostles to the Resurrection of *Jesus*, vouched by a Miracle just then performed by them in his Name, they ordered them to withdraw, and † *conferred among themselves, saying, What shall we do to these Men? for that indeed a notable Miracle hath been done by them, is manifest to all them that dwell in* Jerusalem, *and we cannot deny it. But that it spread no farther among the People, let us straitly threaten them, that they speak henceforth to no Man in this Name: And they called them, and commanded them not to speak at all, nor teach in the Name of* Jesus. Peter *and* John *answered, and said unto them, Whether it be right in the Sight of God to hearken unto you more than unto God, judge ye: For we* cannot

* Acts iv. † Ibid. ver 15—22.

*cannot but speak the Things which we have seen and heard. So when they had farther threatened them, they let them go, finding nothing how they might punish them.* Who, after hearing this Account, could ever imagine that the Disciples stole the Body of *Jesus?* or that the Chief Priests and Elders themselves believed they did? But it may perhaps be objected, that this Account comes from Christian Writers: And could the Objectors expect to meet with it in *Jewish* Authors? We might indeed expect to find in their Writings some Proofs of this Charge upon the Disciples; and had there been any, the Chief Priests, and the other Adversaries of *Christ*, would doubtless not have failed to produce them. But the Progress that Christianity made at that Time in *Jerusalem*, is a stronger Argument than even their Silence, that no Proof of this Charge either was or could be made. Could the Apostles have had the Imprudence to preach, and could so many thousand *Jews* have been weak enough to believe upon their Testimony, that *Christ* was risen from the Dead, had it been proved that his Disciples stole away his Body? An Infidel may,

if

if he pleases, believe this, but let him account for it if he can.

I HAVE dwelt the longer upon the Examination of this pretended Theft of the Disciples, because it is the *only Fact* I know of, that hath been set up in Opposition to the many Facts upon which the Evidence of the Resurrection is founded. How defective it is in point of Proof, whether probable or positive, I need not point out to the Reader. But I cannot help observing, that those, who deny that any Guard was placed at the Sepulchre, take from it the only positive Evidence that was ever brought to support it, *viz.* the Depositions of the *Roman* Soldiers.

AMONG the many extraordinary Particulars related by the Sacred Writers, the Miracles performed by *Christ* and his Apostles, as they were almost without Number, and wrought most commonly in Publick, in the Presence of unbelieving *Jews* and *Gentiles*, yielded the fairest Occasion to the Opposers of the Gospel of overturning the Credit of the Evan-

Evangelical Historians. And yet the pitiful Solutions, which *Pagan* and *Jewish* Writers have been reduced to make use of, in order to take off the Conclusion drawn from these Miracles by the Christians, form a very strong Presumption, that they were not to be disproved. Some, as * *Celsus*, have imputed them to Magick: Others, as the *Jews*, have attributed them to the ineffable Name of God, which, † say they, *Jesus* stole out of the Temple. Both of them have admitted the Facts. I shall not go about to shew the Absurdity of either of these two Ways of accounting for those miraculous Operations: But I must hence take Occasion to beg the Reader to reflect a little upon the strange Perverseness of the human Mind, the Vanity of Reason, and the Force of Prejudice. *Celsus* believed Magick, the *Jews* had Faith in Amulets; and yet both one and the other disbelieved Christianity!

§ 27. The positive Proof of the Veracity of the Sacred Writers is founded on the exact [illegible] [illegible] the con[illegible]

* See Origen contra Celsum.

† See Univ. Hist. Vol. IV. p. 200. Note T.

compliſhment of the Predictions of our Saviour and his Apoſtles recorded in the New Teſtament.

THAT I may not draw out this Article into an exceſſive and unneceſſary Length, I ſhall make no Remarks upon thoſe Predictions, whoſe Accompliſhment is to be found in the Scriptures themſelves; ſome of which I have already taken Notice of. The Scriptures, Infidels perhaps will ſay, were written after theſe Events, and the Predictions therefore probably adapted to them. But they who make this Objection, will gain little by it, ſince if they admit the Events, it will be no difficult Matter to demonſtrate the Truth of Chriſtianity. Beſides, the Reader himſelf may with very little Pains, find out and compare theſe Predictions with their ſeveral Completions.

THE Prophecies I ſhall produce, relate to the different States of the *Jews* and *Gentiles*; different not only from each other, but very different from that, in which they both were at the Time when theſe Prophecies were written:

To have a perfect Understanding of which, it will be necessary to take a general View of the Religious State (for that is principally regarded in these Prophecies) of the Nations distinguish-ed by the Names of *Jews* and *Gentiles*.

FROM the Time of the Covenant (or Compact) which God was pleased to make with *Abraham* and his Descendants, and to renew with the whole Body of the *Israelites* under *Moses*, the *Jews* became the peculiar *People of God*: A Phrase sufficiently justified and explained by the Terms or Conditions of the Covenant; which on the Part of the *Israelites*, were the taking God only for their Lord, and paying Obedience to the Law, the Ceremonial as well as Moral Law, which he had given them. On the Part of God were stipulated Temporal Blessings, and his Almighty Protection to the *Jews*, as long as they should adhere to the Conditions entered into by Them. By virtue of this Covenant, the *Jews* acknowledged God for their King, and God governed them as his Subjects, by his Deputies and Viceroys, the Prophets, Judges, and Kings of *Israel*. *Moses*, the Mediator of this Cove-

nant,

Moses, was the first of these Deputies; and the *Messiah*, who was to be the Mediator of a new Covenant, was to be the last. By Him the New Covenant was to be offered first indeed to the *Jews*, with whom the Covenant mediated by *Moses* was till then to be in Force. But the other was not to be limited to that People only. The *Gentiles*, that is, all the Nations of the Earth, who were no Parties to the former Covenant, were to be invited to accede to this; and all those, of whatsoever Nation they were, who should acknowledge the Messiah, as a King appointed by God to reign over them, were to be admitted into this Covenant, and be reputed thenceforward the *People of God*. But as the Limits of this Divine Empire were to be altered and enlarged, it became necessary to alter and enlarge the Terms of Government. The Ceremonial Law was National and Local: And though, without some such Religious and Political Bond of Union, the *Jews* would not in all Probability have long continued the separate and peculiar People of God, yet as most of the Duties prescribed by that Law were confined to the Holy Land, and even to the Holy City of *Jerusalem*; the *Gentiles*, who were now to be taken into the Covenant, could not possibly comply with it. This therefore was of Necessity to be abolished. But the Moral Law, the Basis and End of the former Covenant, was in like Manner to be the End and Basis of the new one. To this both the *Gentiles* and *Jews* could pay Obedience, as well as to the other Terms super-added to it in the New Covenant, *viz.* the acknowledging the Messiah for their King; and as an outward Token of their Allegiance and Accession to this Covenant, receiving Baptism, and commemorating from Time to Time, by the Celebration of the Eucharist, the sealing this Covenant on the Part of God by the Death of *Christ*. Which Two *Sacraments*, properly so called, may be stiled the Ceremonial Law of the Christians, as Circumcision and other Ritual Duties were of the *Jews*.

Of the twelve Tribes of *Israel*, who were Parties of the *Mosaical* Covenant, ten fell at once from their Allegiance to God under *Jeroboam*; and ceasing from that Time to be the People or Subjects of God, he ceased to be

their

their King; and withdrawing his Protection, suffered them to be carried into a Captivity, from which they never afterwards returned; but being lost and confounded with the Nations, among whom they were transplanted, were thenceforward no more heard of as a distinct and separate People. The two remaining Tribes were then the only People of God; and as such, though often punished by Him for their frequent Transgressions of his Laws, and even carried Captive to *Babylon*, were by his Providence brought back again to the Land of *Canaan*, and restored to a Capacity of complying with the Terms of their Covenant, by the rebuilding the City and Temple of *Jerusalem*. From that Time they were very exact in their Observance of the Ceremonial Law, but had most grossly corrupted the Moral Law, and rendered it, as *Christ* told them, of no Effect, by the Comments and Traditions of their Scribes and Pharisees. This was the State of the *Jews*, when *Jesus* the Messiah, that great Prophet and King foretold by *Moses* and all the Prophets, came to offer them a new Covenant.

THE State of the *Gentiles* was far more deplorable. They had for many Ages transferred their Obedience from the one Supreme God, Creator of Heaven and Earth, to his Creatures, or to Deities of their own devising; under whose imaginary Protection they had ranged themselves by Nations and Communities; and had become almost in the same Sense as the *Israelites* were stiled the People of God, the People of the *Ægyptian Isis*, *Assyrian Belus*, *Athenian Pallas*, *Ephesian Diana*, and *Capitolian Jove*, &c. But there was this farther Difference between them: The God of the *Israelites*, like a righteous and equitable Sovereign, had given his People a Law, to be the Rule of their Obedience, or rather had confirmed and enforced the original Law, which from the very Beginning he had written in the Hearts, *i. e.* the Reason of all Mankind, adding to it such other Institutions, as their particular Situation then required. While the *Gentiles*, having by their Idolatry fallen from their Obedience to that Original universal Law, were left thenceforward, like Out-Laws and Rebels, to frame to themselves such

Rules both Moral and Religious, as the fancied Caprice of their Deities, or their own perverted Reason should suggest; whence it came to pass, that they were over-run with Immorality and Superstition. And though some of the Wisest among them, by following the yet glimmering Light of Reason, had become sensible of many of their grossest Errors, and had endeavoured to reform some Abuses, yet had Superstition taken so strong a Hold on the Majority, that, till that was entirely rooted out, it was impossible to bring them back to what is called the Religion of Nature, *i. e.* the Religion of Reason; were we to allow those *wise Men* to have been as well acquainted with it, in all its Branches, as since Christianity some have pretended to be. But with the Superstition of their Countries, those *wise Men* thought it better to comply than to contend. And had they attacked it with the Intrepidity and Industry of the Apostles, it is much to be questioned, whether with all their Eloquence and Logick, they would have gained the Victory. Such was the dark and hopeless Condition of the Gentiles.



In

In this State of the *Jews* and *Gentiles*, our Saviour, after having represented to the former, under the Parable of a *certain Housholder who planted a Vineyard, and let it out to Husbandmen* *, the righteous Dealings of God to them, and the ill Returns they had made to him, by not only refusing him the Fruits, but murthering the Servants he had sent to demand them; and lastly his Son; and after having extorted from them a Confession that those *wicked* Husbandmen ought to be *miserably punished*, and the *Vineyard* taken from them, and given to *other Husbandmen, who should render him the Fruits in their Season*, spoke to them the following Words: *Did you never read in the Scriptures, The Stone which the Builders rejected, the same is become the Head of the Corner: This is the Lord's doing, and it is marvellous in our Eyes? Therefore say I unto you, the Kingdom of God shall be taken from you, and given to a Nation bringing forth the Fruits thereof: And whosoever shall fall on this Stone, shall be broken; but on whomsoever it shall fall, it will grind him to Powder.* By these Words are plainly signified, 1st, The transferring the

Kingdom

* Matt. xxi. 43, 44.

Kingdom of God from the *Jews* to the *Gentiles*; 2dly, the Obedience of the *Gentiles*; and 3dly, the miserable Punishment of the *Jews*, for their having rejected and murthered the Son of God. There are many other Prophecies relating to each of these Events scattered up and down the Gospels, which I think it needless to produce, this being so very full and explicit. I shall therefore set about shewing the exact Accomplishment of it in it's several Parts.

The *Kingdom of God*, as may be collected from what is said above, denotes the *spiritual* or *moral* Dominion of God over *moral* Subjects, *i. e.* Free Agents; and by the *People of God* are signified such Free Agents, as freely and voluntarily acknowledge the Sovereignty of God, by worshiping him, and receiving and obeying all those Laws, whether natural or revealed, which appear to have been enacted by him. The *Jews* therefore by rejecting *Jesus Christ*, who proved himself to have been commissioned and sent by God, not only from the Testimony of *Moses* and all their Prophets, the Holiness of his Life and

Doctrine,

Doctrine, and the numberless Miracles he wrought among them, but still more plainly, if possible, by his rising from the Dead, and empowering his Disciples to work the same mighty Signs and Wonders in his Name: the *Jews*, I say, by rejecting this Messenger, this Son of God, and refusing to receive the Laws which he proposed to them in his Father's Name, evidently renounced their Allegiance to God, and ceased to be his *People* or Subjects. And the *Gentiles* on the other hand, by renouncing their Vices and Idolatrous Superstitions, returning to the Worship of God, and receiving his Messiah, together with the Laws proposed to them by him in the Name of God, as evidently put themselves under the Dominion of God, acknowledged his Empire, and became the *People* or *Subjects* of God. And hence appears what is meant by the *Kingdom of God being taken from the* Jews, and given to the *Gentiles*. God removed the Throne, whereon *David* and his Posterity had sat as his Substitutes and Viceroys, from among the *Jews*, who renounced his Authority, and from Earth to Heaven; and placing it at his Right Hand, and setting upon it his Messiah, his only

only Son, gave him for his Subjects, not one Nation only, but all *Nations* and *Kindreds*, and People, and all the *Ends of the Earth* for his Dominion. That the Kingdom of God was in this Sense, and in this Manner actually transferred from the *Jews* to the *Gentiles*, is too notorious to need any Proof. The *Jews* as a Nation rejected the Gospel, and persisted in their Refusal of the Messiah, till the final Destruction of their Holy City and Temple; and what is yet more strange, still persevere in their Obstinacy. Whereas the *Gentiles* embraced it so universally, that within a few Centuries after *Christ*, almost the whole *Roman* Empire, that is, almost the then known World, forsook Idolatry, and became Christian. And God on his Part testified that he entered into Covenant with them, and accepted their Allegiance, by pouring upon them the Gifts of his Holy Spirit; as he signified on the other hand his Renunciation of the *Mosaical* Covenant, by not only suffering the Seat of his Empire, the City and Temple of *Jerusalem*, to be utterly destroyed, but permitting the *Jews* also to be banished from the Holy Land, and scattered through all the Nations of the Earth.

And

And thus was this Prophecy most exactly accomplished in all its Parts.

§. 28 But as to the general Change in the State of the *Jews* and *Gentiles* expressed in this Prophecy, many Particulars relating to the Condition of the *Jewish* Nation, were most precisely foretold by our Saviour *Christ*. As first the Destruction of the City and Temple of *Jerusalem*; Secondly, the Signs and Wonders preceding that Destruction; Thirdly, the Miseries of the *Jews* before, at, and after the famous Siege of that City; Fourthly, the Dispersion of that reprobated People; Fifthly, the Duration of their Calamity; and Sixthly, their Restoration.

§. 29 "Our Saviour foretold the Destruction of "the Temple, after it had stood almost 500 "Years, in these Words: *Seest thou these great* "*Buildings? There shall not be left one Stone* "*upon another, which shall not be thrown down.** "And this Prediction was compleated by † *Titus*;

* Mark xiii. 2.

† See for this and most of the following Articles Dr. *Whitby's* general Preface, which, together with his other Preface, I would recommend to the Perusal of all those who read for the Sake of learning the Truth, and not for Amusement only.

“ *tum*, who, saith *Josephus*, commanded his
“ Soldiers *to dig up the Foundations both of the*
“ *Temple and the City*. And both the *Jewish*
“ *Talmud* and *Maimonides* add, that *Terentius*
“ *Rufus*, the Captain of his Army, did with a
“ Plough-share tear up the Foundation of the
“ Temple.

“ With like Exactness and Particularity did
“ our Lord foretell the Ruin of the City of *Je-*
“ *rusalem*: *The Days*, saith he, *shall come upon thee*,
“ *that thine Enemies shall cast a Trench about thee*,
“ *and compass thee round, and keep thee in on*
“ *every Side, and shall lay thee even with the*
“ *Ground, and shall not leave thee one Stone*
“ *upon another*. Now that the Event com-
“ pletely answered the Prediction, is evident
“ from the *Jewish* Historian, who tells us ex-
“ pressly, that *Titus having commanded his*
“ *Soldiers to dig up the City, this was so fully*
“ *done by levelling the whole Compass of the City*,
“ *except three Towers, that they who came to see*
“ *it were persuaded it would never be built again.*
“ The same Historian informs us, that when
“ *Vespasian* besieged *Jerusalem*, his Army *com-*
“ *passed the City round about, and kept them in*

“ *on*

" *on every Side*; and though it was judged a
" great and almost impracticable Work to
" compass the whole City with a Wall, *yet*
" Titus *animating his Soldiers to attempt it,*
" *they in three Days built a Wall of thirty-nine*
" *Furlongs, having thirteen Castles on it, and so*
" *cut off all Hopes, that any of the* Jews *with-*
" *in the City should escape.*

" In the 21st Chapter of St. *Luke*, *Christ*
" speaking of the Destruction of *Jerusalem*,
" says, (*Ver.* 11.) *And great Earthquakes shall*
" *be in divers Places, and Famines, and Pesti-*
" *lences, and fearful Sights, and great Signs shall*
" *there be from Heaven.*

" Now to omit the frequent Earthquakes
" that happened in other Places in the Times
" of *Claudius* and *Nero*, *Josephus* informs us,
" that there happened in *Judea* and *Jerusalem*
" *an immense Tempest, and vehement Winds with*
" *Rain, and frequent Lightnings and dreadful*
" *Thundering, and extreme Roarings of the quak-*
" *ing Earth, which manifested to all that the*
" *World was disturbed at the Destruction of*
" *Men*; and that these Prodigies portended

" no

" no ſmall Miſchiefs. *Joſephus* hath a parti-
" cular Chapter of the manifeſt Signs of the
" approaching Deſolation of the *Jews*; which
" *Tacitus*, a *Roman* Hiſtorian of that Age, al-
" moſt epitomizes in theſe Words: *Armies*
" *ſeemed to meet in the Clouds, and glittering*
" *Weapons were there ſeen; the Temple ſeemed*
" *to be in a Flame, with Fire iſſuing from the*
" *Clouds, and a Voice more than human was*
" *heard, declaring that the Deities were quit-*
" *ting the Place; which was attended with*
" *the Sound of a great Motion, as if they were*
" *departing.* *Joſephus* adds, what *Tacitus* alſo
" touches upon, That the great Gate of the
" Temple, which twenty Men could ſcarcely
" ſhut, and which was made faſt by Bolts and
" Bars, *was ſeen to open of its own Accord*:
" That *a Sword appeared hanging over the City*:
" *That a Comet was ſeen pointing down upon*
" *it for a whole Year together*: And that *be-*
" *fore the Sun went down, there were ſeen Ar-*
" *mies in Battle-Array, and Chariots compaſ-*
" *ſing the Country, and inveſting the Cities*:
" *A Thing ſo ſtrange*, ſaith he, *that it would*
" *paſs for a Fable, were there not Men living*
" *to atteſt it.* So particular an Account have

" we

" we of the *fearful Sights* and *Signs from* " *Heaven* mentioned by our Lord.

" Our blessed Lord is as express in the " Predictions of the Miseries which should be- " fall that sinful Nation; Miseries so great, " as to admit no Parallel. * *There shall be*, saith " he, *great Tribulation, such as never happened* " *from the Beginning of the World to this Time.* " Which Words *Josephus* seems to have tran- " scribed, when he says, *Never was any Na-* " *tion more wicked, nor ever did a City suffer* " *as they did.* Nay, in another Place, he goes " so far as to say, *All the Miseries which all* " *Mankind had suffered from the Beginning* " *of the World, were not to be compared* " *with those the* Jewish *Nation did then suffer.* " And indeed, the Account he gives of the " Number who perished in that Siege is al- " most incredible; and much more so is what " the *Talmud* and other *Jewish* Writers men- " tion of the Slaughter, which *Hadrian*'s Ar- " my made of them fifty-two Years after, " when they rebelled under *Barchochebas*, and " were



* Matt. xxiv. 21.

"were besieged in the City *Bitter*. And yet
" our Saviour having farther said, That
" * *where-ever the Carcass was*, [*i. e.* the *Jews*]
" *there should the Eagles* [*i. e.* the *Roman* Ar-
" mies] *be gathered together*: They were ac-
" cordingly harrassed and destroyed through-
" out the *Roman* Empire. When, saith *Jose-*
" *phus*, the *Romans* had no Enemies left in *Ju-*
" *dæa*, *the Danger reached to many of them living*
" *the remotest from it*: For many of them pe-
" rished at *Alexandria*, at *Cyrene*, and in other
" Cities of *Ægypt*, to the Number of sixty
" thousand, in all the Cities of *Syria*. In
" a Word, *Eleazar*, in *Josephus*, having
" reckoned many Places where they were
" cruelly slaughtered, concludes with saying,
" *It would be too long to speak of all these*
" *Places in particular*.

" AGAIN, our Saviour adds, That *they*
" *should be led Captives into all Nations*. Ac-
" cordingly, *Josephus* informs us, That *the*
" *Number of* Jewish *Captives was ninety-seven*
" *thousand*: That of them *Titus sent many to*
" Ægypt, *and most of them he dispersed into*



* Matt. xxiv. 28.

" *the* Roman *Provinces*; and so exactly ful-
" filled this Prediction."

The Duration of the Calamity of the *Jews*, and their Restoration, are signified in these Words: * Jerusalem *shall be trodden down of the Gentiles, till the Times of the Gentiles be fulfilled.* " This so exactly came to pass, that " *Vespasian* commanded the whole Land of " *Judea* to be sold to those Gentiles that " would buy it; and *Hadrian*, about sixty-" three Years after, made a Law, that *no* " Jew *should come into the Region round about* " Jerusalem, as *Aristo Pellæus*, who was him-" self a *Jew*, and flourished in the very Time " of *Hadrian* relates. *Thus*, saith *Eusebius*, " *it came to pass, that the* Jews *being banished* " *thence, and there being a Conflux thither of* " *Aliens, it became a City and Colony of the* " Romans, *and was in Honour of the Emperor* " [Hadrian] *named* Ælia. *Jerusalem*, saith " *Christ*, *shall be* thus *trodden down*, or subject " to the Gentiles, *till the Times of the Gentiles* " *be fulfilled*; that is, till by the Conversion of " the

* Luke xxi. 24. † The Greek Word is πατυμένη, possessed and trodden by the Feet of the Gentiles.

" the *Jews* to the Christian Faith, the Ful-
" ness of the Gentiles to be converted to it,
" should come in with them: *For Blindness*,
" saith the * Apostle, *hath happened to the*
" Jews, *till the Fulness of the Gentiles shall*
" *come in, and then all* Israel *shall be saved*;
" and with them also the yet *Heathen Gen-*
" *tiles*. *For if*, saith he †, *the Casting away of*
" *the* Jews *was the Reconciling of the World*,
" *what shall the Receiving of them be to it, but*
" *even Life* for *the Dead?* And again ‖, *if the*
" *Fall of them were the Riches of the World*,
" *and the Diminishing of them the Riches of the*
" *Gentiles, how much more shall their Fulness be*
" *the* Fulness *of the Gentiles?* Now here it is
" especially observable, that *Julian* the A-
" postate, designing to defeat this Prophecy
" of *Christ*, resolved on the Rebuilding of the
" City and the Temple of *Jerusalem* in its old
" Station, which was till his Time left in
" Ruins, *Ælia* being built without the Cir-
" cuit of it. For in his Epistle to the Com-
" munity of the *Jews*, he writes thus; *The*
" *Holy City of* Jerusalem, *which you have so*



* Rom. ii. 25, 26. † Ibid. ver. 15. ‖ Ver. 12.

" *long desired to see inhabited, rebuilding by my* " *own Labours, I will dwell in.* This he be- " gan with an Endeavour to build that Tem- " ple, in which alone the *Jews* would offer up " their Prayers and Sacrifices: But the imme- " diate Hand of Providence soon forced the " Workmen to desist from that unhappy En- " terprize. *Ammianus Marcellinus*, an Hea- " then, who lived in those very Times, gives " us the Story thus; That *Julian endeavoured* " *to rebuild the Temple at* Jerusalem *with vast* " *Expence, and gave it in Charge to* Alypius *of* " Antioch *to hasten the Work, and to the Go-* " *vernor of the Province to assist him in it; in* " *which Work when* Alypius *was earnestly em-* " *ployed, and the Governor of the Province was* " *assisting, terrible Balls of Flame bursting forth* " *near the Foundations with frequent Insults, and* " *burning divers Times the Workmen, rendered* " *the Place inaccessible; and thus the Fire obsti-* " *nately repelling them, the Work ceased.*

" The Story is very signal, and remark- " able for many Circumstances; as 1st, The " Persons that relate it, *Ammianus Marcel-* " *linus* an Heathen, *Zemuch David* a *Jew*,

" who

" who confesses that *Julian* was *Divinitus impeditus*, *hindered by God* in this Attempt; *Nazianzen* and *Chrysostom* among the *Greeks*, St. *Ambrose* and *Ruffinus* among the *Latins*, who flourished at the very Time when this was done: *Theodoret* and *Sozomen*, orthodox Historians; *Philostorgius*, an *Arian*; *Socrates*, a Favourer of the *Novatians*, who writ the Story within the Space of fifty Years after the Thing was done, and whilst the Eye-witnesses of the Fact were yet surviving.

2dly, The Time when it was performed; not in the Reign of Christian Emperors, but of the most bitter Enemies of Christians, when they were forced to hide, and had not Liberty of speaking for themselves. Observe,

3dly, With what Confidence Christians urge this Matter of Fact against the " *Jews*, as a convincing Demonstration of the Expiration of their legal Worship, and of the Certainty of Christian Faith against the Heathen Philosophers, inquiring *What the*

" *wise Men of the World can say to these Things* :
" And against the Emperor *Theodosius*, to de-
" ter him from requiring them to rebuild a
" Synagogue, which had been lately burnt by
" a Christian Bishop.

" 4thly and lastly, THE unquestionable
" Evidence of the Thing: *This*, say the
" Christians, *all Men freely do believe and speak*
" *of*; *'tis in the Mouths of all Men*, and is
" not denied *even by the Atheists themselves*;
" *and if it seem yet incredible to any one, he*
" *may repair for the Truth of it both to the*
" *Witnesses of it yet living, and to them who*
" *have heard it from their Mouths*; *yea, they*
" *may view the Foundations lying still bare and*
" *naked*; *and if you ask the Reason, you will*
" *meet with no other Account besides that which*
" *I have given*; *and of this all we Christians are*
" *Witnesses, these Things being done not long*
" *since in our own Time.* So St. *Chrysostom*.

THE Reader, who is inclined to see many Particulars of the Predictions of our Saviour, which relate to this remarkable Catastrophe, and which I have omitted for Brevity's sake,

and

and how they were verified by the Event, will do well to consult Dr. *Whitby*'s Preface, from whence the above Articles are taken.

The Observations I have to make on these Prophecies are as follow:

1st, The common Objection made to Prophecies in general, that they are so obscure and figurative, as not to be expounded but by the Event, cannot be urged against these, which are conceived in Words as simple and intelligible as those made use of by the Historian, who relates the Events corresponding with them.

2dly, It is very remarkable, that of the four Evangelists, St. *John* alone, who is said to have survived the Destruction of *Jerusalem*, makes no Mention either of these Prophecies or their Accomplishment. Of the other three, in whose Gospels they are to be found, St. *Matthew* and St. *Mark* died confessedly before that Period; the Time of St. *Luke*'s Death is uncertain. May we not then from hence very fairly conclude, that this remarkable Silence

 of

of the beloved Disciple, with regard to Prophecies of such Importance to the Credit of his Lord and his Religion, was ordered from above, lest Unbelievers should say, what some had said of the Predictions of *Daniel*, that they were written after the Event?

3dly, As to the Prediction relating to the Duration of the Calamity of the *Jewish* People and their Restoration, though that is the only one of all those above-cited, not yet perfectly accomplished, I beg Leave however to observe, that not only the miraculous defeating of the Emperor *Julian*'s Attempt to rebuild the City and Temple of *Jerusalem*, but the present extraordinary Condition of the *Jews*, is such a Warrant and Proof, that this Prophecy also will have its Accomplishment in due Time, as cannot fail of powerfully striking those who will open their Eyes to view it. To induce the unobserving and unthinking People of this Age to do this, and to assist them in considering this living Evidence of the Truth of Christianity, which lies within their Notice, and even at their very Doors,

Doors; I shall lay before them some Observations of an excellent * *French* Author upon this Subject, whom I chose rather to translate than to give his Arguments in my own Words.

§. 29. " † But neither the Dispersion of " the *Jews* into all Nations, nor the general " Contempt into which they are fallen, are " so extraordinary, as their Preservation for " so many Ages, notwithstanding this their " Dispersion throughout the Earth, and the " universal Contempt which all Nations have " for them.

" Without a singular Providence, a " People disunited, and divided into an infinite Number of distinct Families, banished " into Countries, whose Language and Customs were different from theirs, must have " been mingled and confounded with other " Nations, and all Traces of them must these " many Ages past have entirely disappeared.

" For

* Principes de lay Foy Chrêtienne, tom. i. ch. 16.

† See the preceding Chapter.

"For they not only subsist no longer in "a Body Politick, but there is not a single "City, where they are allowed to live accord- "ing to their own Laws, or to create Ma- "gistrates of their own; neither are they "held together by any publick Exercise of "Religion. Their Priests are without Em- "ployment, their Sacrifices are suppressed. "Their Feasts cannot be solemnized but in "one only Place, and to that they are not "permitted to repair.

"By what Miracle then have they been "preserved amid so many Nations, without "any of those Means which keep other Peo- "ple united? How comes it to pass, that "having been scattered like so many imper- "ceptible Grains of Dust, among all Nations, "they have notwithstanding been able to sub- "sist longer than any, and even to survive the "Extinction of them all?

"Who can at this Day pick out the an- "cient *Romans* from the numerous Crowds of "People, who have thrown themselves into

"*Italy?*

" *Italy?* Who can point out one single Family of old *Gaul*, from those of another Original? Who can make the like Separation in *Spain*, between the ancient *Spaniards* and *Goths*, who conquered it? The Face of the World is changed, both in the East and West; and all Nations are mixed and blended in a hundred different Manners; it is only upon Conjectures, and those oftentimes very frivolous, that a single Family can trace up its Original beyond the publick Revolutions of the State.

" But the *Jews*, by a Tradition which no Calamity, whether publick or private, hath been able to interrupt, can go back as far as the ancient Stock of *Abraham*. They may be mistaken in allotting themselves to this or that Tribe, because since their Dispersion they have not any publick Registers; (which by the Way is a Proof that their Law is abolished, since neither the Priests nor *Levites* can ascertain by any certain Monuments that they are of the Family of *Aaron*, and of the Tribe of *Levi*;) But every Father hath taken Care to tell his Children,

" that

" that he had an Original different from that " of the *Gentiles*; and that he descended from " the Patriarchs, who are celebrated in the " Scriptures.

" The general Contempt into which they " have fallen, should, one would think, have " induced them to confound themselves with " those People, under whose Dominion they " lived, and to suppress every Thing that " tended to distinguish them. By separating " themselves from those who were in Power, " they only drew upon themselves their Ha- " tred and Derision. In many Places they " exposed themselves to Death, by bearing " the exterior Mark of Circumcision. Every " human Interest led them to efface the igno- " minious Stain of their Original.

" They saw every Day their Messiah still " farther removed from them; that the Pro- " mises of their Doctors about his speedy " Manifestations were false; that the Predic- " tions of the Prophets, whom they could " now no longer understand, were covered " with Obscurity; that all the Supputations

" of

"of Time, either terminated in *Jesus Christ*, "or were without a Period; that some a-"mong them lost all Hope, and fell into In-"credulity with regard to the Scriptures.

"And yet notwithstanding all this, they "still subsist, they multiply, they remain vi-"sibly separated from all other People; and "in Spite of the general Aversion, in Spite "of the Efforts of all those Nations who hate "them, and who have them in their Power, "in Spite of every human Obstacle, they are "preserved by a super-natural Protection, "which hath not in like Manner preserved "any other Nation of the Earth.

"One must surely have very little Sense "of what ought to give one Astonishment "and Admiration, if this Prodigy does not "strike one; and one must have a strange "Idea of the Providence of God, to think "he had no Hand in all this.

"But the Holy Spirit was not willing to "leave us under any Uncertainty upon this "Head; and hath declared to us by his Pro-

"phets,

" phets, that the Preservation of the *Jews* is " his Work. *Fear thou not, O Jacob, my Ser-" vant, saith the Lord, for I am with thee; for " I will make a full End of all the Nations, " whither I have driven thee; but I will not " make a full End of thee, but correct thee in " Measure, yet will I not leave thee wholly un-" punished* *.

" This Promise was made to the old Pa-" triarchs, to whom God hath reserved Chil-" dren, Heirs of their Faith, and to the " Remnant of *Israel*, who in the End of the " Ages shall believe in *Jesus Christ*.

" It is for their Sakes that the unworthy " Posterity of the Unbelieving is suffered; " and it is to maintain the Communication " between the first Fathers and their latest Suc-" cessors, that the Nation is preserved not-" withstanding their Iniquity, and in the " midst of Punishments, that threatened to " overwhelm them.

" But

* Jerem. xxx. 10, 11.

"But let it be observed, that this Promise "was made to the Nation of the *Jews* only; "that all others shall be either exterminated, "or so confounded with each other, as to be "no longer distinguished; and that it is the "Efficacy of the Word of God, which pre-"serves the *Jews* amidst every Thing, that "in all Appearance would otherwise have "sunk them entirely, and swallowed them "up.

"*Thus saith the Lord, if my Covenant be not* "*with Day and Night, and if I have not ap-*"*pointed the Ordinances of Heaven and Earth*; "*then will I cast away the Seed of* Jacob *and* "David *my Servant*;—*for I will cause their* "*Captivity to return, and have Mercy on them**. "This I say is the Promise, and the End of "the Promise. The *Jews* shall one Day be "recalled through Mercy; and for the Sake "of Those who shall one Day be recalled, "the Patience of God suffers all the rest, and "his Power preserves them.

"*Thus*

* Jerem. xxxiii. 25, 26.

" *Thus saith the Lord, which giveth the Sun*
" *for a Light by Day, and the Ordinances of the*
" *Moon and of the Stars for a Light by Night,*
" *which divideth the Sea, when the Waves*
" *thereof roar; the Lord of Hosts is his Name.*
" *If those Ordinances depart from before me,*
" *saith the Lord, then the Seed of* Israel *also*
" *shall cease from being a Nation before me for*
" *ever. Thus saith the Lord, If Heaven above*
" *can be measured, and the Foundations of the*
" *Earth searched out beneath, I will also cast*
" *off all the Seed of* Israel, *for all that they*
" *have done, saith the Lord*.*

" THAT is to say, Heaven and Earth shall " pass away sooner than the *Jews* shall cease " to be a distinct People. The same Power, " which hath given Laws to Nature, watches " over their Preservation. And the unheard-" of Crime, which they have committed in " crucifying the Saviour promised to their Fa-" thers, and which hath filled up the Measure " of their former Iniquity, will not move " God to retract his Promise, and to reject " entirely,

* Jerem. xxxi. 35, 36, 37.

" entirely, and without Resource the Posterity of *Jacob*.

" With what Light were the Prophets " illuminated, to presume to speak in so great " and lofty a Strain of a Thing so little probable as the Duration of a People, weak, " dispersed, universally hated, and guilty of " the greatest of all Crimes ?

" Who would question the other Prophecies, after seeing the Accomplishment of " this ? What more astonishing Proof can " any one desire of the Truth of the Christian " Religion, than these two Events joined together, the Dispersion of the *Jews* into all " Nations, and their Preservation for sixteen " hundred Years ? One of these Things taken " separately and by itself was incredible ; and " they became still more so by being united ; " but both these Prodigies were necessary to " prove that *Jesus Christ* was the Messiah.

" It was necessary that those who had rejected him, should be banished into all Regions, should into all Parts carry with them

" the Scriptures, and should every where be
" covered with Ignominy.

" But that the Promises made their Fathers
" might be accomplished, it was necessary
" that their banished Family should be recall-
" ed, and that their Blindness being dissipat-
" ed, they should adore him, whom * *Abra-
" ham* had desired to see, and whom he had
" adored with a holy Transport of Joy and
" Gratitude.

" The *Jews* punished and dispersed, bear
" Witness to *Jesus Christ*. The *Jews* recalled
" and converted, will render him a Testimo-
" ny still more awful and striking. The *Jews*
" preserved by a continual Miracle, that they
" may preserve to *Jesus Christ* the Stock and
" Succession of those who shall one Day be-
" lieve in him, bear Witness to him conti-
" nually.

" Had they been only punished, they
" would have proved his Justice only: Had
" they

* John viii. 56.

" they only been preserved, they could have " proved nothing but his Power. Had they " not been reserved to worship him one Day; " they could not have proved his Mercy and " Fidelity, nor have made him any Reparation " for their outrageous Crimes.

" THEIR Dispersion proves that he is " come, but they have rejected him: Their " Preservation demonstrates that he hath not " rejected them for ever, and that they shall " one Day believe in him; and they declare " by both that he is the Messiah, and the pro- " mised Saviour. That their Miseries proceed " from their not having known him, and that " the only Hope they have left is, that they " shall one Day come to the Knowledge of " him.

" WE ought not to demand why God sup- " ports them so long without enlightening " them; and why he leaves so great an Inter- " val between the faithful Fathers, and the " Children that will hereafter become so too. " To pretend to examine the impenetrable " Judgments of God, and the Abysses of his

" Wiſdom, is to pretend to *meaſure the Height* " *of Heaven, and to ſearch out the Foundations* " of the Earth. * God hath ſet Bounds to " the Incredulity of the *Jews*, and to the In- " gratitude of the *Gentiles*: His Mercy and " his Juſtice ſucceed each other; and no one " knows at what Time he will execute what " he hath promiſed to the lateſt Poſterity of " *Iſrael*, although his Promiſes are infallible.

" † Thus *ſaith the Lord that created thee*, " O Jacob, *and he that formed thee*, O Iſrael: " *Fear not, for I have redeemed thee: I have* " *called thee by thy Name; thou art mine.* " *When thou paſſeſt through the Waters, I* " *will be with thee; and through the Rivers,* " *they ſhall not overflow thee. When thou* " *walkeſt through the Fire, thou ſhalt not be* " *burnt, neither ſhall the Flame kindle upon* " *thee. Fear not, for I am with thee: I will* " *bring thy Seed from the Eaſt, and gather thee* " *from the Weſt. I will ſay to the North, Give* " *up; and to the South, Keep not back: bring my* " *Sons from far, and my Daughters from the*

" Ends

* Rom. xi. 32, 33.
† Iſaiah xliii. 1—8.

" *Ends of the Earth: even every one that is " called by my Name. For I have created him " for my Glory, I have formed him, yea I " have made him. Bring forth the blind Peo- " ple that have Eyes, and the Deaf that have " Ears.*

" THIS Prophecy, truly admirable in all " its Parts, is addressed to *Jacob*, the Head " of the Tribes of *Israel*, and the Heir of the " Promises of the Messiah and Salvation.

" HIS Posterity is dispersed into all the " Quarters of the World. This is the State " of the *Jews* since the Coming of *Jesus Christ*.

" THEIR Dispersion is the Punishment of " their Spiritual Deafness and Blindness. And " with how great a Blindness, with how great " a Deafness may one not deservedly reproach " the *Jews*, for not having known *Jesus* " *Christ*, and not having heard him, though " he proved his divine Mission by an Infinity " of Miracles!

" THEIR Condition seems desperate: The
" Waters are ready to over-whelm them;
" the Flames surround them on all Sides:
" But the Protection of God follows them
" throughout, and delivers them.

" THIS Protection is vouchsafed to the
" whole Body of the Nation, in favour of
" those, who shall one Day call upon that
" Name, which the rest have dishonoured
" with their Blasphemies.

" GOD out of mere Mercy will give a do-
" cile and faithful Heart to those, who shall
" renounce their former Incredulity. They
" will be the Creatures of his Grace, to which
" alone they will stand indebted for their Re-
" pentance and Return.

" THEY will not then begin to see a new
" Object, but an Object which their Blindness
" had concealed from them. They will not
" then hear a Teacher, who began but a few
" Days before to make his Appearance, but
" one whom their voluntary and obstinate

" Deafness

" Deafneſs had kept them from hearing be-
" fore.

" The Change will be in their Perſons, " and not in his Religion; that will remain " what it is, but they will then begin to ſee " it. *Jeſus Chriſt* will take away the Veil that " is upon their Eyes; but he will be the ſame. " He will cure their Deafneſs; but he will " ſpeak the ſame things.

" It is evident, then, that the *Jews* are " preſerved for him; and that the whole Body " of the Nation ſubſiſts only by the Efficacy " of that Promiſe, which is to lead the Re- " mains of *Iſrael* to *Jeſus Chriſt*: *Bring forth* " *the blind People that have Eyes, and the Deaf* " *that have Ears.*"

Can any one, after reading theſe ſeveral Prophecies above quoted, queſtion the Veracity of the ſacred Writers; who, by publiſhing them in this manner, put their Maſter's Credit, and their own upon Contingencies very remote, and ſeemingly improbable? And doth not the exact Accompliſhment of theſe, and several other Predictions, which might have been produced, sufficiently establish the Authority of the Scriptures, and ascertain the Truth of all the Facts related in them.

§. 30. I COME now to consider the second Argument to induce us to believe that *Christ* rose from the Dead, *viz.* The Existence of the Christian Religion.

FROM the Existence of the Christian Religion, may be drawn the same kind of Evidence of the Resurrection of *Jesus Christ*, and the Wonders attending it, as is exhibited to us of the Deluge by the many Petrifactions of Shells and Bones of Fishes, and other Animals of distant Regions, &c. found often in the Bottoms of the deepest Mines, and the Bowels of the highest Mountains; for, as it is impossible to account for those various Petrifactions being lodged in so many Parts of the Earth, some many Leagues distant from the Sea, others very much above the Level of it, without admitting such a Subversion and Confusion of this Globe, as could not have been occasion'd by a less violent Cause than the

the *Breaking up the Fountains of the great Deep*, and the *Waters flowing above the Tops of the highest Hills*; so will it, I apprehend, be extremely difficult to account for the Propagation and present Existence of Christianity in so many Regions of the World, without supposing that *Christ* rose from the Dead, ascended into Heaven, and enabled his Disciples, by the miraculous Gifts of his Holy Spirit, to surmount such Obstacles as no mere human Abilities could possibly overcome. In the former Case, a Cause superior to the ordinary Operations of Nature must be assign'd for the Production of Effects plainly above, and contrary to those Operations: And for a Solution of the latter, Recourse in like manner must be had to an Agent of Power and Wisdom transcending and controlling the natural Faculties and Wisdom of Man; and this Cause, this Agent, can be no other than the great Law-giver of Nature, the All-wise, and All-mighty Creator of Heaven and Earth. He alone could *break up the Fountains of the great Deep, open the Windows of Heaven*, and *cover the whole Earth with Water*; that is, bring on that universal Deluge, which alone furnishes

furnishes us with a Solution of many Phænomena, otherwise unaccountable; and He alone could break the Jaws of Death, and the Prison of the Grave, *open the Kingdom of Heaven*, and shower down upon Mortals such mighty Gifts and Powers, as are the only adequate Causes that can be assign'd of the astonishing and præter-natural Birth and Increase of Christianity. This will not appear exaggerated, if we consider the Difficulties the Gospel had to struggle with at its first Appearance, and the Inabilities, the human Inabilities I mean, of its first Preachers, to oppose and overcome those Obstacles.

THE Difficulties they had to encounter were no less than the Superstition, the Prejudices, and the Vices of the whole World; Difficulties of so much the harder Conquest, as being derived, though by Corruption, from good Principles; namely, the Religion, the Nature, and the Reason of Mankind. How powerful an Opposition all these form'd against the Gospel, will best appear from a short View of the State of the World under the first Ages of Christianity.

THE *Jews*, though possess'd of a Body of Laws fram'd, as they acknowledg'd, by God himself, had however, by listening to the Comments and Traditions of the Scholastick and Casuistical Scribes and Rabbins, so far departed from the Spirit and Intention of their Law-giver, as to place almost the Whole of their Religion in the Observance of ritual Purities and Ceremonies, to the Neglect of the * *greater and weightier Matters of the Law, Judgment, Mercy, and Faith*; which, as our Saviour told them, they ought to have regarded, and not to have disregarded the others: That is, the *Jews* were fallen from true Religion into a Superstition, which differ'd from that of the *Gentiles* principally, in that the *Gentiles* worshiped a Number of Deities, the *Jews* acknowledg'd and worshiped One alone; but still they worshiped him superstitiously, with exterior Services only, Ablutions, Sacrifices, Observation of Days, and other ceremonial Duties; not perceiving, or not remembering, the great and wise End of those ceremonial Institutions; which, by not allowing any Forms

* Matt. xxiii. 23.

Forms of Worship, but those prescribed by the Law, and not admitting to that Worship any, but those, who by Circumcision would become perfect *Israelites*, not only tended to keep them from being mingled with the *Gentiles*, and learning from them their idolatrous Polytheism; by which Means that fundamental Article of all true Religion, the Belief of one God, though lost in all other Nations, was for many Centuries preserved among the *Jews*; but by the Fasts and Festivals, the Purifications, Offerings, and propitiatory Sacrifices appointed in the Ritual, put them perpetually in Mind of the Duties of Prayer and Thanksgiving to God; of the Importance of moral Purity, the Obligation of Repentance, and the Necessity of an Expiation for Sin. But as Holiness of Life was of more difficult Practice than the Observation of Ceremonies, numerous and burthensome as they seem to have been, they soon became willing to commute; and reposing their chief Hopes of obtaining the Favour and Protection of God in their Compliance with the ceremonial Law, they turned their Attention principally to that, and attached themselves to it so strongly, that tho'

they

they did not scruple to commit a thousand Immoralities, they would sooner die than eat any unclean Meats, or suffer their Temple to be profaned.

From this Attachment to what they esteemed the Law of *Moses*, they presumed upon the special Favour and Protection of God, and looked upon themselves as sole Heirs of the Promises made to *Abraham* and *David*, and repeated and confirmed by all their Prophets. But the same Blindness that with-held them from seeing the spiritual Intent and Meaning of the ceremonial Institutions, kept them likewise from understanding the spiritual Sense of those Prophecies. The Blessing therefore promised through the Seed of *Abraham*, to *all the Nations of the Earth*, and the *Kingdom* stipulated to the *Posterity of David*, they preposterously interpreted to belong to themselves alone; and expounding the Deliverance of *Israel* intimated by the Prophets, and the Victories and Dominion of the Son of *David* in a carnal Sense, they expected, at the Time of *Christ's* Coming, a Messiah, who should not only deliver them from their Subjection to the

*Romans*, but even conquer and subdue *them*, and all the other Powers of the Earth, to the Empire of the *Jews*, the sole Favourites of Heaven, and destin'd Lords of the Universe, under their invincible glorious King. These Expectations, so flattering to the whole Nation, had so infected the Minds of all Orders and Degrees, that even the Disciples of *Jesus*, who were (some of them at least) of the lowest of the People, were a long while tainted with them, notwithstanding the spiritual Instructions, and plain Declarations of their Master to the contrary. And though, soon after his Ascension, they seem to have given up all Thoughts of a temporal Kingdom, yet could they not for some Time, nor without an express Miracle, be convinced that the Gentiles had any Title to the Mercies of God, or any Share in the Kingdom of the Messiah. Such was the Superstition, and such the Prejudices of the whole *Jewish* Nation.

To these national Prejudices may be added others arising from the peculiar Tenets of the different Sects, that divided among them almost the whole People of

the

the *Jews*. The most powerful of these were the *Pharisees* and *Sadducees*: Of whose chief Doctrines some Notice is taken by the Evangelists, as well as of their rancorous Opposition to the Gospel of *Christ*. The Reader, who is desirous of seeing a more particular Account of the Opinions of these, and the other Sects, may consult the * *Universal History*. It may be sufficient to observe here, that they had all of them many Followers, had great Authority with the People, and had, especially the *Pharisees*, a large Share in the Government of the *Jewish* State. And though there was a constant Hatred and Rivalry between them, and consequently so great a Zeal in each for the Advancement of their particular Opinions, that they *would compass Heaven and Earth to gain one Proselyte*, yet they all agreed with the same Ardour to oppose the Progress of Christianity.

THE idolatrous Superstitions of the Heathen World, and the zealous Attachment of every Nation and City to the Worship of their respective tutelary Deities, are too well known

so

* Vol. IV. p. 169, & seq.

to be enlarged upon in this Place: But I muſt observe, that beſides the Prejudices of the ignorant and bigotted Multitude, there ſprung up from theſe Superſtitions other Obſtacles to Chriſtianity no leſs formidable, though of a different Kind: For many Religious Rites and Ceremonies having, either by Preſcription, or the Policy of Legiſlators, been mixed and interwoven with the Adminiſtration of Civil Affairs, the Worſhip of the Gods was become not only an eſſential Part of the Conſtitution, but the great Engine of Government in moſt States and Kingdoms. Thus, among the *Greeks* and other Nations, Omens and Oracles; among the *Romans*, Auſpices, Auguries, and Sacrifices, either of Thanſgiving, or Propitiation, were often very ſucceſsfully employed upon great and important Occaſions: On which Account, all the *Roman* Emperors, who had appropriated to themſelves the Authority of the whole Empire, formerly divided among ſeveral Officers, after the Examples of *Julius Cæſar* and *Auguſtus*, either actually took upon them the Office, or at leaſt the Title of *Pontifex Maximus*, Chief Prieſt; that is, according to the Definition of *Feſtus*, *Judex at-*

*que*

*que arbiter rerum humanarum divinarumque*; the Judge and Arbitrator of human and divine Affairs. And hence those wise, as well as humane Emperors *Trajan*, and the Two *Antonines*, might possibly think themselves under a double Obligation, as Chief Magistrates and Chief Priests, of persecuting the Christians, whom they apparently consider'd as Innovators with regard to the Constitution, as well as Religion of the Empire. This, tho' no sufficient Excuse for such barbarous and inhuman Proceedings, may serve however to lessen the Astonishment we are apt to fall into, upon hearing that so virtuous a Religion as that of the Christians was persecuted by so virtuous a Prince as *Antoninus the Philosopher*; tho' it must at the same time be acknowledged, that there was in him a great Mixture of Superstition, however incompatible that is thought to be with Philosophy. This may also serve to shew us the distressful Situation of Christianity, against whose Progress not only the Superstitious Zeal of the Multitude, the Laws and Policy of almost every State and Kingdom, but the seeming Duty of even good and just Magistrates were fatally combined.

If to politick and pious Princes, Religion and the Laws of the State might serve for a Reason or Pretence for opposing Christianity, to wicked Emperors there was yet another Motive distinct from any Consideration either of Duty or Policy, or even of their Vices; and that was, their own *Divinity*. After all the Power and Dignity of the *Roman* People, and their several Magistrates, was devolved upon the single Person of the Emperor, the Senators, by a Transition natural enough to Slaves, from Counsellors becoming Flatterers, had not only established by Law the absolute Authority of their Tyrants; but so far consecrated their Persons, even in their Life-time, as to erect Altars to their Names, to place their Statues among those of the Gods, and to offer to them Sacrifices and Incense. Though these impious Honours were conferred upon all alike without any Distinction of Good or Bad; yet the latter, not being able from their own Merit to acquire to themselves any Respect or Veneration, had nothing to stand upon but the Power and Prerogatives of their Office; of which therefore

they

they became so jealous, as to make it dangerous for any one to neglect paying them those outward Honours, however extravagant and profane, which either the Laws, or their own mad Pride required. And hence adoring the Image of the Emperors, swearing by their Names, *&c.* became a Mark and Test of Fidelity, with which all who sought their Favour, or feared their Power, most religiously complied; all those especially who held any Magistracy under them, or governed the Provinces. And these, by their Offices, were yet farther obliged to take care, that within the Limits of their Jurisdiction, that most essential Part of the Duty of Subjects to bad Princes, exterior Respect and Veneration, was most punctually paid. Now, as the Doctrines of *Christ* were entirely opposite to all kinds of Idolatry, Christians were by this Test, with which they could by no means comply, rendered liable to the Guilt of that kind of Treason, which Tyrants and their Ministers never pardon, how apt soever they may be to overlook Crimes against Religion or the State. And that this Test was, among others, made use of against the Professors of

 Chri-

Christianity, even in the best Reigns, is evident from a Passage in the famous Epistle of *Pliny* to *Trajan*, in which he relates his Manner of proceeding with those who offered to clear themselves of the Charge or Suspicion of being Christians, in the following Words.*

" *Propositus est libellus sine autore, multorum nomina continens, qui negant se esse Christianos, aut fuisse: Cùm præeunti me Deos appellarent, & imagini tuæ (quam propter hoc jusseram cum simulacris numinum afferri) thure ac vino supplicarent; præterea maledicerent Christo; quorum nihil cogi posse dicuntur, qui sunt revera Christiani. Ergo dimittendos putavi. Alii ab indice nominati, esse se Christianos dixerunt, & mox negaverunt; fuisse quidem, sed desiisse; quidam ante triennium, quidam ante plures annos: non nemo etiam ante viginti quoque. Omnes & imaginem tuam, deorumque simulacra venerati sunt; ii & Christo maledixerunt.* A Paper was set forth, without a Name, containing a List of many People, who denied that they either were, or ever had been Christians. Now these Persons having, after my Example, invocated the Gods, *and with Wine and Incense payed their Devotions to your Image (which I had caused to be*

* Epist. xcvii. l. 10.

" *be brought forth for that Purpose, with the*
" *Images of the Gods)* and having moreover
" blaſphemed *Chriſt* (*any one of which Things*
" *it is ſaid no real Chriſtian can be compelled to*
" *do)* I thought proper to diſmiſs them. O-
" thers, who had been informed againſt, con-
" feſſed that they were once Chriſtians, but de-
" nied their being ſo now, ſaying they had quit-
" ted that Religion, ſome three Years, others
" more, and ſome few even twenty Years ago.
" All theſe *worſhiped both your Image, and thoſe*
" *of the Gods, and did alſo blaſpheme* Chriſt."

To theſe powerful Patrons of Superſtition, and Enemies of the Goſpel, may be added others, whoſe Authority, tho' inferior and ſubſervient to the former, at leaſt within the Limits of the *Roman* Empire, was however of very great and extenſive Influence; I mean the Prieſts, Diviners, Augurs, and Managers of Oracles, with all the ſubordinate Attendants upon the Temples and Worſhip of almoſt an infinite Number of Deities; and many Trades, if not intirely depending upon that Worſhip, yet very much encouraged and enriched by it, ſuch as Statuaries, Shrine-makers, Breeders of Victims, Dealers in Frankincease, *&c.* All of whom were by Interest, to say nothing of Religion, strongly devoted to Idolatry.

It may not be improper also, under the Article of Religion, to mention the *Circensian*, and other Spectacles exhibited among the *Romans*, the Four Great Games of *Greece*, the *Olympian*, *Pythian*, *Isthmian*, and *Nemean*; with many others of the same Kind, celebrated with great Magnificence in every Country, and almost in every City of *Greece* both in *Europe* and *Asia*; all of which were so many religious Festivals, which by the Allurements of Pomp and Pleasure, not to mention the Glory and Advantages acquir'd by the Conquerors in those Games, attached many to the Cause of Superstition.

But Superstition, universal and powerful as it was, by its Union with the Interests and Pleasures of a considerable Part of Mankind, was not the only nor the greatest Obstacle that Christianity had to contend with. Vice leagued against it a still a greater Number. The Ambitious and Luxurious, the Debauched and Lewd,

Lewd, the Miser and Extortioner, the Unjust and Oppressive, the Proud and the Revengeful, the Fraudulent and Rapacious, were all Foes to a Religion, that taught Humility and Moderation, Temperance and Purity even of Thought, Liberality and Clemency, Justice, Benevolence and Meekness, the Forgiving of Injuries, and *the doing that only to others, which we would have them to do to us.* Virtues agreeable indeed to Reason, and discoverable in Part by the clear Light of Nature; but the Difficulty lay in the bringing those to hear Reason, who had abandoned themselves to Superstition; And how was the almost extinguished Ray of Nature to be perceived, among the many false and glaring Lights of Religion, Opinion, and Philosophy, which recommended and sanctified many enormous Vices? The Gods, like dissolute and despotick Princes, who have often been very properly compared to them, were themselves the great Patrons and Examples of Tyranny, Lewdness and Revenge, and almost all Kinds of Vice. And Opinion had magnified *Alexander*, and deified *Julius Cæsar* for an Ambition, which ought to have rendered them the Object of the Detestation and Curses of all Mankind.

NEITHER was Philosophy so great a Friend to Virtue or Enemy to Vice as she pretended to be. Some Philosophers, on the contrary, denied the Being, at least the Providence of God, and future Rewards and Punishments, and, as a just Consequence of that Opinion, placed the Felicity of Mankind in the Enjoyments of this World, that is, in sensual Pleasures. Others affecting to doubt and question every thing, took away the Distinction of Virtue and Vice, and left their Disciples to follow either, as their Inclination directed. These were, at least indirectly, Preachers of Vice: And among those who undertook to lead their Disciples to the Temple of Virtue, there were so many different, and even inconsistent Opinions, some of them so paradoxical and absurd, others so subtilized and mysterious, and all of them so erroneous in their First Principles, and so defective in many great Points of Religion and Morality, that it is no Wonder that Philosophy, however venerable in her Original, and noble in her Pretensions, degenerated

rated into Speculation, Sophistry, and a Science of Disputation, and from a Guide of Life, became a pedantick President of the Schools; from whence arose another Kind of Adversaries to the Gospel: A Set of Men, who from seeing farther than the Vulgar, came to fancy they could see every thing, and to think every thing subject to the Discussion of Reason; and carrying their Inquiries into the Nature of God, the Production of the Universe, and the Essence of the human Soul, either framed, upon each of these, or adopted some quaint or mysterious System, by which they pretended to account for all the Operations of Nature, and measure all the Actions of God and Man. And as every Sect had a System peculiar to itself, so did each endeavour to advance their own upon the Ruins of all the rest; and this engaged them in a perpetual War with one another; in which, for want of real Strength and solid Arguments, they were reduced to defend themselves and attack their Adversaries with all those Arts, which are commonly made use of to cover or supply the Deficiency of Sense and Reason; Sophistry, Declaration, and Ridicule, Obstinacy, Pride, and

and Rancour. Men of this Turn, accuſtomed to reaſon upon Topicks, in which Reaſon is bewildered; ſo proud of the Sufficiency of Reaſon, as to think they could account for every thing; ſo fond of their own Syſtems, as to dread Conviction more than Error, and ſo habituated to diſpute pertinaciouſly, to aſſert boldly, and to decide magiſterially upon every Queſtion, that they were almoſt incapable of any Inſtruction, could not but be averſe to the receiving for their Maſter a crucified *Jew*, and for Teachers a Parcel of low obſcure Perſons of the ſame Nation, who profeſſed to *glory in the Croſs of* Chriſt, *to know nothing but Him crucified*, and to neglect and deſpiſe the ſo much admired Wiſdom of this World; and who moreover taught Points never thought of by the Philoſophers, ſuch as the Redemption of Mankind, and the Reſurrection of the Dead, and who, though far from forbidding the due Exerciſe of Reaſon, yet confined it within its proper Bounds, and exhorted their Diſciples to ſubmit with all Humility, and to rely with all Confidence upon the Wiſdom of God, inſtead of pretending to arraign his Proceedings; *whoſe Judgments are unſearchable, and whoſe Ways are paſt finding out.*

FROM

FROM this View of the *Jewish* and Gentile World, it is evident that every Thing that most strongly influences and tyrannizes over the Mind of Man, Religion, Custom, Law, Policy, Pride, Interest, Vice, and even Philosophy, was united against the Gospel: Enemies in their own Nature very formidable and difficult to be subdued, had they even suffered themselves to be attacked upon equal Ground, and come to a fair Engagement. But not relying upon their own Strength only (for Prejudice and Falshood are always diffident and fearful) they intrenched themselves behind that Power, which they were in Possession of, and rendered themselves inaccessible, as they imagined, to Christianity, by planting round them not only all Kinds of Civil Discouragements, but even Torments, Chains and Death: Terrors, which no one could despise, who had any Views of Ambition or Interest, and who was not even contented to resign, what he might otherwise have enjoyed in Peace, and without a Crime, his Reputation, his Ease, his Fortune, and his Life. These were the Difficulties, which Christianity had to struggle with

with ſor many Ages, and over which ſhe at length ſo far prevailed, as to change the whole Face of Things, overturn the Temples and Altars of the Gods, ſilence the Oracles, humble the impious Pride of Emperors, thoſe earthly and more powerful Deities, confound the preſumptuous Wiſdom of Philoſophers, and introduce into the greateſt Part of the known World a new Principle of Religion and Virtue. An Event apparently too unwieldy and ſtupendous to have been brought about by mere human Means, though all the Accompliſhments of Learning, all the inſinuating and perſuaſive Powers of Eloquence, joined to the profoundeſt Knowledge of the Nature and Duty of Man, and a long Practice and Experience in the Ways of the World, had all met in the Apoſtles. But the Apoſtles, excepting *Paul*, were ignorant and illiterate, bred up for the moſt part in mean Occupations, Natives and Inhabitants of a remote Province of *Judea*, and ſprung from a Nation hated and deſpiſed by the reſt of Mankind. So that allowing it poſſible, that a Change ſo total and univerſal might have been effected by the natural Powers and Faculties of Man,

yet

yet had the Apostles none of those Powers, St. *Paul* alone excepted, who was indeed eloquent and well versed in all the Learning of the *Jews*, that is, in the Traditions and Doctrines of the Pharisees, (of which Sect he was ;) a Learning, which, instead of assisting him in making Converts to the Gospel, gave him the strongest Prejudices against it, and rendered him a furious Persecutor of the Christians. Yet of this Eloquence, and of this Learning, he made no Use in preaching the Gospel ; on the contrary, † *When I came to you*, (says he to the *Corinthians*) *I came not with Excellency of Speech, or of Wisdom, declaring to you the Testimony of God ; for I determined not to know any thing among you, save* Jesus Christ, *and him crucified : And I was with you in Weakness and in Fear, and in much Trembling ; and my Speech and my Preaching was not with enticing Words of Man's Wisdom.* And in the preceding Chapter, comparing the Insufficiency of the Preachers of the Gospel with the Success of their Preaching, he attributes the latter to the true Cause, the Wisdom and Power of God, in these expressive Words :—* *For* Christ *sent me*

*to*

† 1 Cor. ii. 1—4. * 1 Cor. i. 17, 18.

*to preach the Gospel, not with Wisdom of Words, lest the Cross of* Christ *should be made of none Effect. For the Preaching of the Cross is to them that perish Foolishness; but unto us, who are saved, it is the Power of God.* * *For it is written, I will destroy the Wisdom of the Wise, and will bring to nothing the Understanding of the Prudent. Where is the Wise? Where is the Scribe? Where is the Disputer of this World? Hath not God made foolish the Wisdom of this World? For after that in the Wisdom of God the World by Wisdom knew not God, it pleased God by the Foolishness of Preaching to save them that believe. For the* Jews *require a Sign, and the* Greeks *seek after Wisdom. But we preach* Christ *crucified, unto the* Jews *a stumbling Block, and to the* Greeks *Foolishness; but unto them which are called, both* Jews *and* Greeks, Christ *the Power of God, and the Wisdom of God; because the Foolishness of God is wiser than Men, and the Weakness of God is stronger than Men: For you see your Calling, Brethren, that not many Wise Men after the Flesh, nor many Mighty, nor* [illegible] *many* [illegible]

* Is. xxix. 14.

*many Noble, are called. But God hath chosen the foolish Things of the World to confound the Wise; and God hath chosen the weak Things of the World to confound the Things that are mighty; and base Things of the World, and Things which are despised, hath God chosen; yea, and Things which are not, to bring to nought Things that are, that no Flesh should glory in his Presence.*

THIS is a true Representation of the Condition of the first Preachers of the Gospel, and their Opposers. The latter were possessed of all the Wisdom, Authority, and Power of the World; the former were ignorant, contemptible, and weak. Which of them, then, according to the natural Course of human Affairs, ought to have prevailed? The latter, without all doubt. And yet not the Apostle only, but all History and our own Experience assure us, that the Ignorant, the Contemptible, and the Weak, gained the Victory from the Wise, the Mighty, and the Noble. To what other Cause, then, can we attribute a Success so contrary to all the Laws, by which the Events of this World are governed, than

to

or the Interpolition of God, manifested in the Resurrection and Ascension of *Jesus Christ*; and the miraculous Powers conferr'd upon his Apostles and Disciples? A Cause adequate to all the Effects, however great and astonishing. For, with these ample Credentials from the King of Heaven, even a poor Fisherman of *Galilee* might appear with Dignity before the High Priest and Sanhedrim of the *Jews*, assert boldly that *God had made that same* Jesus, *whom they had crucified, both Lord and Christ*; and make good his Assertion by proving, that He was risen from the Dead, strange and supernatural as it might seem, not only by his own Testimony, and that of his Brethren the Apostles and Disciples of *Jesus*, by whom he was seen *for forty Days after his Passion*, but by innumerable Instances of a Power, superior in like manner to Nature, derived upon *Them* from *Him*, aad exercised by them in his Name. From the Scriptures also might the same ignorant and illiterate *Galileans* shew against the Traditions of the Elders, the Learning of the Scribes, and the Prejudices of the whole *Jewish* Nation, that the humble suffering *Jesus* was the

the mighty triumphant Messiah, spoken of by the Prophets; since if, with reference to the Interpretation of those Prophecies, any Doubt could have arisen among the People to whose Expositions they should submit, to those of the Scribes and Elders, or those of the Apostles; the latter had to produce, in Support of their Authority, the Attestation of that Holy Spirit, by whom those Prophets were inspired, now speaking through their Mouths in all the Languages of the Earth. And with regard to that other Point, of still harder Digestion to the *Jews*, namely, the calling the uncircumcised Gentiles to an equal Participation of the Kingdom of God, and consequently the abolishing Circumcision, and the whole Ceremonial Law, the Apostles were furnished with an Argument, to which all the Rabbins were not able to reply; by the Holy Ghost bestowing upon the Gentile Converts to Christianity, the same heavenly Gifts as he had conferr'd, at the Beginning, upon the believing *Jews*.

INVESTED with such full Powers from on high, might these same obscure *Jews*, notwithstanding the Contempt and Hatred which all other Nations had for that People, undertake and accomplish the arduous and amazing Task of preaching the Gospel to all the World. The Belief of One God is the fundamental Article of all true Religion; and the Unity of the Godhead is certainly discoverable, and even to be demonstrated by Reason. But this Article of Belief (as I have said before) was not to be found in the Religion of any Nation, besides the *Jews*; and long Arguments and Deductions of Reason, by which it was to be demonstrated, were above the Capacity of the greatest Part of Mankind. To prove this important Truth, therefore, in a Manner easy to be comprehended by the weakest, and yet not to be refuted by the strongest Understanding, the Apostles and their Followers were for many Ages endow'd, besides all their other miraculous Gifts, with a Power over Devils or Dæmons, (the only Deities of the Pagans that had any real Being)

per-

permitted perhaps to ſhew themſelves at that Time in extraordinary Operations, for the ſake of illuſtrating and proving this great Truth. By this Power they caſt them out of many, who were poſſeſſed by them, drove them from their Temples, Groves, and Oracles, obliged them to confeſs their own Inferiority, to acknowledge the Dominion of *Jeſus Chriſt*, and to declare his Apoſtles to be * *the Servants of the moſt high God*, ſent to *ſhew* Mankind *the way of Salvation*. This Power they exerciſed in the Name of *Jeſus Chriſt*, in order to prove his Mediation and Interceſſion between God and Man, the ſecond Article of the Chriſtian Creed. And as by this Power, thus exerciſed in the Name of *Chriſt*, the Apoſtles and their Followers were enabled to prove, even to the Senſes of all Mankind, that there is but One God, and One Mediator; ſo from that and other miraculous Gifts of the Holy Spirit, healing all manner of Diſeaſes, ſpeaking with various Tongues, propheſying, *&c.* did they



* Acts xvi. 17. See, for many other Inſtances, *Whitby*'s General Preface to the Epiſtles.

derive to themselves Authority to teach the great Doctrines of Christianity, Repentance, Remission of Sins, Holiness of Life, future Rewards and Punishments, and the Resurrection of the Dead: Of which last, the Resurrection of *Christ* was both an Instance and a Pledge; as the Effusion of the Holy Ghost upon Believers was a clear Evidence of the Efficacy of Repentance, and the Remission of their Sins. And of the Necessity of a holy Life, and the Certainty of future Rewards and Punishments, nothing could afford a stronger and more convincing Argument, than the Lives and Deaths of these Ambassadors of God, who were apparently guided into all Truth by his Inspiration; and who, upon the Assurance of a blessed Immortality, not only practised all the Virtues they preach'd, but chearfully underwent all kinds of Sufferings, and even Death itself.

After this manner were the first Preachers of the Gospel, weak, ignorant, and contemptible as they were, furnished with Strength sufficient to overthrow the *strong Holds*

*Holds of Satan*, the Superstitions, Prejudices, and Vices of Mankind; and by the *Demonstration of the Power of God*, an Argument whose Conclusiveness was visible to the dullest Capacity, enabled to confound the Subtilties of the most disputatious, and surpass the Wisdom of the wisest Philosophers, in establishing Religion upon the Belief of One God, grounding the Obligation to Virtue upon it's true Principle, the Command of God; and deriving the Encouragement to Holiness of Life from the Promises of God, to reward those who should obey his Will with eternal Happiness, obtained by the Sacrifice and Mediation of *Jesus Christ*. Which last Point, together with the Doctrine of Providence, the free Agency of Man, and assisting Grace, how much soever beyond the Ken of Reason, yet could not but be admitted by all reasonable Men for certain Truths, as standing upon the Authority of Persons visibly commissioned and inspired by God. For what Conclusion of Reason, what Maxim in Philosophy is more evident, than that *Men speaking by the immediate Inspiration of God, cannot lie?* And is not the Divine Inſpiration of the Apoſtles to be inferr'd with as much Certainty, from the mighty Wonders they performed, as the Divine Creation of the World from the ſtupendous Beauty, Order, and Magnificence of the Univerſe? Every Effect muſt have a Cauſe; and a ſupernatural Effect muſt have a Cauſe ſuperior to Nature; and this Cauſe can be no other than God. There may be, indeed, and we are authoriſed by the Scriptures to ſay there are many Beings both good and bad, endued with Faculties and Powers exceeding thoſe of Man. But theſe Beings are, doubtleſs, limited as well as Man in the Exerciſe of thoſe Powers, and ſubjected to Laws preſcribed to them by their great Creator; which, in reſpect to them, may be likewiſe ſtiled the Laws of Nature. From whence it follows, that they cannot break in upon or diſturb the Laws of any other Syſtem of Creatures, though inferior to them, without the Permiſſion of the Univerſal King; who, nevertheleſs, may certainly make Uſe of them as Inſtruments to bring about his

2 wiſe

wise Purposes, even beyond the Bounds of their proper Spheres. Thus, in establishing Christianity, he thought fit to employ the Ministration not of Angels only, but of Dæmons, though in such a manner as to leave no Doubt of their Subjection to his Sovereignty. The Angels were, upon many Occasions, assisting to *Christ* and his Apostles; the Dæmons trembled, and fled at their Command; and both of them, those by their Subserviency, and these by the Servility of their Obedience, manifestly declared *Christ* and his Apostles to be vested with an Authority and Power derived from their Lord and King. So that Mankind, seeing the Apostles possessed of a Power plainly paramount to the Powers of all other known Beings, whether Angels or Dæmons, could no more question their being commissioned and inspired by God, than doubt whether the magnificent Frame of the Universe, with all the various Natures belonging to it, was the Workmanship of his Almighty Hands.

Thus by arguing from Effects, notorious and visible Effects, to Causes, the surest Method of investigating and proving some Kinds of Truths, I have endeavoured to demonstrate (if I may speak without Offence) the Certainty of the Resurrection of *Jesus Christ*, upon which the whole System of Christianity depends. For if *Christ* is not risen from the Dead, then, as St. *Paul* says, vain is the Hope of Christians, and the Preaching of the Apostles vain; nay, we may go still farther, and pronounce vain the Preaching of *Christ* himself. For had he not risen, and proved himself by many infallible Tokens to have risen from the Dead, the Apostles and Disciples could have had no Inducement to believe in him, that is, to acknowledge him for the Messiah, the *Anointed of* God; on the contrary, they must have taken him for an Impostor, and under that Persuasion could never have become Preachers of the Gospel, without becoming Enthusiasts or Impostors, in either of which Characters it is impossible they should have succeeded, to the Degree which we are assured

they

they did, considering their natural Insufficiency, the strong Opposition of all the World to the Doctrines of Christianity, and their own high Pretensions to miraculous Powers; about which they could neither have been deceived themselves, nor have deceived others. Supposing therefore that *Christ* did not rise from the Dead, it is certain, according to all human Probability, there could never have been any such Thing at all as Christianity, or it must have been stifled soon after its Birth. But we know on the contrary, that Christianity hath already existed above seven hundred Years. This is a Fact about which there is no Dispute, but Christians and Infidels disagree in accounting for this Fact. Christians affirm their Religion to be of divine Original, and to have grown up and prevailed under the miraculous Assistance and Protection of God; and this they not only affirm, and offer to prove by the same kind of Evidence, by which all remote Facts are proved, but think it may very fairly be inferred from the wonderful Circumstances of its Growth and Increase, and its present Existence. Infidels, on the other hand, assert

Christia-

Christianity to be an Imposture, invented and carried on by Men. In the Maintenance of which Assertion, their great Argument against the Credibility of the Resurrection, and the other miraculous Proofs of the divine Original of the Gospel, founded in their being miraculous, that is, out of the ordinary Course of Nature, will be of no Service to them, since they will still find a Miracle in their Way, namely, the amazing Birth, Growth, and Increase of Christianity. Which Facts, though they should not be able to account for them, they cannot however deny. In order therefore to destroy the Evidence drawn from them by Christians, they must prove them not to have been miraculous, by shewing how they could have been effected in the natural Course of human Affairs, by such weak Instruments as *Christ* and his Apostles (taking them to be what they are pleased to call them, Enthusiasts or Impostors) and by such Means as they were possessed of and employed. But this I imagine to be as much above the Capacity of the greatest Philosophers to shew, as it is to prove the Possibility of executing the proud Boast of

*Archimedes*

*Archimedes* (even granting his Poſtulatum) of moving and wielding the Globe of this Earth, by Machines of human Invention, and compoſed of ſuch Materials only, as Nature furniſhes for the ordinary Uſe of Man.

A TABLE

A

# TABLE of CONTENTS.

omitted by the other. 2*dly*, Of ſuch as they both agree in. 3*dly*, Of ſuch as ſeem to claſh and diſagree with each other. 1*ſt*, Circumſtances mentioned by St. *Matthew* only: Earthquake, Deſcent of the Angel, his rolling away the Stone, ſitting upon it, Terror of the Soldiers, Appearances of *Chriſt* to the Women, and to the Eleven in *Galilee*. Flight of the Soldiers into the City; Tranſactions between them and the High Prieſts. Circumſtances mentioned only by St. *Mark*: Of the Women's having brought Spices; Of *Salome*'s being one of thoſe Women; Of their entering into the Sepulchre, and ſeeing there a young Man ſitting on the right Side, cloathed in a long white Garment; Of the Appearance of *Chriſt* to *Mary Magdalene*, to the two Diſciples who were going into the Country, and to the Eleven as they ſat at Meat.

§. 4. *p*. 35. Circumſtances in which the two Evangeliſts agree. 1*ſt*, The Women's going to the Sepulchre early in the Morning on the firſt Day of the Week. 2. Their being told by an Angel that *Chriſt* was riſen, &c. 3. The Terror and Flight of the Women.

§. 5. *p*. 41. Circumſtances which ſeem to claſh and diſagree with each other. Different Accounts of the Time when the Women came to the Sepulchre, adjuſted. Date of the Reſurrection ſettled. Remarks on the Word Πϱωϊ. Signifies not only *early*, but *over-early*, *before the appointed Time*. Importance of the Words, *went to ſee the Sepulchre* in St. *Matthew*, and *Who ſhall roll away the Stone for us* in St. *Mark*,

*Mark*, pointed out. Women knew nothing of the Guard at the Sepulchre.

§. 6. *p.* 49. Obſervations on the firſt Part of the 24th Chapter of St. *Luke.* Particulars in Saint *Luke*'s Account differing from thoſe of the other Evangeliſts noted. St. *Peter* ſhewn to have gone twice to the Sepulchre; the firſt Time upon *Mary Magdalene*'s firſt Report, the ſecond Time upon the Report of *Joanna* and thoſe with her. *Peter* preſent when *Joanna* made her Report. Reaſon for St. *Luke*'s naming *Mary Magdalene* and the other *Mary*, with *Joanna* and thoſe with her, who told theſe Things to the Apoſtles. Reports of the Women farther ſhewn to have been made ſeparately, and at different Times. Women went to the Sepulchre at different Times. Reaſons for their going at different Times. Conduct of *Joanna*, &c. conſider'd.

§. 7. *p.* 66. Obſervations on the latter Part of the 24th Chapter of St. *Luke.* Connexion of this Chapter pointed out.

§. 8. *p.* 74. Appearances of *Chriſt* to the Women ſhewn to be diſtinct and different, and to refer to two different and diſtinct Events, *viz.* the Aſcenſion of Chriſt, and his meeting his Diſciples in *Galilee.* Recapitulation of the ſeveral Points proved in the foregoing Section. 1*ſt*, That the Women came at different Times, and in different Companies to the Sepulchre. 2. That there were ſeveral diſtinct Appearances of Angels. 3. That the Angels were not always viſi-

[illegible] ble,

ble, but appeared and disappeared as they thought proper. 4. That these several Facts were reported to the Apostles at different Times, and by different Women. 5. That there were two distinct Appearances of *Christ* to the Women. 6. That St. *Peter* was twice at the Sepulchre. Observations of a very eminent and judicious Person on *Mary Magdalene*'s being named by all the Evangelists, &c.

§. 9. p. 84. The several Incidents in the History of the Resurrection, set down in the Order in which they appear to have arisen.

§. 10. p. 97. Two Reflections upon the Order of the several Incidents. Three Points proposed to be considered. 1st, The Manner (i. e. the Method and Order) in which the Proofs of the Resurrection arising from the foregoing Incidents were laid before the Apostles. 2. The Matter (i. e. the Facts) of which those Proofs consist. 3. The Characters and Dispositions of the Apostles; and first of the Characters and Dispositions of the Apostles at the Time of *Christ*'s Death.

§. 11. p. 103. The Method and Order in which the several Proofs of the Resurrection were laid before the Apostles. *Mary Magdalene*'s first Report. Report of *Joanna* and those with her. *Mary Magdalene*'s second Report. Report of the other *Mary* and *Salome*. Appearance of *Christ* to the two Disciples at *Emmaus*. Appearance of *Christ* to the Eleven as they sat at Meat. Difference in the Accounts of *Mark* and *Luke* reconciled. Appearance of *Christ* to St.

St. *Thomas*. Appearance of *Christ* to the Disciples in *Galilee*. *Christ*'s Ascension. Descent of the Holy Ghost at *Pentecoste*. Miracles wrought by the Apostles, *&c*.

§. 12. *p*. 135. The Facts which constitute the Evidence of the Resurrection considered under three Heads. 1*st*, The Appearances of the Angels. 2*dly*, The Appearances of *Christ* to the Women. 3*dly*, The Appearances of *Christ* to the Disciples and Apostles. Four Appearances of Angels: 1*st*, To the *Roman* Soldiers. 2. To the other *Mary* and *Salome*. 3. To *Mary Magdalene*. 4. To *Joanna*. Of the Appearance to the *Roman* Soldiers. Propriety and Necessity of this Appearance. The Miraculousness of it, no Objection to its Credibility.

§. 13. *p*. 144. The Appearance of the Angels to the Women (1*st*, To the other *Mary* and *Salome*; 2. To *Mary Magdalene*; And, 3, To *Joanna* and those with her) examined, and shewn to have been real, and not the Effects of a distemper'd Imagination, or the Operations of Artifice and Fraud.

§. 14. *p*. 162. Of the Appearances of *Christ* to the Women; the Words of *Christ* to *Mary Magdalene*, *Touch me not*, &c. explain'd. Different Behaviour of *Christ* to *Mary Magdalene*, and to the other *Mary* and *Salome* accounted for. Import of the other Words spoken by *Christ* to *Mary Magdalene*, viz *But go to my Brethren, and say to them, I ascend to my Father*, *&c*. Observations on the Word *ascend*.

§. 15.

§. 15. p. 186. Of the Appearances of *Christ* to the Apostles and Disciples. Appearance to the two Disciples at *Emmaus* consider'd. Two Objections to this Appearance: 1st, That these Disciples knew not *Jesus* during the whole Time of his walking, conversing, &c. with them. 2. That after they are said to have known him, he vanished so suddenly out of their Sight, that they had not Time sufficient to satisfy their Doubts, &c. answered. Prov'd that these Disciples had sufficient Reason to be assured that it was *Christ* himself who appeared to them.

§. 16. p. 196. Of the Appearances of *Christ* to the Eleven and those with them.——To Saint *Thomas*. The Proofs arising from the Appearances of *Christ* to the Women and Apostles, or referred to by *Christ* himself, proposed to be consider'd under four Heads. 1. The Testimony of those who had seen him after he was risen. 2. The Evidence of their own Senses. 3. The Accomplishment of the Words he had spoken to them, while he was yet with them. 4. The Fulfilling of all the Things which were written in the Law of *Moses*, and in the Prophets, and in the *Psalms*, concerning him. For the first, see the two preceding Sections. The second, *viz.* the Evidences of their own Senses considered. Two Objections: 1. That *Christ*'s Body was a spiritual Body, and consequently incapable of being handled, &c. 2. That the Apostles were imposed upon by Sensations miraculously imprinted on their Minds, examined and answer'd.

§. 17. *p.* 211. Of the Accomplishment of the Predictions of *Christ* relating to his Sufferings, Death, and Resurrection. Several Particulars of the Passion and Death, &c. of *Christ*, and the Prophecies corresponding to them produced. Proof of the Death of *Christ* from the 19th Chapter of *John*, 33d and 34th Verses, *viz.* One of the Soldiers pierced his Side, and forthwith came thereout Blood and Water. Proofs of *Christ*'s rising precisely on the Third Day. Cavils on the Phrases *three Days and three Nights*, and *after three Days*, answer'd.

§. 18. *p.* 229. Of the Prophecies and Types, &c. contained in the Law of *Moses*, the Prophets, and the Psalms, concerning the Sufferings, Death and Resurrection of *Christ*, and their Accomplishment. Prophecy from the third Chapter of *Genesis*, 15th Verse. Quotation from *Sherlock*'s Discourses on Prophecy, &c. Prophecy from the 53d Chapter of *Isaiah*. Prophecies from the other Prophets and the *Psalms*. Particular Accomplishment of the Prophecy from *Isaiah*, relating to the Burial of *Christ*. Prophecy of *David* concerning the Resurrection of *Christ*, cited by St. *Peter*, from *Acts* ii. 25, &c. Of Types and Figures.

§. 19. *p.* 268. Reflections on the Evidence arising from the exact Accomplishment of the Prophecies of *Moses*, &c. and the Predictions of *Christ* himself relating to his Sufferings, Death, and Resurrection.

§. 20. *p.* 282. Of the Departure of the Disciples into *Galilee* after the Resurrection of *Christ*, and of their Return to *Jerusalem* at the Feast of *Pentecost*.

*Pentecost*. Reasons for their going into *Galilee*, and for their returning to *Jerusalem*, assigned. All the Appearances of *Christ* to his Disciples, from that to St. *Thomas* related by St. *John*, to the Time of his Ascension, were probably in *Galilee*. All the latter Part of the 24th Chapter of St. *Luke*, from the 49th Verse to the End, relates to what happened at *Jerusalem* after the Return of the Apostles from *Galilee*.

§. 21. *p*. 294. Short Recapitulation of the Proofs of the Resurrection. Reasons of *Christ*'s appearing so often to his Apostles, *&c*. Cavils about *Christ*'s not appearing to the *Jews*, and forbidding *Mary Magdalene to touch him*, answer'd.

§. 22. *p*. 305. Reasons for our believing at this Time that *Christ* rose from the Dead. These are Two: 1. The Testimony of the Apostles contained in the Scriptures: 2. The Existence of the Christian Religion. Proofs of the Genuineness of the Scriptures: 1. The concurrent Attestation of all the earliest Writers of the Church: 2. The Probability of the Apostles having left in Writing the Evidences and Doctrines of Christianity: 3. The Improbability of any Books forged in the Names of the Apostles escaping Detection. Probability of the Apostles having left in Writing the Evidences and Doctrines of Christianity, moved thereto either by the Holy Spirit, or by their Care for the Church, or by the Sollicitation of their Children in *Christ*, who not having in themselves the Words of eternal Life, must naturally have endeavoured

to obtain them from the Apoſtles themſelves in Writing, or have wrote them down from their Mouths, or under their Inſpection; or laſtly, have tranſcribed from their own Memories what they could recollect of the Preaching of the Apoſtles. Many Writings of this Kind extant when St. *Luke* wrote his Goſpel: All loſt, ſuperſeded by the Writings of the Apoſtles, which muſt have been preferred to all the other Writings, and preſerved, *&c.* with the utmoſt Care and Fidelity.

§. 23. *p.* 319. Improbability of any Books forged in the Names of the Apoſtles eſcaping Detection. Importance of diſtinguiſhing between the true Writings of the Apoſtles and others forged in their Names. Means of knowing the genuine from forged Writings. No Motive can be aſſigned for any Chriſtian's being guilty of ſuch a Forgery. Books acknowledged by the earlieſt Chriſtians to have been written by the Apoſtles, ought to be admitted for ſuch. Scriptures come down to us pure and uncorrupted in all Matters of Conſequence.

§. 24. *p.* 335. Arguments for giving Credit to the Teſtimony of the Apoſtles and Evangeliſts. Two Qualities requiſite to eſtabliſh the Credit of a Witneſs, *viz.* a perfect Knowledge of the Fact he gives Teſtimony to, and a fair and unblemiſhed Character: Both found in the Apoſtles. Characters of the Apoſtles collected from their Lives and Doctrines.

§. 25. *p.* 341. Internal Marks of the Veracity of the ſacred Writers, obſervable in the Scriptures. Diſagreement, a Proof that they did not write

in

in-Concert. Agreement, an Evidence that they wrote after the Truth. Their naming the Time, the Scene of Action, the Actors, and the Witnesses of most of the Facts related by them, another Mark of their Veracity; Instance, the Story of guarding the Sepulchre. Their Attachment to the Truth manifested by their relating Things of themselves and their Brethren tending to their own Dishonour. What they say of the low Condition, Infirmities, Sufferings, and Death of *Christ*, a most unexceptionable Evidence of their Veracity. Their Integrity farther illustrated by some Reflections on the Stile of the Scriptures.

§. 26. *p* 363. External Proofs of the Veracity and Inspiration of the sacred Writers, two; One Negative, the other Positive. Negative Proof, That no one Fact related by them hath ever been disproved or falsified. That the Disciples stole the Body of *Jesus*, the only Fact set up in Opposition to the many Facts, which constitute the Evidence of the Resurrection, never proved, nor so much as inquired into. Miracles performed by *Christ* and his Apostles never disproved: Admitted by *Celsus* and the *Jews*.

§. 27. *p*. 370. Positive Proof of the Veracity of the sacred Writers, founded in the exact Accomplishment of the Prophecies recorded by them. Prophecy of the different (Religious) State of the *Jews* and *Gentiles*, and its Accomplishment.

§. 28. *p.* 382. Prophecies concerning the Destruction of the City and Temple of *Jerusalem*, the Misery and Dispersion of the *Jews*, and the Duration of their Calamity, with their Accomplishments. Observations on the foregoing Prophecies.

§. 29. *p.* 395. Observations on the Prophecies relating to the present State of the *Jews*, translated from the *French*.

§. 30. *p.* 410. Argument from the present Existence of Christianity considered. Nature of this Argument. Difficulties Christianity had to struggle with at its first Appearance and for a long time after, the Superstition, Prejudices, and Vices of the whole World. Short View of the State of the World under the first Ages of Christianity. Superstition and Prejudices of the *Jews*. Religion, Custom, Law, Policy, Pride, Interest, Vice, and Philosophy, united the whole Heathen World against Christianity. Representation of the different and unequal Condition of the first Preachers of the Gospel, and their Opposers. The latter possessed of all the Wisdom, Power and Authority of the World; the former ignorant, contemptible, and weak; yet triumphed over their Opposers, by the Interposition and Assistance of God, manifested in the Resurrection of *Christ*, and the miraculous Powers conferred on the first Christians. Apostles enabled by those miraculous Powers to prove that *Christ* was risen from the Dead----- that he was the *Messiah*-------that the *Gentiles* were to be admitted into the Kingdom of God-----

God------that there was but one God-----and one Mediator; together with the ſeveral peculiar Doctrines of Chriſtianity. God in eſtabliſhing Chriſtianity, thought fit to employ the Miniſtration of Dæmons as well as Angels, and why. Concluſion.

*FINIS.*

Lightning Source UK Ltd.
Milton Keynes UK
172262UK00005B/25/P